THE SOUL'S CRITICAL PATH

Waking Down to the Soul's Purpose, the Body's Power, and the Heart's Passion

John P. Davidson

HeartWorks
PUBLISHING

Raton, New Mexico

HeartWorks Publishing is a trademark of HeartWorks Publishing Company

Cover Art: Daemys/123rf.com and Levengenil Skryzhak/123rf.com

Cover design: Ann Lowe

Interior Book Design: Booknook.biz

Davidson, John P. (John Philip), 1947-

    The soul's critical path: waking down to the soul's purpose, the body's power, and the heart's passion /John P. Davidson. – Raton, NM.: HeartWorks Pub. Co., c2013.

    p. ; cm.

Summary: Drawing on experiences with heart-centered meditation, vision questing, Peruvian shamanism, conscious relationship, and entheogenic plants, the author identifies five stages through which all souls can evolve in one lifetime. This new approach to an ancient mystery describes how an experiential soul perspective speeds the process by which a soul skillfully transcends fate and creates a unique destiny while remaining richly connected to both the earth and the other-dimensional intelligences that support the soul's journey. – Publisher.

    1. Soul. 2. Ayahuasca. 3. Ethnobotany. 4. Spirituality. 5. Evolutionary psychology. 6. Consciousness. 7. Peru. I. Title

BD503.5.D38 2013   2013939246
253.5/3—dc23   1308

ISBN: 978-0-9882557-0-8

Library of Congress Control Number: 2013939246

HeartWorks Publishing Company
P.O. Box 6
Raton, New Mexico USA 87740
www.heartworkspublishing.com

For Darlene, Jack, Quinn, and Abuela

CONTENTS

CHAPTER THREE

PART TWO: THE BODY
STAGE TWO: THE SOUL PERSPECTIVE IS LOST

CHAPTER FOUR

PART THREE: THE BRIDGE
STAGE THREE: CAPTURING CONTROL OF ATTENTION AND REMEMBERING WHO WE ARE

CHAPTER FIVE

PART FOUR: THE GATEWAY
STAGE FOUR: RE-VISIONING THE PAST AND OPENING TO OUR DESTINY

CHAPTER SIX

PART FIVE: THE ARC
STAGE FIVE: SKILLFUL EMBODIMENT OF DESTINY

CHAPTER SEVEN

FINDING THE HEART OF THE EARTH

PROLOGUE

ONE DAY YOU AWAKEN TO a new sensation.

Something beckons, but the *beckoner* remains out of sight.

The feeling may seem to depart for a time, but it always returns, quietly tugging at your attention. Your senses quicken in its presence. You are drawn to follow, but you have no idea where you are called to go, or how you are going to get there.

The beckoning persists. In time, you sense that your own ever-present yearning is turning to meet it.

There may come a singular moment. It does not come for everyone. But for you, it comes. In that moment, the yearning merges into a crescendo of *knowing*. Deep in your heart, you *know* that you have to follow this call. To your surprise, the mere idea of not going, even into an utter unknown, now hovers about you like a dark, suffocating cloud.

So you have to respond. Even so, your first step forward is cautious, tentative. The yearning soon senses its object and changes into an attraction—subtle at first, struggling to push past your persistent doubt. This insistent sense of attraction magnetizes you in this direction instead of that—toward *this* relationship, or *this* teacher, or *that* place or work, or even *this* notion or idea.

Time passes. The attraction grows, compelling you now. You watch its play and discover a paradox. Time and again, the attraction brings you to experiences that are not what you have projected them to be. With each new experience, there is an element of surprise—disappointment, rejection, pain, sorrow, a sense that you have made a mistake, ironic laughter. You question this attraction and the choices you have made in response to it. You remain drawn, yet you hesitate to trust it. Still, you find yourself learning valuable lessons. You become more discerning. You see more deeply into the circumstances and people that attract you. You trust more and more in yourself. You feel less a victim in the world. Life circumstances begin to feel less a struggle and more an opportunity for connection and growth. Nevertheless, mystery remains.

You persist. The lessons begin to illuminate a thread that extends from your experiences in the external world to your own internal sense of yearning. You begin to ask, *Why have I made these choices? From where does this yearning come?*

You realize that the journey has entered an internal landscape. The sense of attraction has turned in on itself. You find yourself talking to yourself more and more. You ask, *Who is asking these questions?* Finally, the question *Who am I?* explodes into your consciousness with all the subtlety of a neon billboard flashing in the dark night of your journey. That question is quickly followed by another. *And why am I here?*

There comes a magic moment in which you suspect the presence of your own soul. You suspect that the beckoner is *there*—some *something* in some *somewhere* distinct from your personality, ego, thoughts, emotions, distinct even from your heart.

Your search deepens. You look for ways to know this soul, to reveal it to your own eyes. In time, you suspect that *your* attention is the *soul's* attention. You sense, now and again, that the soul's eyes are looking out upon the world through your eyes.

That strange sense—that you are looking out upon the world through the soul's eyes—gives way to a deeper exploration. You find that the soul's attention can be anywhere. It may be fragmented or it may be focused. You encounter unusual experiences, some that you hesitate to share with others. Mysterious memories may arise—memories that may seem to come from another life.

And at some magical crossroad of your internal journey, you find that the soul finds itself looking out upon the world through the *heart*—that organ of perception than which no sight or sense is more powerful. There is a new and powerful sensation—a distinct joy that attends this simple heart-looking.

The question *Who am I* begins to have an answer. You hear, *I am the soul*. Then, simply, *I am*. The soul has infused the personality, and the former indistinct identity of the personality—the ever-shifting amalgam of thoughts and feelings—has merged into a clear and singular sense of identity.

As the soul explores this new heart-sight, your own body comes again into view, but in a different light than before. There is a strange and new resonance. The soul senses an attraction for the body that was not present before. Sensing into the body, the soul senses that the body feels also an attraction for the soul. In time, this mutual attraction grows, even as it is apparent that the body is hesitant and perhaps fearful as though the body feels the discomfort of an outsider looking in.

As the body becomes more and more at ease with the presence of the soul, the senses of the body become more available to the soul, allowing the soul to navigate the world of matter with increasing skill. The attention that moved inward and found itself to *be* the soul now begins again to move outward. And, as the soul deepens even further into the heart's vast field, it finds itself able to connect at will with subtle dimensions beyond the body and time and space—fields made of the frequencies that we have called *heaven* and *angels* and *guides* and *spirits*, fields encoded with information that come to us as voices, insights, intuitions, visions, extraordinary sensory experiences, and knowings. Tuning that connection carefully through the extraordinary lens of the heart, the soul finds those very particular fields that seem to await the soul's own attention—fields that speak directly to the soul's purpose in the world.

As the soul gazes out from its new home in the heart, it sees a dimly lit path. The path disappears into darkness, but the soul knows that it must follow, if only it can find the means. The soul calls out—a prayer to heaven, a prayer for its mate to appear, a prayer for guidance. The prayers become a burning desire. *Come my love*, it cries out.

Desire resonates with desire. So many respond. The soul may become confused, distracted. And yet the soul settles down once more, anchoring itself in the heart and calling all of its attention back to itself. And there, the soul listens more carefully, more skillfully.

Across the vast expanse of the heart's field, the soul senses the approach of a golden thread of the most pure tone, the deepest resonance. Can it be? *Come my love*, the soul hears. It is the voice of the body itself.

Like a wild horse that has fallen in love with the one—the only one—it would consent to ride it, the body races also to the heart, where awaits the soul. In the body, the soul finds its legs, its partner, its first and most true mate—matter, *mater,* the means of manifestation—the one that powers the soul's purpose.

Like the strike of a serpent, the body arcs to the soul and soul to body, igniting the altar of the heart into a burning *passion.*

And, as magic follows magic, heaven arcs in a lightning-like stroke, cutting a brilliant path through soul and body and across the burning altar of the heart. As soul has penetrated the body, heaven penetrates deeply now into the waiting earth, following the luminous pathway the soul has forged, moving through the embodied soul itself. Electrified and magnetized by heaven and earth, the soul's former trickling sense of its purpose surges, now a great river—a cascading free fall of passion powering down Creation's ever-deepening escarpments, a standing wave that connects heaven to earth. The subtle light of the soul's path explodes into brilliance—laser-like, focused, strong, and brilliant.

The body's nostrils flair with a sudden, deep in-breath. Destiny insists. The soul responds. There is a new confidence. The soul cannot see the end, but looks out through the heart, and heart senses the way one bold step at a time. A deep sense of adventure floods the soul, and excitement fills the body.

Now, beneath the body's feet, the earth heaves, calling to the awakening soul. Soul-sight turns to the earth, finding there the heart of the earth gaping open—inviting the now embodied and behearted soul to enter and explore the earth's own mysteries. The soul surrenders, and earth pulls it into herself, turning with her intimate embrace the secret key that opens the door to the myriad earth fields—the mother fields of waters, winds, plants, stones, mountains, animals, and all other living beings on the planet—that now offer their treasures in support of the soul's journey and its ultimate work. Energies pour themselves into the soul's open heart. Everything is alive. Everything is connected. Everything awaits the soul's invitation for relationship. Everything stands ready to support the quickening journey of the soul.

And all of that is prologue. The soul has awakened to the process that reveals the soul's own purpose, a means of partnering with the body's power, and access to the heart's passion. Now the dance can truly begin.

PREFACE

In this Preface . . .

The Soul's Critical Path
Plato's Story of Er
Our Own Soul Stories

The Soul's Critical Path

EVERYONE HAS HEARD IT SAID—our experience of the world depends on how we look at it.

There is no richer life you can experience than the one seen through the eyes of your own soul living out the fullness of its destiny. But there is nothing inevitable about the onset of one's destiny. Destiny can define our lives only if we learn to locate our souls within our hearts, focus our attention there, and look out upon the world with the eye of the soul gazing through the lens of the heart. I call that way of looking a *soul perspective*. Getting your own soul perspective in control of your life will make more difference than you can imagine—one that will become radically apparent in your relationship with yourself, with others, and with those powerful spirit helpers arrayed from heaven to earth who await for you to awaken to the alliances they offer to support your soul's journey.

Getting your soul perspective in control of your life is a process of skill development. Getting that skill involves disciplined work. Few of us understand that how we look at the world depends on learning two things: how to control our own attention and where to put it. Most of us have given control of our attention almost completely away—far away from the heart that provides both a home for the soul in the body and the basic guidance system for the soul's navigation of its journey.

This book tells the story of how I came to a soul perspective in my own life. The soul's desire led to decades of meditation from both Eastern and Western traditions, years of yoga and qi gong practice, sitting in ceremony with spiritual teachers and shamans across a variety of traditions, vision questing gifted with unanticipated experiences of unconditional love and clairaudience, sweat lodges that provided a sense of community and an opportunity for emotional and physical release, medicine wheel practice that emerged into an ironically modern change map, pilgrimage to sacred mountains of the Andean Cordillera in southern Peru, and a course of cross-cultural and scientific readings that attempted to herd all of these experiences into a coherent understanding for a modern mind. Occasionally, I would find some affirmation or clue in my reading, but I found that my own direct experience continually trumped reading as a means of discovering my own soul nature.

My soul destiny is unique to me, as yours is to you. Yet, I sense that my journey revealed the shape of a fundamental soul trajectory that is common to all souls sojourning on the planet. There appears to be common terrain that all earthbound souls must navigate, along with identical stages through which soul consciousness evolves toward that more skilled soul perspective. And, with hindsight, I can see that a somewhat more direct path across this terrain was possible. I call that more direct path—the one with less meandering and backtracking than is inevitable—*the soul's critical path.*

A *critical path* is the shortest distance between two points, the sequence of dependent steps that determine the minimum time needed to carry out an operation. The *soul's critical path* is the shortest distance between the point at which the soul first touches into the dense consciousness of the body and the point at which the soul becomes fully and consciously embodied, begins to control the personality, successfully partners with the body, and then—and only then—becomes capable of an open-ended and co-creative collaboration with heaven and earth. In that collaboration lies our absolutely unique destiny.

My method is to describe what I perceive to be the core essence of this process as illustrated by the events that have marked my own soul evolution and by the frame provided by Plato's story of Er, a soldier who got a brief but powerful soul perspective by the fortuitous accident of a near-death experience on the battlefield. My story picks up where Er's leaves off, telling of gradual soul awakenings that came for me over time, as they come for every embodied soul that begins the process of remembering who it is and where it came from.

That core essence is present most strongly in a fusion of very divergent traditions that have migrated to American shores, primarily in the forms of Asian meditation and indigenous shamanic practices. Both of these huge containers provide valuable soul tools. At the same time, they do not translate easily into our own postmodern culture, one that is very different from the cultures in which those traditions arose. Yet, America provides a perfect opportunity to fuse the core essences of those traditions into a new and powerful synthesis that defines a critical path for these times.

My own experience suggests that the adoption of a soul perspective together with a sense of the soul's critical path are the most practical and efficient steps we can take to bring our souls forward amidst the cultural complexity of a postmodern world. The notion of a critical path may help you to emerge through that complexity to a new simplicity. Simple is not necessarily easy, but it remains easier than the challenge presented by trying to navigate complexity without a soul perspective. Without that perspective, we are left to navigate by means of mind, emotions, and the default personality they largely control. These were not designed to adapt to rapid change, and they are not faring well as the rate of change increases.

This introduction will set the stage for the story of a soul journey that emerges in the chapters that follow. The story that unfolds over the balance of this book is a story of that first journey. As the book ends, we find ourselves looking out over the threshold of a second journey. The first journey takes us over the terrain of our fate. The second journey is itself the life of destiny—with all of its purpose, passion and power—for which our souls ultimately make this rigorous sojourn to the planet.

Plato's Story of Er

Though left for dead on the battlefield, Er was not dead. The body had become, for the moment, inhospitable to Er's soul. Separated by the shock of an injury to the body, Er's soul awakened to find itself in a place between heaven and earth. There, in what appeared as a meadow, Er saw souls gathering.

In the meadow, souls were being prepared for joining with bodies on the earth. Er watched as each soul received a guardian angel that would assist the soul on its earth journey. The souls were then instructed to choose the kind of life each would lead. Some souls chose the mantel of power or the allure of riches in the life to come. Others chose, in Plato's telling of the story, more wisely.

That choice made, the souls were led away from the meadow. In four days time, the souls arrived at a broad and beautiful column of light that extended from heaven to earth. There, Er saw the whirling Spindle of Necessity suspended from the column of light. As souls were led beneath the Spindle, the three sisters of Fate wove the fate and destiny of each. Their fate fixed, and their destiny securely veiled, the souls were led to the River of Forgetting and instructed to drink. Er observed that some souls drank more. Some drank less. As they slept, the souls were swept away and into bodies awaiting them on the earth.

Our Own Soul Stories

From Er's time, fast forward two and a half millennia.

Each of our souls is taking a sojourn upon the earth, a brief appearance in time compared to the timeless nature of soul continuity. Like the souls that Er observed, we also drank from the River. Arriving here on planet earth, each of us has forgotten to lesser or greater degree who we are, where we came from, and why we came. Who can know who drank more and who drank less?

Either way, soul remembrance tugs urgently at the soft underbelly of our consciousness. That insistent tug is the nascent soul trying to muster enough energy and traction to move the dead weight of our forgetfulness into a momentum of soul purpose that can travel at the speed of passion. The story of that purpose has its own life force, and the nascent soul yearns to live that story. While we think we may make our own stories, it is really the other way around. There is a story in each of us, one might say, trying to find its way out, trying to shape our lives. It is a soul story.

Each of our soul stories is absolutely unique in its detail and the potential of its purpose, passion, and power. Yet, there is a universal structure to the narrative of those stories. There is a beginning, an end, and many mysterious adventures in the middle. In every story, fate holds destiny in its tight grip. The process of wrestling our destinies free from that grip provides far more drama than most of us would prefer. For every story, there is an initial set and setting—the mind-set of the surface personality that filters and attempts to organize our life experience, and the physical, cultural, and geographical setting that provides the resistance against which our stories unfold. And in every story, there is a dual question that lies at some depth below the surface personality that sits atop a slumbering soul: *Who am I, and why am I here?*

The question seldom arises directly until it has already come to us in myriad indirect ways. For example, there comes a point when we cannot resist wondering about the persistent voices in our heads, the yearnings in our chests, and the feelings in our guts. At some point, we wonder whether there is a meaning or purpose beyond the never-ending scramble for security and sustainable, nurturing relationship. Some of us use words like *soul path, spirituality,* or *personal growth*—even *I just want to have more fun* or *I want to feel better* or *I want a relationship*—like files that contain our dreams, efforts, and aspirations. All of these are questions that hint of the bigger and persistent questions: *Who am I, and why am I here?*

You know that you are a person who can feel better, who can have more fun from life, who has some important role to play, who has love to give if only someone could appreciate it. Yet the person who aspires is often also identified with the personality that feels blocked. The person who aspires may wonder what she would prefer to do if she didn't always give in to and go along with what others want. Embedded in these feelings is the soul's rather more muted voice, seeking to express its own preferences to a personality whose attention is distracted by voices and events outside itself.

Soul preferences may be as basic as *what color I like, what food I prefer, who my favorite musician is,* and *how my body wants to be touched.* Such individual preferences do not reflect the depth of the soul's nature, but they do hint at the soul's ultimate desire. For all of us, the soul's greatest desire is to combine its special gifts with a clear life purpose that is quite distinct from the dreams that our parents and a consumer culture have projected upon us, dreams that our personalities have often embraced because the dreams of the nascent soul remain hidden.

At some point your personality may experience an overwhelming soul imperative bursting forth, dislodging the personality's hold on your consciousness, long before you are able to see the shape of the personality that will eventually emerge to reflect this powerful soul force. At such times, you may feel outright diagnosable. And you may be. Diagnosis can be culture's way of imposing its story on yours, trying to pull you back from the edgy unique to the fat middle that is *normal.*

We all need some help from time to time, but the help needs to be about getting our soul story up and balanced on its own legs, so that it can overwrite the old stories of victimization and the tragic surrender to culture's preferred story. It does not help to tranquilize the soul's story. Quieting the soul's voice with pharmaceutical strength suppressants risks soul death even as careful use might create a little breathing room from the chaos of culture so that we can feel more deeply into our soul natures. Yet, it is important to remember that the pain we feel in our lives—both physical and emotional—is the soul reaching out in the only way to which the personality will finally pay attention.

The question of *identity—who am I?*—is present at every moment in our lives. It is not enough to say that I am a mother, or a woman, or a lawyer, or a Buddhist/Christian/Pipe Carrier/roller derby champion, or an addict, or a person who likes dogs. These are things that we do or feel or believe, but they do not reach so far as to describe who we *are.* And if we cannot know who we are in a very general sense (*I am a soul*), we will not find ourselves in any specific sense (*and my destiny is to . . .*). Without that soul sense, we are little likely to *choose* to face fate down and wrest our destiny from fate's tight grip.

Answering the identity question in postmodern America is quite different than in Er's time. My own eclectic soul journey may not be typical of Americans, but it is quintessentially present-day American—one that smacks of the chase to realize the American dream in the setting of the shopping mall. Amidst more than three decades of active participation in the life of a small community where I practiced law and raised a family, I also gradually gave vent to a soul desire that my conventional life could not satisfy. That desire pulled me along a path parallel to that of my more conventional life, a path that I have only in retrospect seen simultaneously as both an archetypal and absolutely individual soul journey. In time, I began to understand how the soul journey included my conventional life and was not separate from it. What I thought to be the conventional part was a critical part of my own soul evolution waged by means other than what we often put into the category of "spiritual."

During these years of parallel processing, peak "spiritual" experiences began to accumulate like stars emerging in the darkening sky of my conventional life. Yet, it was difficult to make sense out of these experiences relative to the momentum of my conventional life. I didn't recognize those peaks as my soul peeking out from beneath layers of unconscious cultural conditioning. Later experiences began to provide the information that would connect the dots into an understanding of how each experience in some way built upon or related to an earlier one, and that each was relevant to a process of soul maturation.

That evolving understanding eventually gave way to a sense of identification with my own soul, and a growing partnership between soul and body. It was as though I had dived deep and recovered pearls—each beautiful on its own—long before awakening to the notion of stringing them together into a powerful and beautiful statement of my own soul identity that could define its place within the frame of my body and personality. What was consistent and apparent throughout that time was an unyielding soul desire that pulled me forward, sideways and, it sometimes felt, backwards.

During this time, I experienced many visions. These visions occurred over a period of about eleven years. Taken together, I ultimately saw them as a process that began with various *healing* experiences. By *healing,* I mean anything that more finely tunes the receptive capacities of the body by releasing the unconsciously held trauma that holds our physical sensitivities in a defensive posture that cannot be present to the world. The process continued with *direct transmissions of information* that we can access only when our receivers have been tuned finely enough to hear that other-dimensional information despite the cultural din and chaos that surrounds us. And sometimes we tune to that other-dimensional information without the benefit of a healing because the depth of our trauma has so driven our attention out of the body that it connects on its own in the vast elsewhere. Psychologists call this latter condition *dissociation*. Sometimes, dissociation is the only form of respite that our struggling souls and bodies can find in the moment.

That same soul desire, combined with the more noisy desires of the body, also led me to the most powerful of spiritual techniques: *the intense mirroring found in intimate relationships*. The powerful mirroring of relationship provides feedback that is essential to any personal change and to integrating that change into the day to day of our lives. Ram Das quipped that relationship is the "fast path" to awakening—too hard for him, he said, with only small humor and great insight. Because all relationship—conscious or not—invites mirroring, relationship reliably provides the challenges that serve up the insights we call *awakenings*—if we are ready to receive them. If peak experiences are the occasional nights when the soul escapes to dine out on more exotic fare, intimate relationship provides the daily bread of our dining in.

This mirroring of relationship includes far more than human relationships. We are in constant *connection* with our environment, whether we are awake to that connection or not. Because of that connection, we are also inevitably in relationship with the changing elements in our environment that invite us to adapt, or else. The environment is itself an infinite variety of subtle fields that both make up and hover about the dense reality of time and space. Our relationships—conscious or unconscious—with these fields also invite the awakenings that give rise to insight. Like our human relationships, the outcomes of these other relationships constitute constant feedback that informs us whether our presence and action in the world is skillful, or not.

Awakenings invite our personalities to become aware of the presence of our souls, and to an understanding that we need more *skill* in *all* relationships—between each other, between soul and body, between body and earth, between earth and soul, and between soul and heaven—so that our relationships provide more than a series of projections, heartaches, disappointments, crashes and a tragic waste of the opportunities that this life presents. A relationship crash is just a crash unless our skill of attention renders it into a gift of insight that magnetizes a growth toward soul potential. It was in the jungle experience of the visionary plant medicines that I began to suspect that *the whole of human experience can be expressed as an exercise first in becoming aware of the inherent connection of all things, and second in creating skillful relationship* (although we routinely try to get it the other way around). As the plant medicine began to impart information, it succinctly set forth a few simple rules of relationship by which we can more skillfully navigate this rough and fated terrain in order to put our feet firmly on the path of our destiny. I share that information in the chapters that follow.

If we are to ignite the passion that fuels our own soul journeys, we have first to overcome our forgetting, restore the fullness of our attention to the soul field, attend to the process of how the soul *connects through the heart,* and then attend to how it *relates,* starting with the relationship between soul and body. Then the soul's attention can go anywhere and everywhere, and there is little more interesting, breathtaking, supportive, or powerful than that.

In sharing the story of my own journey here, it feels as though I take my place around the ancestral fire where also sat Er. Er sits in the fire circle still, where he and I will pass the talking stick back and forth throughout this book. I hope both stories will help you to learn how to ignite and navigate your own soul story.

INTRODUCTION

In this Introduction . . .

America's Spiritual Mall
The Paradox of the Mall
The Paradox of Science
A Soul Perspective
The Dangerous Imbalance of Parallel Perspectives
New Soul Challenges, New Soul Opportunities
The New American Fusion: A Stereoscopic Vision

America's Spiritual Mall

AMERICA—AND THE POSTMODERN CULTURE that is America's primary export throughout the world—largely determines both the *set* and *setting* of our soul stories and journeys. That set and setting are characterized by a spiritual confusion and distractions present nowhere more than today's America and to a degree perhaps unparalleled in human history.

America has become a literal mall of spiritual teachings, with all of the materialistic undercurrents and overtones that also define secular American consumption in general. The economic prosperity of America, and the relative openness of its popular and spiritual culture—in contrast to its increasingly conservative political, legal, and religious culture—has largely encouraged the importation of all of the world's spiritual traditions. The presence of so many choices provides an incredible opportunity for soul exploration in ways simply not possible for an individual in earlier times, as well as an opportunity for incredible confusion.

In any of the largest of America's cities, one can access every Asian spiritual practice, of which perhaps Buddhism is the most familiar. Having gotten through *vipassana* boot camp makes you a member of an exclusive club. Words like *Tai Chi, Zen* and *yoga,* along with *meditation,* have come to the front row of American vernacular. Zen and the less familiar Mahayana form have morphed into the singularly American form called *mindfulness.* This meditation technique has become the focus of much research, the sanitizing American gateway into the conventional and mainstream, and has been found to foster many positive health benefits.

The Institute of HeartMath has also morphed an ancient form of heart-centered meditation into a stress-management technique that may feel more relevant and accessible to a postmodern culture that is more assailed by stress than the conscious desire to discover compassion or one's own soul. As with mindfulness, this heart-centered technique has also been scrutinized by research sufficient to demonstrate its positive impact upon health outcomes. Similarly, Richard Davidson's research at the University of Wisconsin-Madison has demonstrated that a compassion-focused meditation technique has direct and positive effects on both the neurological system and emotional states.

xx The Soul's Critical Path

There are many other spiritual practices that hold a growing attraction for Americans. Various forms of shamanism are taught all across America, from Native American to Celtic to African and Meso- and South American. Traditional forms are morphing in response to their integration into an American culture. In America, everyone can aspire to be a shaman, never mind that shamans in indigenous cultures do not become recognized as such by the possession of a credit card and attendance at a few workshops. Few of us would choose the means by which the Q'ero of southern Peru recognize the selection of a shaman, which is to be struck three times by lightning and to survive, after which the more difficult training begins.

In America, Judaism, Islam, and Sufism are also present, along with various approaches to Christianity. Wiccan and Pagan practices are on the rise. Indeed, all of the world's religions are present here, alongside the growing demographic of "spiritual but not religious." Atheism is a strong religious force in America, devoted to the belief in scientific reductionism as the highest form of epistemology and based in the faith that absence of objective evidence is objective evidence of absence.

Medicinal plants that accelerate our efforts to break through ordinary states of consciousness—such as mushrooms, ayahuasca, and mescaline—are used in America despite a general legal prohibition that brooks only minor exceptions for sanctioned religious use. On the other hand, tobacco, also regarded as a medicinal plant in the jungle, has been poisoned and diluted with hundreds of addictive additives and is regarded, consequently, as a poison.

The spread of many of these spiritual programs and plant experiences is now made possible by workshops and retreats. For many people, these gatherings have taken the place of long-term family and ethnic affiliation with traditional religious organizations or village-based indigenous traditions. This new delivery system, aided by the marketing engine of technology, has allowed for mixing and matching of these traditions, just as I have experienced, without the requirement of identification with a particular religious or ethnic group.

While this mixing and matching encourages evolution of practice and belief, the mixing and matching also leads to melding. Melding tends to cause the very real cultural differences among these traditions to disappear. The mixing and matching also has the potential to reveal core essences present in each that are common to all—core essences that invite a new synthesis or fusion that may be available to more people in American than elsewhere. At the same time, those core essences are still largely hidden beneath persistent cultural veneers. Those cultural veneers make it difficult to penetrate to a core essence without years of diligent practice within the frame of a single tradition, making a valuable synthesis across several traditions difficult to achieve. The deep dive into a single tradition, while extraordinary and valuable in itself, may deny the opportunity to make the cross-tradition comparisons that reveal a common core essence. I suspect that no single tradition contains the rich essence that mixing of traditions offers. My personal preference and inclination has been to taste several traditions and to look for the synthesis amidst the change that is challenging those traditions.

Despite the availability of so many shifting opportunities for the exploration of traditional spiritual systems, there are challenges within the richness of that opportunity. And there is another challenging shift that is not commonly recognized—one that is also very specifically American.

The Paradox of the Mall

At the same time America has become the beneficiary of multiple spiritual traditions, it has begun to explore them in a setting entirely different than the settings that have spawned those traditions. Like our own Native American traditions, the Asian and indigenous traditions now presenting themselves to the American spiritual consumer arose entirely in cultures that were—as an everyday practical fact—*earth connected.*

America is the first country in the history of humans not to be earth connected. We have taken the last step necessary to accomplish that remarkable threshold by leaving small-scale family farming behind, a process that was substantially complete shortly after World War II. There were earlier and other forms of earth connection that preceded farming, but the family farm was the last that larger numbers of Americans experienced. Most of the family farms that have not disappeared have been effectively turned over to the control of corporations that are now global in their reach. Those corporations are destroying small-scale farming around the world—and very likely food sustainability—by focusing on the bottom line of the quarterly shareholders' statement instead of the very dangerous consequences of their policies and practices.

Even as this tragic trend is moving around the world, it happened first and most dramatically in America. Because of this, America has become a kind of laboratory that allows us to observe what happens when people are separated on a large scale from a connection with the land. While there is much being written about how this revolution of disconnection with the land is affecting health, food security, and prospects for human viability on the planet, I am aware of little written about how this disconnection affects spiritual practice.

As we Americans sit to practice our mindfulness meditation or stand to do our Tai Chi, we do so in a culture that is no longer earth connected in any meaningful, practical, day-to-day manner. Earth connection for Americans has itself become an arcane spiritual practice—something that would-be shamans and Wiccans and progressive Buddhists do, often on weekends, retreats, new moons, or the changing of seasons. I've laughed at myself for paying hundreds of dollars to a teacher to "put me out" on a vision quest—just sitting on the side of a hill for days. Of course, I'm grateful I did—the experience was life changing for me. In a city where I lived, I heard of a woman who, for a modest sum, will let her customers gather eggs from her henhouse, milk her goats, pick her tomatoes, and make soft mozzarella cheese in her kitchen before dining on her farm side deck. I think this is wonderful, but I find it ironic that such simple processes have been lost to a culture so quickly that we find ourselves buying it back from well-intentioned facilitators in bits and pieces.

I did not grow up on a farm, but I did grow up in the 1950s in a neighborhood where my elderly neighbor let me dig my imaginary fort beneath her lilac bush and eat from her garden. I played with my childhood friends from an early age in the nearby foothills of the Rocky Mountains. We rode our bikes away from adult super-vision for hours or a day at a time. We built fires in those hills to cook our Boy Scout dinners years before we were old enough to have drivers' licenses, and we let our imaginations guide our daylong treks into those hills. We grew up *in the dirt*. And the earth's dirt nurtured us and held us in its unconditional embrace. That experience is gone for most children in our industrial and technological culture, and that not insignificant fact is directly related to the rapid rise of childhood attentional and other health and emotional disorders.

Because the day-to-day agrarian connection with the earth was a reality pres-ent—in the background, as it were—for the traditions now imported to America, there is often little taught by those traditions about the importance of the daily con-nection with earth, even as those same traditions expressly honor Mother Earth in ceremonies that we dutifully learn to practice on our available weekends. But as we honor Her, we often also fail to see Her in the pavement, brick, plastic, and steel of our everyday lives. We have disconnected from the omnipresence that matter— *mater*—also represents in the lives. We live unconscious of the mater in our own bones and blood. Consequently, the teaching of meditative traditions in a culture disconnected from the earth may have a paradoxical and unintended consequence.

Let us consider the example of mindfulness meditation. This form encourages the de-enmeshment of our attention from thoughts and emotions. However, when we have pulled our attention back from the turmoil within and around us, our atten-tion does not rest in a default relationship with the nurturing environment of the earth, as more likely occurred in the Zen monasteries and Mahayana ashrams where the practice developed. In a typical American context, the attention begins to float more freely from a body whose consciousness is already dissociated from the body and the earth.

In a dissociated state, a person already feels disconnected from and unable to sense his own body. It may feel as though the consciousness is projected outside the body, and that is literally the case. Television helps to induce this state, as do alcohol and other drugs. Projection and fantasy are forms of dissociation. If we are dissoci-ated, we do not experience pain as intensely. We do not have access to our powerful bodily sensors. We do not have access to our heart's subtle guidance. We can't feel the earth beneath our feet. In a spiritual context—and it is ultimately all a spiritual con-text—we may use this dissociation to trip out in the form of "shamanic journeying" or "deep meditation," but it is still a dissociation unless the destination of those trips is skillfully connected to one's own heart-centered and body-grounded soul.

I was interested to hear recently of an emerging group within the Transcendental Mediation community of Fairfield, Iowa, that has adopted a new theme of "waking down" in an apparent acknowledgement of the ungrounding effect of the "waking up" that is the object of that common and powerful meditation form. Zen and mind-fulness can easily have the same ungrounding effect. There are teachers of mindful-ness and Zen who have incorporated the additional element of a heart or body focus of attention, but that is a step added by insightful and grounded teachers, not neces-sarily a strict application of either the traditional practice or the transitional form by which it is being brought to Americans.

While we might intentionally dissociate in order to explore the infinite realms of consciousness, that is not the usual objective of the typical American who might resort to mindfulness meditation. Dealing with stress, depression, illness, or PTSD is a more likely motivation. We know that stress is epidemic in this culture, and that its presence is an early marker for virtually all of the primary diseases with which the health care system is already overwhelmed. In addition to the growing epidemics of "physical illnesses," one in six children is taking a prescription for an attention disorder. Attention disorders, whatever else they represent, are a form of dissociation. An estimated one in five American adults has a "diagnosable mental illness," most of which is or includes depression. Chronic depression, whatever else it may represent, is a state of dissociation from what is going on in the body. PTSD, however defined, is also dissociation. Dissociation by meditation can deepen that separation, even while it improves the health markers that are negatively affected by stress.

What is unclear from a conventional psychotherapeutic view is what is dissociated from what, because conventional culture simply does not have a theory that includes the soul or otherwise explains the nature of the missing attention. As I will discuss in the chapters that follow, the indigenous peoples have a clear view on that. Trauma, a shaman would likely say, fragments the soul. I would translate that to say that trauma disinclines the body to tolerate the presence of the soul and its consciousness, preventing the soul from its necessary engagement with the body. A primary shamanic tool is to retrieve that dissociated attention and restore it to the soul and the soul to the body, so that the soul can again operate on full power—a state most people seldom if ever experience. It is not clear that mindfulness helps to heal soul-level dissociation, and it appears to me that it can exacerbate it. I am not discounting the value of meditation or mindfulness, but we do need to look more closely at how to use these valuable techniques more skillfully relative to the body.

A second example can be drawn from shamanism itself. Many Americans have embraced the practice of shamanic journeying. Until some time after the arrival of Americans and Europeans in indigenous villages, one did not find shamans holding classes on how to journey, as is now commonplace in America. Taking an out of body journey when the consciousness is already dissociated from the body does not necessarily bring the soul into a constructive relationship with the body. To the contrary, it can simply enhance the pre-existing dissociation and any troublesome psychological states that accompany it. And it is not the village shamans who are cashing in on this new American demand. There are probably more shamanic entrepreneurs than real shamans, and it is these entrepreneurs who are using the village shamans as the attraction that captures the credit card. Like corporate marketers, these folks have little motivation to watch for the side effects of what they are selling. On the other hand, while I have concern about such negatives of this new spiritual business, I also see that something of deep value is getting to America that would not otherwise have arrived. Just as is the case with meditation, shamanic journeying is a valuable tool for supporting the emergence of the soul, but it needs to be approached with some understanding of the complexities of using these techniques skillfully in a dissociated culture.

There is a flip side to the easy availability of spiritual programs in America. With those programs have come teachers that now operate in a culture unlike their own. More than one traditional guru has found that the practice which elevated and sustained him in his home culture did not protect his "higher" consciousness from crashing into the complexity of postmodern American culture, including its rampant materialism and sexuality. Sexual and financial exploitation of students by teachers is not uncommon. It is also true of "shamans" and "gurus," and it is certainly true of many entrepreneurs of spirituality.

This is not a criticism of meditation or shamanic practice, both of which I regard to be important if not essential tools for bringing attention into the heart as a means of bringing the soul into control of the personality. It is simply an observation that we must pay attention to our assumptions about the transferability of the wisdom traditions of other cultures that have now presented themselves for our "consumption."

Here is the paradox. The off-migration from American farms has contributed to the availability of labor to fuel the new American prosperity. That prosperity has afforded us the time, money, and cultural freedom to explore new spiritual avenues. Yet, the off-migration from the earth has made it difficult to get the benefit of those new spiritual programs without a much deeper and perhaps newly American understanding of how to use them.

And that same off-migration and the prosperity that has followed have been further fueled by advances in science and technology, wherein lies another paradox that affects our ability to access the smorgasbord of spiritual offerings.

The Paradox of Science

A mere hundred and fifty years ago, someone living in rural America might have identified more with the life of Er or many of today's transitional indigenous cultures than with the life of today's twenty-five-year-old. The major difference is the emergence of science and technology. In the blink of an evolutionary eye, science and technology have come into their own as very powerful forces.

The methodology of science is to separate and reduce in order to observe more finely the separate elements of a thing. The hopeful assumption of many scientists is that the ultimate nature of the thing can be understood by reduction. Because the methodology of science is limited to observing by separating, it is not surprising that science has difficulty with observing wholeness, which is the hallmark of a soul perspective. Like those scientists who have naively adopted the method of science as dogma—that there are no wholes but only parts—it is a frequent step for those of us who *believe* in science to believe also that reality is simply a pile of parts, and that everything is, ultimately, separate.

One cannot experience one's own soul by a process of separation. Whatever else a soul may be, it is defined by its direct connection to the whole of consciousness. Consciousness itself cannot be understood from a parts perspective, since it is the very fabric of the whole. Matter, which is the domain of science, is a particular manifestation of consciousness, not the other way around, although those scientists who believe in science as dogma rather than method argue just the opposite despite the absence of scientific evidence to support their position. For those who connect experientially with consciousness and without the presumption that everything is reducible, it is almost inevitable to accept the possibility that *everything is consciousness, because our direct experience with consciousness connects us to everything.* Souls operate within the frame of the whole of consciousness, which includes both matter and those realities that transcend matter. Souls can reduce *and* transcend—be and see the part, while being and seeing the whole. These are simply different motions of attention along a single continuum.

Science, by its emphasis on an "everything is parts" perspective, engages in another important and dangerous presumption, which is that consciousness and intelligence arise in the brain, rather than the other way around. It does seem that the brain is the situs of rationality and logic—the highly touted critical thinking emphasized in our educational system. Consequently, the belief that brain is the center of intelligence makes it a rational leap to conclude that intelligence and rationality are one and the same. Such a perspective, on the other hand, causes us to neglect a rigorous scientific examination of the other alternatives, including the apparent intelligence of the heart. How many people have you heard say "follow your head"?

The gold standard of scientific inquiry is the randomized double blind study. It is thought to provide *objectivity,* which is the hallmark of rationality and detached scientific observation. Such a study may tell us something about a hypothetical average human. It tells us what *might* happen if someone takes an aspirin, but tells us little about what happens when *you* take an aspirin. It might tell us whether a government program is working to achieve its intended objective or not. It might suggest whether a new heart medication is killing more people than it saves. But, while such a study might be scientific and objective, it tells us little or nothing about an individual. And there is nothing more individual than a soul and its unique design. The only way to study a soul is to *be* that soul, and the only way to be that soul is to bring our attention fully back to it.

Science can say nothing about souls. There is no objective evidence that the postmodern, scientific American mind can find to support the truth of Er's story (or put the lie to it either). Souls do not submit to science, even though soul insights often inform the process of science. Subjective experience is the only means of exploring the soul, but we have to learn to pay attention to experience it.

Our American setting has cultivated a particular *set*: a mind-set dominated by a scientific- and brain-centric perspective that—unintentionally but nevertheless effectively—tends to steer us away from the experience of consciousness. The consequences of this mind-set contribute to dissociation of consciousness from the body and its variety of expressions of intelligence that are among the many manifestations of consciousness. Our *setting* is a landscape polluted with toxins and distractions that separate us from a direction connection with dirt, trees, natural grasses and plants, clean waters, and a deep awareness of our own bodies. Bringing more dissociation to that circumstance, even with a spiritual motivation, doesn't necessarily improve our lives, much less bring our souls forward, even if it lowers the body's blood pressure.

That many scientists cannot grasp a notion of consciousness in its wholeness is not a criticism of scientific method. Science, at its shining best, is simply a perspective. Science has provided the practical means of technological advancement. Now, the insights of quantum physics have begun to offer a new language and vision that help us explore the vibratory mechanisms by which consciousness operates. However, science is not and never will be a complete perspective. American culture is confronted by the challenge of the dogmatic religion of science, which has managed to overshadow the other perspectives humans naturally have, including those of the heart, the gut, the more visual/holistic right brain, and the absolutely unique perspective of the heart-connected soul. This overshadowing almost defines America.

The paradox is simple. Science has contributed greatly to the American prosperity that accounts for the availability of so many spiritual traditions and has introduced a *quantum* language that reaches toward a broader view of reality that has stretched scientific thinking. At the same time, its overshadowing of the other approaches to consciousness diverts our attention from the very perspective necessary to use those traditions in support of our soul exploration.

A Soul Perspective

Er's story is told from the *perspective* of a soul. The perspective of a soul is not the common belief that "I have a soul," or an openness to the possibility of the soul's existence. These are mental approaches, more akin to scientific hypothesizing. The soul perspective is far more than that. It is a perspective that arises from a full-on identification: *I am the soul.* If you could hear the soul speak, its primary message would be an emphatic *I am!* A soul perspective becomes a powerful driver of behavior when that full-on identification subsumes the personality, so that our day-to-day behaviors flow directly from the soul's clear and self-aware purpose for being on the planet.

Er's story related the individual, personal *experience* of Er's soul. The personal experience of *being the soul* is not a matter of belief, or faith, but a full-on merger of the focus of consciousness—attention—into the soul and its experience. It is a *knowing* that arises only from direct experience and that has nothing to do with information that comes to us from some external source, such as books or the narratives of the experiences of other people, or from scientific studies. It cannot be objectified, nor reproduced in any lab. It is the experience from which the statement *I am the soul* becomes a direct statement of our personal truth, fully and subjectively experienced without the need for any external affirmation of that experience.

With that full identification and merger, there comes a knowing that the terrain of the body and the earth are necessary destinations for the soul on this journey. The body and earth are the partners with whom the soul will dance if the necessary preliminaries can be successfully negotiated.

In our post-modern scientific culture, this necessarily individual experience is often denigrated as *merely* subjective. By subjective, we mean *personal.* In a culture that has a preference for *objective evidence based upon scientific and detached observation*, personal experience is typically regarded as unreliable for use as evidence of any general truth. Scientists worry about their work being tainted by personal perspectives. Soul work is the ultimate in personal perspectives. The scientific search for general truths has come to trump the importance of personal truth, and it has denied to some scientists—and to those of us who have subordinated ourselves to a dogmatic scientific perspective—a conscious and personal encounter with soul.

To encounter the soul, we must bring our attention fully to it. We do that by bringing attention to the heart. Though little recognized as such, the heart is an organ of perception. There is nothing more subjective than the heart. That is its strength, not its weakness. By "heart" I mean not the physical heart, or the heart chakra, but a field of intelligence that operates by connecting, by feeling into. This is precisely the opposite of the way the mind works. The mind gathers information by disconnecting, distancing, and separating. The heart-field seems to operate as a portal between time/space, on the one hand, and the dimensions beyond time/space, on the other. It is what allows the infinite soul to come into connection with the finite body. With the soul on one side and the body on the other, the heart-field acts as a doorway through which infinity can communicate with the finite.

When it comes to living one's own life, uncovering and developing your own soul gifts, overcoming the struggle of fate, and opening the door to your own destiny, it turns out that a heart-based soul perspective is more important than scientific theories or the brain's vaulted rationality. The most effective way of dealing with dissociation is to bring attention to the heart-field, which returns the dissociated attention to the soul itself. That is why, when a shaman performs a "soul retrieval" for a client, the retrieved soul is blown into the client's heart. The shaman is restoring attention to the soul and the soul to the heart.

A soul perspective and a scientific perspective are compatible. The two offer the potential of a powerful collaboration. But, if the voice of a dogmatic, reductionist, brain-centric science dominates the scientific community and permeates American culture, then a dangerous imbalance can result. And it already has, decades ago.

The Dangerous Imbalance of Parallel Perspectives

Writing almost one hundred years ago, Sri Aurobindo—the Oxford-educated Indian freedom fighter, poet, and prodigious author of yoga philosophy—saw this challenging soul context emerging. He wrote, in essence, that the prodigious capacity of the mind to create in the external world was, even then, overpowering the capacity of the immature soul to bring attention to itself:

> At present mankind is undergoing an evolutionary crisis in which is concealed a choice of its destiny; for a stage has been reached in which the human mind has achieved in certain directions an enormous development while in others it stands arrested and bewildered and can no longer find its way. A structure of the external life has been raised up by man's ever active mind and life-will, a structure of an unmanageable hugeness and complexity, for the service of his mental, vital, physical claims and urges, a complex political, social, administrative, economic, cultural machinery, an organised collective means for his intellectual, sensational, aesthetic

and material satisfaction. Man has created a system of civilisation which has become too big for his limited mental capacity and understanding and his still more limited spiritual and moral capacity to utilise and manage, a too dangerous servant of his blundering ego and its appetites. [*Life Divine*, Sri Aurobindo Ashram Press, Pondicherry, India, Eleventh impression 1996, 1053–54].

Aurobindo died in 1950. These words were published between 1914 and 1919. He wrote long before American culture became a caricature of the trend Aurobindo earlier observed, before television and pharmaceuticals began to dominate the consciousness, before technology became the pre-eminent means of manipulating consciousness and stimulating consumption, before a heart-disconnected mind brought the study of war to a nuclear level, and before people separated so radically from the land that food had become a dangerous instrumentality in the hands of an unregulated industry. The picture painted by his commentary, if not more true now, is at least far more apparent.

Aurobindo saw the domination of consciousness by an externally oriented mind without the balancing influence of an equally skillful soul-based consciousness to be possibly fatal for humankind. America's current economic and political system—based in a notion of consumerism that demands infinite and unending growth to accommodate growing population and lifestyle expectations—will fail, and our illusions of the reliability of a material security with it. Although it only recently seemed unimaginable in the prosperous America that had become a new normal for a couple of generations of Americans, this fragile bubble is on the verge of bursting. That burst will be followed by suffering on a scale we don't want to imagine.

Reductionist science and the heart-disconnected mind that have fueled American prosperity now largely contribute to America's system failure in all of its economic and political structures. Following our off-migration from the land, in a period of about six decades, America has found and then dropped its industrial capacity, lost the capacity to grow its own food, commodified the natural resources (the forest, food, water) that belong to humans as a whole, allowed the patenting of seeds, become the primary consumer in the world, become a debtor nation instead of a creditor nation, reversed a positive trend in life expectancy, become dependent upon foreign investment, poisoned itself with processed foods and the pollution that has accompanied an unregulated agricultural and energy economy, transferred its wealth predominately to a tiny proportion of its citizens, given political institutions over to demagogues, diminished our constitutional rights, lost the capacity to educate its young despite the prodigious amounts spent, given control of our economy over to the barons of technology and finance, begun to raise our children fearfully and indoors, given our rather understandable emotional responses over to the pharmaceutical and alcohol industries, and quietly embraced pornography—itself a powerfully addictive engine of dissociation—as a partner in the drive to finance the continuing development of communications technology. We medicate ourselves and our children and imprison more adults than any other country.

I would suggest that the most immediate cause of these changes is the separation of people from farming, which is tantamount to separating people from the earth. The deeper cause and context of this separation has been the emergence of narrow-minded scientific- and brain-centric culture. The limitation of science and the culture it has spawned has been the reliance on the lens of perception found in that aspect of human consciousness that we call the *mind,* and its neglect of the lens of perception found in the aspect of human consciousness that we call the *heart,* where resides our access to our own souls.

America has lost its soul.

Soul Challenges, Soul Opportunities

We face paradoxical challenges to the soul's earth sojourn in postmodern America. Today, almost the entire spiritual wisdom of the world is laid before us like an endless buffet. Ironically, filling one's plate from this abundance is as difficult as filling it from scarcity. With this feast before us, Americans have followed our usual gustatory practice—piling our plates, sampling this and that, mixing it up, and often finding it to be more than we can digest.

The circumstance of America's immanent system failure simply suggests that we may want to eat and drink from this spiritual smorgasbord somewhat more efficiently than the typically long apprenticeship that comes with traditional approaches. If we are focused on the soul work that can be accomplished in *this* lifetime, one might no longer choose to sit at the guru's gate for years before our ardor earns us entry, or to apprentice to the shaman for a similar time—even if we can find a good and wise teacher. We must learn how to import wisdom traditions into American culture without making fast food of them and, at the same time, not get caught in unnecessary traditional practices that stop the faster forward movement of the soul emergence that our times now invite so strongly. Indeed, it is time to move forward from the system of master teachers and gurus and learn how to use the tools that allow us to teach ourselves through the resources directly available to our own recovered soul consciousness.

I know that this brief commentary seems to contain some huge negatives. For those not in touch with the soul, the rapidly emerging changes will mean more fear. Religious fundamentalism will grow upon the promise of saving "souls" for a better life after death. Fearful personalities, not souls, are concerned with being saved.

From the perspective of an individual soul, these observations are not negatives at all. The soul thrives on challenge of any flavor, and our cultural transition is simply one of them. In the mysterious and unfathomable process by which souls choose to come to the planet, the presence of a greater challenge is attractive, and your own soul may have already responded to the opportunity that now presents itself. You are here for a reason—a soul reason. American culture will provide endless opportunities for your soul in the days to come.

From the perspective of the evolution of consciousness of humankind as a whole, however, the trend remains as Aurobindo observed. It seems tragic that we humans should be the very means of our own demise, which seems quite possible now. Yet, in each of our souls resides the impulse to counter that likelihood. As Aurobindo also observed, the awakening soul responds to this crisis with "the feeling that there is no other solution than the spiritual cannot but grow and become more imperative under the urgency of critical circumstance." [*Life Divine*, 1060] In other words, while the surface personality may want to hide from the darkness that appears to lie ahead, the maturing soul is called to awaken itself through the facility of that very challenge—whatever presents itself—and to continue to look through that awakening for the means of forwarding the evolution of consciousness. We must simply do the work that is in front of us, and that is the soul's natural inclination as it gathers itself to move forward in pursuit of its own purpose.

What is in front of us is a particular opportunity presented by America's spiritual mall. We can do just as the elder Peruvian shaman Don Umberto suggested in his speech to a small gathering of Americans that I attended in 2004. "Our children will not learn our traditions," he said. "You white people need to learn them, take them back to your homes, mix and match them, and evolve them. Let the eagle fly with the condor."

We can synthesize. We can distill the essences. We can, as I heard Swami Rama suggest as he spoke of the multiplicity of spiritual traditions, eat the seeds and throw away the shells. We can, as Peruvian shamans say of the hummingbird, drink the nectar from many flowers. This is the face of the emerging and particularly American fusion of spiritual traditions into a wide open embrace of core process—a trimmed-down, streamlined process that arises from a soul perspective and stands respectfully on the shoulders of our ancestors without imposing upon ourselves the robes or feathers of their traditions.

The New American Fusion: A Stereoscopic Vision

The widespread importation of spiritual models from other cultures has not resulted in a clear way to guide the soul's engagement with its fate in American culture. I am aware that the mere suggestion that traditional spiritual models do not fully address a radically different American culture may be read to dishonor the beauty and wisdom of those traditions. Yet, it is clear to me that these traditions are quickly losing appeal, if not relevancy, for souls that must cope with an environment quite unlike those traditions. I understand that I am taking a position rather than reciting an accepted fact. I am comfortable with my own felt sense that changing times demand a new approach for growing numbers of awakening souls on the slippery slope of rapid cultural change.

The critical path approach draws upon precisely the same functions of consciousness that the traditional approaches attempt to cultivate. But there are very important differences in how I propose to address the richness of these traditions. Postmodern circumstances create for the first time the imperative of learning how to look with soul consciousness through the lens of the mind and the lens of the heart simultaneously.

America is now quickly stepping beyond a mere mixture of spiritual traditions to the possibility of a synthesis, an emerging *pragmatic, direct spiritual path*—what I call *critical path spirituality*. This new path is beyond the bounds of the guru/priest/minister/shaman system of spiritual teaching. It is about individuals breaking free, taking what is valuable, leaving the rest, and empowering the forward movement of consciousness, one soul at a time.

The challenge before us is to merge the parallel perspectives. It is not enough to look at the world through the heart alone, and far too dangerous to regard the world through the mind alone. We need to learn to see ourselves as souls, and look with soul eyes through the lens of mind and heart simultaneously.

That learning is a soul path. And on that path, there are stages.

CHAPTER ONE

THE SOUL TRAJECTORY IN
SIX PARTS AND STAGES OF CONSCIOUSNESS

In Chapter One . . .

Near Death Reveals the Soul's Presence
A Common Soul Trajectory
An Overview of the Parts and Stages
The Four Stages of Soul Competence
Summary of the Parts and Stages
A Visual Schematic of the Soul Journey

To INTRODUCE A SKELETAL STRUCTURE of the progressive stages of consciousness of both the critical path and the soul perspective that emerges from it, I'll start with an experience from the middle of my journey—one that was a critical juncture in my own soul process that I could not understand without several more years of integrating work. I believe this part of the story illustrates the kind of confusion that can arise even from a clear soul-level experience in the absence of some helpful context of understanding. With due respect for the absolute inevitability and necessity of confusion on the soul path, I sense that the understanding I am calling *a soul perspective* shortens the time that it takes to integrate powerful experience into a more skillful soul presence.

Near Death Reveals the Soul's Presence

Several years ago, I had a near death experience.

It did not come in a life-threatening way. Like so many Americans who pursue a spiritual path, I was in a workshop. Although the event that triggered my death experience was designed to create a death experience, the experience itself was a complete surprise. The year was 2003.

I was one of about six or seven people instructed to enact a deathbed scene as though it were a play. *Psychodrama* is a term associated with this process. Its purpose is to use the realm of imagination and the tool of role-playing to induce an experience that approximates reality while in a "safe mode." The idea is that, if we can get the approximate experience, we might be able to sense how we would respond to the real thing. So, the theory goes, the purpose of engaging an imaginary experience with death was to confront our real fears of death, as well as to explore the unknown that both the notion and experience of death represent.

The common usage of the word "imagination" in American culture describes something typically regarded as "not real." This belief—itself a lack of imagination—fails to grasp the larger dimensions of imagination that have been long recognized and more recently articulated by such authors as James Hillman and Stephen Buhner.

As thinking is the lens of the mind, imagination is the lens of the heart. Thinking sees by separating something into steps or parts. Imagination sees by connecting with the parts in full awareness of the whole. The heart lens of imagination provides the means for the soul to discover and navigate its destiny within a context that cannot be reduced to parts. Just as critical thinking is an acquired skill, the soul's ability to hold attention within itself and to see through the lens of the heart is an acquired skill.

In preparation for the deathbed exercise, my companions and I had spent some time writing our own obituaries and talking about personal views and experiences of death. In a "kitchen talk" exercise, we listened to our companions read our obituaries and speak of us while we lay quietly in attendance at our own "wakes." Becoming an observer of others talking about death as though it had already occurred helped to bring the prospect of our own deaths into the immediacy of the moment. (American culture encourages just the opposite, placing death into a remotely unreal future that discourages any practical preparation for death's inevitability.)

We explored the question of how we would want to have lived our lives. Did we feel satisfied with what had occurred prior to this moment? Could we leave the earth feeling that our business had been finished? Were things left in a state that felt undone? What would be the most important way to spend the time we have left, particularly when the time had become short? What emotions might attend the moment of death? Could we remain present? Were there words that needed to be said to those we were leaving behind?

As we worked to shift perspective in these ways, it was common for insights to arise, for tears to be shed, for old memories to be evoked, and for fears to surface from the places we had hidden them. Our attention became increasingly focused on the present. The "bucket list" of things to accomplish became more apparent in the moment, and then began to shorten. What was most important to accomplish began to push itself to the surface.

Yet, coming to the climax of the training—the deathbed scene itself—I felt underwhelmed. I had spent a career as an attorney, and one portion of my work was writing wills and advance directives. The experienced lawyer mind is purposely and habitually skeptical. I wasn't skeptical of the possibility that consciousness continued beyond the body and after death. I was skeptical that this psychodrama could offer a "real" experience of a consciousness separated from the body. It was, after all, "imaginary"—an indictment the rational mind of dogmatic science hands down to the subjective and personal. My own mind was not above a little dogma.

My skepticism had deepened after two prior events when I had participated in analogous attempts to journey out of the body during late-night ceremonies on the death stone at the top of the Machu Pichu village in Peru. My consciousness didn't leave the body then. What I took away was the incredible experience of two nights spent with fellow travelers doing a death chant under a full moon while indigenous shamans attempted to rattle the spirit out of the body.

In contrast, our present attempt was unfolding on a sunny morning at a retreat center in Glendale, California, without a shaman. Our own teacher was somewhere else, having imparted instructions before leaving us to our own experience. The sole stage prop was a massage table on a patio in the shade of a tall eucalyptus tree. My job, as the dying person, was to assign to each of my companions the role of a person from my life. My companions had to quickly and spontaneously assemble their scripts from the sparse information I provided. Among those roles would be a master of ceremonies. In our poly-religious culture, that could be the priest, minister, shaman, lama, sheik, guru, rabbi, best friend, family member, or other such functionary.

As the preparation was completed, the massage table became my deathbed. I chose Peter, a Canadian massage therapist with a very gentle demeanor, to be my shaman. My instruction to Peter added a borrowed piece of ritual. Our teacher, Alberto Villoldo, had spoken of traveling with his teacher to attend the death of his teacher's teacher high in the mountains. The master's students had gathered to be present at the moment of his death. In that tradition, Villoldo had said, it was customary for the eldest student to breathe in the dying exhalation of the master's breath, then to share it—student to student and mouth to mouth— until the last student exhaled it through the window of the stone hut in which the master had lived.

I had been taken by the story when I heard it, and I asked Peter to take my last breath in our drama. Even though I expected nothing to come of the process, I wanted it to be done with style and with a tip of the hat to some ritual. I genuinely wanted to give it every chance to succeed.

To the rest of my companions, I assigned particular roles. My daughter and son would be present, along with my spouse and a former spouse. I omitted my parents, who were still alive, and my sisters—feeling that I had pretty well resolved any outstanding issues with them or that I would outlive them anyway (as we so often presume). And there was one special role. I wanted someone to enact my best and first childhood friend, who died when she was thirty years old, thus creating an even more imaginary role within an imaginary play. For all of the actors and myself, the anticipated dialogue would consist of the classic deathbed fare: the *thank you*'s, *I forgive you*'s, *please forgive me*'s, and *I love you*'s. With those preliminaries done, I laid back on the table expecting only that nothing would happen and we could get on to lunch. It was now late in the week of this workshop, and I was tired.

My children came first. Each of my companions held my hand, and some stroked my face. Words were brief and to the point. Quickly, the imaginary morphed into the real. Deep feelings welled up. Sobbing followed. My tears flowed at such a volume as to cause a little choking. Within moments, I was exhausted, both emotionally and physically. I was absolutely engaged and deeply present, fully drawn into the drama.

By the time the last actor withdrew, I had quite forgotten my instruction to Peter, who shocked me into even deeper presence with a gentle kiss by which he enacted the ritual of taking my last breath. That done, he performed the shaman's critical work, using a rattle to spin my *chakras* in reverse direction. The purpose was to disconnect—at least to some significant degree—the resonate vibratory connection by which the soul field attaches to the body field. We intended to induce a soul-level dissociation. As Peter completed his duty, the California morning faded suddenly. Darkness and death seemed to overtake me. In this moment, there was no difference between the imagined and the real.

In that moment, I became aware of the presence of my childhood friend at my left shoulder. I could not see or hear her, but knew without doubt that she was there. I had never had the experience of a dead person becoming tangible to me in such a way. I had had many experiences of other dimensional presences in various ways, but never one that I had known as a person from my lifetime. Although I say "she" of this presence, I experienced no particular quality of gender nor vision of an ethereal body. I simply knew her to be the one I had known.

Together, my friend and I—"I" being the now-disembodied consciousness with which I identified naturally and immediately—left this deathbed scene and sped away. I was entirely oblivious to my other companions and gave them not a single thought. In retrospect, I think it was significant that I found it natural to identify myself as a disembodied consciousness. The alternative in this moment of dying—identifying with the body—is also possible, and possibly common.

Instantly, my friend and I arrived at a platform of sorts, as though at the top of the proverbial tunnel of light that is often identified as a central element of near death experiences. The tunnel or ramp itself was not, however, an element in my journey. There was only the presence of an intense light. In that same instant, she was gone. There was no emotion for me in this. I was completely absorbed in the immediacy of the experience.

I then became aware of being buffeted, as if by wind. The light had diminished substantially, leaving me in dimness. In another instant, I sensed that the buffeting was coming from sound, or vibration without sound. I could not hear so much as feel a chorus of voices pushing through me, as though tuning or cleansing me in some way.

Everything that happened to this point seemed to come instantly, as recognitions, and without a context of time but for the sequence in which they happened. During this sequence, I had no awareness at all of the body—my body—that continued to lie in state on that table back in Glendale. I was not there.

The wind-voices stopped. I then experienced a sense of descending, as though in an elevator, with a distinct sense that I was moving within a torus. The word *torus* describes the shape of an electromagnetic field. Viewed from the outside, it would be roughly the shape of an apple. I was moving down through the core of the field, then up a side, when the words "Did you get it?" appeared in my awareness. Although it was as clear as though I had heard words spoken in my ear, I would say that they just pushed into my mind. I was far too occupied with the narrative force of the journey itself to be writing imaginary dialogue on my own.

And I *did* get it. As soon as I heard this question, I understood that I needed to change an unresolved and self-limiting pattern of behavior in my life. The pattern involved a failure to tell the truth at a deeper level than I had previously learned to say it. I knew in that instant that I needed to tell the truth, and tell it to my spouse. And I needed to do it now. This seemed to become the most important priority in my life in this moment in time.

Immediately upon the arrival of this insight, I emerged into what I can only call a place of luminous whiteness, even though that description feels inadequate as I write it here. In that "place"—the notion of place is not accurate either, implying a time/space kind of dimension, when some other kind of dimension seemed to be the occasion of this experience—I had a sense of being home, in the deepest way that the notion of *home* is meaningful to humans. Although I could "see" nothing but the whiteness, I knew—simply *knew*—that others were present, that I recognized them in some non-specific way, and that I too was recognized and welcomed. This sense of home was accompanied by some deep knowing—an experience of connecting, of belonging, of oneness without loss of a sense of self. One might call it a homecoming of the soul that was characterized by a sense of separate identity without loss of an equal sense of connective identity with the whole. This was not a merger into a sense of oneness, but a sense of personal and individual wholeness existing within a larger wholeness.

In the midst of this experience, I knew that I had the option to stay "there" in the extraordinary comfort of an almost unbounded sense of connection. And I also knew that I had work to do back in the life I had just left, even though the nature of the work was not at all clear to me apart from a next step connected with the insight that had just arisen. I had no sense of fear or anxiety in these realizations. I did, however, have a simple desire to return to the work of my own soul that was to be enacted in the body temporarily left behind.

In the instant of experiencing and acknowledging that simple desire, I felt a rush of movement unlike any I had yet felt on this short journey, and I—"I" being the disembodied consciousness that was experiencing—pushed back into the body. The re-entry was not gentle. Think of a large airplane hitting the runway on a hot day—the kind of landing that throws passengers forward in their seats. I felt like I had landed hard upon the runway of my body.

Skidding to a stop at the end of that runway, I felt my body jerk upright, and I burst into loud and uncontrolled sobbing and laughter. My joy was immeasurable. As my eyes refocused on my surroundings, it was apparent that my companions were as surprised as I.

Of course, words cannot convey this experience to someone who has not had it, but that is not my purpose.

My purpose is to say that, when we experience ourselves as souls and begin to see from the perspective of the soul, everything changes.

A Common Soul Trajectory

It is one thing to say everything changes when we begin to see from a soul perspective. It is quite another to perceive the nature of that change in the very midst of our first powerful taste of this radically new way of looking. In the midst of this breathtaking psychodrama experience, there was no neon flashing on the back of my forehead that said *you are a soul*.

Here I was, with this incredible near death journey now on my plate. I knew it was important. I sensed in some tangible way that to deny or neglect the import of the experience would risk the death of something fundamental in my being. It had brought a new exhilaration that pulled me now toward an unknown, and it had brought an equally urgent sense of confusion. Thrown back into my ordinary, day-to-day consciousness over the next several days, I literally had no idea what to do with this experience. While the notion of *soul* was not alien or obnoxious to my thinking, I did not have a soul frame of reference to easily explain the experience, even though I was studying shamanic techniques that included the notion of "soul retrievals." My conceptual framework was simply not large enough to contain this new experience.

After I returned home, I began to research near death experiences. I found Plato's story of Er among similar accounts that can be found in the folklore and literature of most cultures. I already knew that the shaman's ability to make similar journeys is the bread and butter of shamanic practice. I found a report of surveys indicating that perhaps 15 percent of adults have had a journey of the same nature as my own near death experience—most of these the spontaneous result of an unintended encounter with the real possibility of physical death, and some the result of an intentional "spiritual" effort like my own. Many who have had a near death experience acknowledge it as the most significant one of their lives, and express hope that it never happens again. I would not wish for the real encounter with death, but I could not possibly wish away my own experience, even though it was beginning to create havoc to the relative comfort of my conventional life.

That impending sense of havoc, of course, is the purpose of that taste of our own *soulness*. It announces the great magnitude of the change that is possible if we choose to surrender our surface personalities upon the altar of change where we pray for our larger selves to appear and take charge of the trajectory of our lives.

As it turned out, this *was* a critical turning point of particular significance in my soul journey, but it was a turning point that my mind could apprehend as such only in retrospect. Afterwards, I could see that the visit to my soul home was the end of what I call Stage Three Consciousness and the beginning of Stage Four. Only in retrospect could I see that the death experience was the gift of a particularly intense taste of *soulness*—of viewing life and myself for just a few moments *purely through the eyes of the soul*—seeing through what I have subsequently come to call a *soul perspective*. Only by looking back could I see that the peak experiences that had preceded this death experience were also moments of soul seeing that came and faded, leaving important markers on a pathway that would not emerge into clearer view until the accumulation of experiences reached a certain tipping point of intensity.

The word *perspective* is derived from linguistic roots that mean *looking through*. When we look at life through the soul's eyes, we get a different view than when we do not. The familiar, ordinary American cultural reality is not one viewed through the soul's lens. The conventional view is one heavily modulated by the rational, linear brain—a brain-centric lens. There are many other body lenses, but the soul at home in the heart naturally looks outward with its own eyes through the lens of the heart.

It has taken many years for my retrospective view of the death experience to integrate with prior and subsequent peak experiences and to form up into a more constant soul perspective operating in the present. This book emerged when I could look back and see that my earlier experiences formed a pattern unlikely to be unique to me.

An Overview of the Parts and Stages

My own experience suggested to me that the terrain over which the soul's trajectory travels might be sensibly divided into six parts, along with six corresponding stages of consciousness that are roughly associated with those parts. These six parts and stages constitute what I have called the critical path of the soul.

1. PART ONE / STAGE ONE

Terrain of the Soul Journey	Stage of Consciousness	Perspective
Part One: The gathering place of souls intermediate between heaven and earth	**Stage One:** The soul knows that it is a soul and knows that it is called upon to choose another round on the planet.	The earth journey is the soul's opportunity to learn.

The terrain that is Part One of the soul journey is the "place" described by Er as the meadow.

In this gathering place, the nature of the soul's consciousness is that it knows itself to be a soul seeing directly through its own eyes. This is a soul perspective. Although a self-aware soul perspective, it is not necessarily a developed or mature perspective. Whatever the level of development, this is Stage One Consciousness.

In that self-aware state, the soul chooses a life. The Sisters imprint a fate upon that life—a fate that is not disclosed. The soul drinks from the River of Forgetting. The soul is swept away to be born upon the earth, carrying a secret that it will keep even from itself until the skillful means of discovery of that secret has been acquired. The secret is that soul's destiny and how that destiny is embedded in the soul's fate.

2. PART TWO / STAGE TWO

Terrain of the Soul Journey	Stage of Consciousness	Perspective
Part Two: The dense body field and the earth	**Stage Two:** Attention is captured by the body, held in a provisional personality, and entrained outward by culture. The soul has lost control of the ability to control its own attention.	Life is a struggle. I (the personality) am a victim of circumstances. Things that happen to me are either good or bad. The bad is my fate. I can't control my fate or emotional reactions because those depend on what happens to me. Life is out of my control unless I outsmart it.

Part Two of the terrain of the soul's trajectory is the body. Coming to the earth for the birth of the body represents the beginning, but not the end, of a process of merger. That merger first involves a mutual entrainment of the respective fields of the body and the soul to a degree sufficient to sustain life in the body. The further progress of this entrainment is not automatic. The initial stages of this entrainment are unconscious to the soul. Further entrainment requires skillful attention, which represents the work of the ensuing stages of consciousness at the soul level. If the soul experiences the body to be alien territory, that's because it is. And the body, similarly, may experience the soul as an invader.

This second stage of consciousness is characterized by the inability of the soul to control attention, thereby defaulting attention to culture's control of an immature personality—a default personality that reflects the stronger identification with the body, an attention directed outward, and an almost total absence of awareness of the soul. Modern culture takes advantage of that opportunity intentionally, mercilessly, and skillfully. In this environment, particularly without the presence of a nurturing connection with the earth, the surface personality often feels out of control. For the personality that arises from this preliminary merger of soul and body in a challenging environment, this is the stage of victim mentality and an engagement with the external world that excludes the inner. Dissociation, depression, and a deeply felt sense of disconnection are common as the personality finds itself unable to make sense of the world or navigate skillfully in it.

3. STAGE THREE / PART THREE

Terrain of the Soul Journey	Stage of Consciousness	Perspective
Part Three: The terrain includes the body and the earth, but also includes the other dimensions beyond time/space. There is a move from the exclusively external to include the internal.	**Stage Three:** A battle for control of attention begins, with culture on one side, and the nascent soul on the other. The soul is now working, even below the level of conscious awareness, to capture control of the attention that has been taken by the personality and culture during the soul's forgetfulness.	Life remains confusing even as a sense of purpose has begun to form. I begin to shift from seeing everything as good or bad, to seeing what happens as *just is*. Reactivity begins to diminish as I learn to reclaim the projections that are the basis of my victim perspective.

Part Three of the terrain has now expanded in the same way that the soul's awareness has also begun to expand. The soul is aware not only of the density of its body but also of the heaven dimensions that call out to it, helping the soul to awaken and emerge. We may feel these as awakenings—stirrings, intuitions, knowings, and peak "spiritual" experiences.

Within Stage Three Consciousness, small awakenings may occur many times until they form the critical mass sufficient to shift from a personality perspective that excludes the soul to one that begins to contemplate the presence of the soul. Even though the ultimate work of the soul involves a full partnership with the body, with attention in the control of the soul, this preliminary part of the soul work is about remembering itself. This step carries the attention back away from the body—including the its thoughts, feelings, and sensory attachments—to a remembrance of the fundamental sense of connection that is the mature soul's natural state.

Like my own near-death experience, there is a return to a consciousness of the heaven dimensions. For some religions, that return would be the end of the journey and possibly—from some perspectives—the end of a punishment that the earth journey has represented. But from the soul perspective that I am suggesting here, this gradual return to awareness of the heaven dimensions and the increasing access to "peak" experiences are only a preparation for the next stage. Stage Three Consciousness is about re-cognizing something we've known, but from a much different perspective. In that remembrance, we know heaven for the first time from the soul's perspective of being in the body. We begin to acquaint ourselves with the body from the perspective of the soul's connection to heaven. Remembering that we are souls that left heaven allows us to get to work on the question of why we left that place and came to the earth journey to work in an unfamiliar body. This remembrance may occur in a dramatic manner, as occurred for me with the near death experience, or in the variety of ways we will discover as we begin to focus on achieving a soul perspective. With this remembrance restored firmly in the soul's consciousness, the soul is ready to move forward to the deeper work of embodiment.

In short, Stage Three Consciousness involves the process of learning how to control attention, learning how wrest it from the grasp of the body and culture, placing that attention in the heart-field where the soul's awareness of itself is cultivated, and ultimately shifting identity from the personality to the soul.

4. PART FOUR / STAGE FOUR

Terrain of the Soul Journey	Stage of Consciousness	Perspective
Part Four: Anywhere that the empowered soul now directs its attention, including the body field, the other dimensions, or the soul itself	**Stage Four:** The soul has now captured control of attention and is able to direct attention, with some effort, to itself, to the body, and to other dimensions that contain information for the soul's further journey, setting the stage for learning how to engage more deeply with each of those destinations.	Life and its challenges are neither good nor bad, nor "just is." Life's challenges are now a gift of opportunity for soul development. "I" is now characterized increasingly by my identification with soul rather than with the personality. The soul now assumes responsibility for creating a partnership with the body in the service of the emergence of soul destiny. I no longer project responsibility for my fate or destiny on everything and everyone else. I am no longer a victim.

The peak experiences encountered during Stage Three Consciousness now provide meaning for our day-to-day experience of life in Part Four of the journey. While the terrain of Part Three and Part Four is the same, our experience with it becomes more intentional, intense, and skillful during Stage Four Consciousness. My landing onto the runway of my body was a second landing within the same lifetime—a second coming of the soul in a moment of awakening that begins a purposeful effort by the soul to partner with the body in service of soul's work.

This fourth part of the trajectory is less familiar in our culture, or in any culture for that matter. Aurobindo made it his life's work to talk about its beginning and its potential for bringing consciousness to the very cells of the body, even as he acknowledged that he did not accomplish it. This is the stage to which the notion of Tantric practice—*Vajrayana*—is introduced even though its potential is explored only in Stage Five. In Stage Four Consciousness, we begin to use the soul's growing control over attention to discover and engage the variety of dimensions of reality, including the fields of body, earth, heaven, fate, destiny, and the soul itself. Stage Four also represents a looking back upon the prior stages as we identify and resolve the dysfunctional patterns that have blocked the soul's emergence. So Stage Four represents the time of healing the body-based consequences of a victim perspective and developing the skills of soul attention, both of which are necessary to power the soul toward its destiny.

5. PART FIVE / STAGE FIVE

Terrain of the Soul Journey	Stage of Consciousness	Perspective
Part Five: The body is now the temporary home base of the soul as it explores the density of time/space in the context of its connection with the other dimensional fields that provide constant support for the soul journey.	**Stage Five:** The soul's ability to focus attention grows as it goes increasingly into the other dimensions, and as it explores the density of matter. The soul's control of attention is no longer simply conscious and intentional, but increasingly automatic and, one might say, becoming more *skilled*.	Life is often joyful and full of energy, yet even more challenging in new ways. The soul's work is at the edge of the evolution of consciousness through the expression of its own purpose through the power of the body and the passion of the heart. I identify both with the whole of consciousness and with my particular soul role as a co-creator of the play of consciousness.

The terrain remains cosmic, including every possible field that soul consciousness can visit, but the focus is upon deepening the soul's relationship with the body and earth, which is the frontier of human conscious. We have called the stage that follows death the frontier, but that is only because we have failed to see the frontier that lies more immediately before us in this lifetime. The death stage is well traveled, but the exploration of the body/earth fields by a soul fully grounded in the heart with skillful control of attention is the very definition of the frontier of human consciousness. This is the exploration that we have come to do. We cannot leapfrog over the earlier stages and start our work here. We must all pay our dues and gain admission to Stage Five by working through the prior stages.

6. PART SIX / STAGE SIX

Terrain of the Soul Journey	Stage of Consciousness	Perspective
Part Six: The bridge between body and the heaven dimensions that forms upon the death of the body	**Stage Six:** If the soul has managed to control attention, then this is a direct and smooth transition. If the soul remains in Stage Two or Three Consciousness, the transition is more complex because of the personality's confusion about the process of death.	Death is a transition back to a self-aware soul state, although that remembrance may not occur immediately, and a soul confusion that occurs during life may persist for some time beyond death.

Part Six terrain is the short bridge to the heaven dimensions, to which we journey upon death without prospect of return to this body. Stage Six Consciousness is a wide-awake approach to the transition of dying. All of our preparation for this transition occurs in earlier stages of consciousness as the skill of attention and the experience of using it develops and matures. That maturation may define our ability to focus attention into the death transition itself. Without that preparation, a transition from body to the heaven dimensions will occur, but it may occur in the midst of an earlier stage of consciousness. Many people experience this transition from a consciousness that is characterized by Stage Two Consciousness, a lucky few in Stage Three, fewer in Stage Four, and a smaller number in Stage Five. I suspect from my reading and the felt sense that is emerging in me that coming to Stage Six from Stage Five may present other opportunities, but that is beyond the scope of this book.

The Four Stages of Soul Competence

There are four stages, my young Pilates teacher said, in learning a new body-based skill. Bringing soul into collaborative partnership with the body is the ultimate body-based skill.

I found her description of the stages of learning Pilates a helpful way of looking at the skill progression required of the soul in its effort to partner with the body and take control of attention back from culture and the personality. Her description comes from a learning sequence that emerged several decades ago of unknown origin, although variously attributed to Abraham Maslow, Noel Burch, and others. Wikipedia lists it as the *Four Stages of Competence.* There is an interesting correspondence to what I have identified as soul consciousness stages Two through Five.

- **1) Unconscious/incompetent:**
  Before coming to Pilates, I had heard of the program but certainly didn't know how to do it or even what it looked like, so the whole idea of how it worked laid outside my awareness (unconscious). My body couldn't comply in the moment even if I had some idea about it, so I did not have the skill to do it (incompetent).

  In Stage Two Consciousness, when the soul has forgotten itself and entered into the density of the body/mind field, it is unconscious of the fact that it is a soul in a body and that it has chosen this life as an opportunity to learn a lesson. Without the ability to skillfully control attention and bring it to the soul's agenda, the unconscious soul is simply tossed about by fate, and the struggle commences. The soul is both unconscious and incompetent.

- **2) Conscious/incompetent:**
  Now I've shown up for the Pilates class. My intention is to learn, and I'm motivated, even though I'm a little unsure if this program is for me. I watch my teacher demonstrate the positions and movements, so I have some idea of what I'm supposed to do, but I can't do it yet.

  In Stage Three Consciousness, there has been an awakening of the mind/body field to the idea of the soul, if not its presence. At the level of the personality, I'm beginning to get the idea of a soul, but my own soul doesn't know how to overcome the momentum of my immature personality. The soul is beginning to be conscious, but is still incompetent when it comes to controlling the personality.

- **3) Conscious/competent:**
  Now that I have practiced the Pilates movements for several months, I can begin to feel my body dropping its resistance, leaving its old habits, and finding strength and fluidity in the new movements. I know I've reached a new stage in both my collaboration with the body and its response to my intention and agenda, and I'm feeling excited about how I'm feeling. Intention and practice are starting to come together.

  In Stage Four Consciousness, the soul has managed to gain a modicum of control over attention, bringing attention increasingly to the heart, the soul itself, and the body, as well as the beyond dimensions. There is substantive and observable progress in moving along the soul trajectory. This is a stage of both extraordinary exploration of new experiences and attention skill development in which the soul gradually learns how to control attention within the body field and beyond it. Old habits of behavior and thinking are addressed and left behind. There are new and extraordinary "peak" experiences that occur during this time. The soul is both conscious of itself and competent in moving its agenda forward, at least to a point.

- **4) Unconscious/competent:**

After a year or two of practice, I have persisted with the Pilates program to a point of preliminary mastery (Disclosure: This isn't true; I haven't accomplished this with Pilates and am using this as an example only. I know that the generality of it is true from playing tennis and riding my bike). The body is now strong enough to partner with my intention, offering exploration of the territory of the body in far greater depth. I no longer have to think about it, and my intention quickly translates into movement. It is as though the body and I are one, ready to explore new ways of strengthening the body and stretching the mind together.

In Stage Five Consciousness, the soul now has effectively recovered control over attention. The attention automatically moves in accordance with the soul's agenda, which is about exploring the frontiers of consciousness with the soul's own unique gifts. I no longer have to think about it. In that way, the soul is highly competent, but its process is now able to operate unconsciously, below the level of thought. Imagination powers the movements.

Summary of the Parts and Stages

Putting the parts and stages of consciousness model together with the stages of competence model, the summary in chart form looks like this:

Terrain of the Soul Journey	Stage of Consciousness	Perspective
Part One: The gathering place of souls intermediate between heaven and earth	**Stage One:** The soul knows that it is a soul and knows that it is called upon to choose another round on the planet.	The earth journey is the soul's opportunity to learn.
Part Two: The dense body field and the earth	**Stage Two:** Attention is captured by the body, held in a provisional personality, and entrained outward by culture. The soul has lost control of the ability to control its own attention.	Life is a struggle. I (the personality) am a victim of circumstances. Things that happen to me are either good or bad. The bad is my fate. I can't control my fate or emotional reactions because those depend on what happens to me. Life is out of my control unless I outsmart it.

Part Three: The terrain includes the body and the earth, but also includes the other dimensions beyond time/space. There is a move from the exclusively external to include the internal.	**Stage Three:** A battle for control of attention begins, with culture on one side, and the nascent soul on the other. The soul is now working, even below the level of conscious awareness, to capture control of the attention that has been taken by the personality and culture during the soul's forgetfulness.	Life remains confusing even as a sense of purpose has begun to form. I begin to shift from seeing everything as good or bad, to seeing what happens as *just is*. Reactivity begins to diminish as I learn to reclaim the projections that are the basis of my victim perspective.
Part Four: Anywhere that the empowered soul now directs its attention, including the body field, the other dimensions, or the soul itself	**Stage Four:** The soul has now captured control of attention and is able to direct attention, with some effort, to itself, to the body, and to other dimensions that contain information for the soul's further journey, setting the stage for learning how to engage more deeply with each of those destinations.	Life and its challenges are neither good nor bad, nor "just is." Life's challenges are now a gift of opportunity for soul development. "I" is now characterized increasingly by my identification with soul rather than with the personality. The soul now assumes responsibility for creating a partnership with the body in the service of the emergence of soul destiny. I no longer project responsibility for my fate or destiny on everything and everyone else. I am no longer a victim.
Part Five: The body is now the temporary home base of the soul as its explores the density of time/space in the context of its connection with the other dimensional fields that provide constant support for the soul journey.	**Stage Five:** The soul's ability to focus attention grows as it goes increasingly into the other dimensions, and as it explores the density of matter. The soul's control of attention is no longer simply conscious and intentional, but increasingly automatic and, one might say, becoming more *skilled*.	Life is often joyful and full of energy, yet even more challenging in new ways. The soul's work is at the edge of the evolution of consciousness through the expression of its own purpose through the power of the body and the passion of the heart. I identify both with the whole of consciousness and with my particular soul role as a co-creator of the play of consciousness.

Part Six: The bridge between body and the heaven dimensions that forms upon the death of the body	Stage Six: If the soul has managed to control attention, then this is a direct and smooth transition. If the soul remains in Stage Two or Three Consciousness, the transition is more complex because of the personality's confusion about the process of death.	Death is a transition back to a self-aware soul state, although that remembrance may not occur immediately, and a soul confusion that occurs during life may persist for some time beyond death.

A Visual Schematic of the Soul Journey

In short, the potential of this journey is that we jump "down" from heaven, hopefully recover from the fall, do the work of waking up by which we find our way "upward" to the experience that refreshes the memory that we came from heaven on purpose, do some wide-ranging healing and practice with our newly growing soul consciousness, then focus that awakening consciousness back down into the body and the density of matter as far as we can with the help of the other dimensional fields (frequency encoded with information), all before the soul leaves the body and returns to heaven—a down, then an up, then another down before the last up when the body dies. A picture of that trajectory might look like this (the numbers refer to the six stages of consciousness):

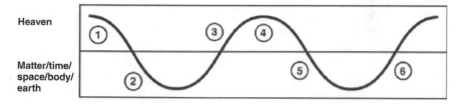

Associating labels with a line drawing doesn't give you a meaningful experience. Nevertheless, these conceptual tools help to organize what is otherwise chaotic and constantly moving information into a framework that may be helpful until your own internal territory is familiar and your movement within it becomes increasingly intuitive. The linear map helps a linear mind—and we need that linear mind even if it's a mistake to let it rule our lives—to chart some progress over longer time frames than a moment or a day. More importantly, it may help the linear mind open to a partnership with the soul through the heart.

Although it may be helpful to have a kind of rough visual of this up-and-down process divided into parts and stages, such a schematic is far too simplistic and linear to be an accurate representation of the progression of the soul in a day-to-day way. It is, after all, only a map; it is not the territory. And, even though the map shows an idealized trajectory in the form of a critical path, we sometimes stand still, hesitate, go backwards, or sideways, and forget what we are up to. Even if I am living mostly in Stage Four, I may spend a particularly difficult week in Stage Two until my partner reminds me that I have regressed.

None of us is completely in Part Two/Stage Two to the exclusion of Part Three/Stage Three. Within each stage, there is a beginning, middle, and emergence into the beginning of the next. When I speak of being in one stage or another, it is really more accurate to say that the stage represents the nature of challenges with which our consciousness is faced at a particular time. To say that we are in a particular stage of consciousness is simply to say that a particular form of identity and relationship with attention is a predominant, though not exclusive, state of consciousness at a particular point in time. We routinely go back and forth between stages in particular moments, but the trend—if we persist—is to move in an arc that has identifiable benchmarks, such as the parts and stages that I am identifying here.

The signs I'm posting along the way—*parts* and *stages*—are ways of marking the milestones on the journey by saying "this is different than that," "there's a direction to the journey," and "there's a purpose embedded in this experience." Noting milestones allows us to mark a position or sense a movement and understand that something a little different is significant even if it is subtle. If we were talking about a roadmap laid out on the geography of the earth, it would be easier to see. It's more challenging to talk about consciousness. The tools are metaphor and similes, feelings, experiences, knowings, and partial understandings that we abandon when we get better understandings—much tougher territory to navigate than learning math or driving the Interstate.

Our ultimate spiritual work on this journey is to get soul consciousness into the body and become the agents of consciousness through which heaven collaborates with earth to co-create at the edge of the evolution of consciousness itself. The challenge is not merely to experience consciousness beyond the body in the heaven dimensions, but to bring it into the body and to experience it fully there—here, now. No one knows where that process will lead. That is both its delight and challenge. There may be spiritual work beyond this journey, but we won't likely know what that is until we have lived this one out.

Now, to the details of each Part and Stage, starting with more of Er's story of what the souls experienced in the gathering place that prepared them for their earth journey.

CHAPTER TWO

In Chapter Two . . .

Er's Story of the Fates
Stage One Consciousness
The Soul Perspective
The Difference Between Fate and Destiny
The Spindle: How Destiny Is Hidden in Our Fate
(and How an Astrological Psychology Can Help Find It)

Terrain	Stage of Consciousness	Perspective
Part One: The gathering place of souls intermediate between heaven and earth	**Stage One:** The soul knows that it is a soul and knows that it is called upon to choose another round on the planet.	The earth journey is the soul's opportunity to learn.

Er's Story of the Fates

ER TOLD OF HOW SOULS emerged from both above and below into a meadow that was the staging area for the souls' impending earth journey.

Those that came from earth showed the wear and tear of their earth journey, while those that came from heaven were free of the grime and dust of toiling on the earth. All were grateful to arrive here, and there was a greeting among souls that reflected long acquaintance.

The souls remained in the meadow for seven days, after which they were led upon a journey of several days. On the fourth day of their journey, they saw a pillar of light that extended from heaven through the earth. The light included the colors of the rainbow but was more luminous. It took another day of travel to reach the pillar itself. Arriving there, the souls could see that the pillar held the heavens and earth together.

Stretching down from the light's source was the spindle of Lady Necessity. The whorl on Necessity's spindle consisted of eight concentric hollow half-globes. These half-globes spun in their own orbits, some opposite to the others, and at different speeds. Er related that each of the orbiting whorls was the vehicle for a Siren. Each Siren emitted a single pitch, and the eight together made up an harmonious scale.

No longer familiar to most Americans, a *spindle* is used for creating a yarn from animal or plant fibers. The spindle is a stick. One end of the stick may have a hook, and the other end is inserted through a disc called a "whorl," weighting the spindle so that it can be spun like a top. By Googling "whorl spindle," you can find a modern demonstration of a spindle at work on YouTube, and you will find numerous pictures of a variety of the bottom whorl spindles that furnished the analogy for Er's mythical spindle. Er's spindle, however, had a bottom with multiple orbits.

Arriving in the meadow where the spindle had come into view, the souls were instructed to choose a life from many different possible lives offered them. The souls were warned that they themselves were responsible for the outcome of the life chosen. A soul could choose a life as a man or a woman, or as an animal. The lives available to choose were of all conceivable kinds.

Er watched as the souls chose their lives. Some chose without considering fully what might be the consequences of the choice. Many chose based upon the habit of former lives. Others chose more wisely, taking into account the lessons of a prior earth journey. In any event, the choice was irrevocable. The life, once chosen, had to be lived out.

When all the souls had chosen, each was led before the Fates. The first was Lachesis, whose name means "she who alots." In the encounter with Lachesis, souls each received a guardian angel, or daemon. The guardian was to follow the soul throughout its life on earth to assist the soul to live out the life it had chosen.

This done, the guardian led the soul to Clotho, whose name means "weaver." The souls passed under her hand and the orbits of the spindle, which wove the fabric of the life chosen by the soul. With that, the soul was led before Atropos, whose name means "implacable." Atropos made the web woven by Clotho fixed and unalterable.

Then the souls were led to the Plain of Oblivion, through which ran the River of Forgetting. The souls were instructed to drink. Some drank more. Some drank less. Upon drinking, the souls fell asleep. Then, amidst an earthquake and thunder, the souls were swept away to bodies being born upon the earth.

Stage One Consciousness

When the soul emerges into the gathering place, the soul experiences itself as a soul. It recognizes other souls as souls. Stage One Consciousness is the soul's temporary remembrance that it is a soul. It holds that awareness for this preparatory time in the meadow and beneath the spindle. It forgets that it is a soul at the River. The forgetting, in turn, is the beginning of the setup that contains the soul's lesson.

In Stage One Consciousness, the soul may not have the big picture yet. Those souls that begin to get the lessons of prior journeys may make wiser choices when they pick the manner of life that will form the soul's experience in the next journey. A wiser choice does not mean that the life to come will be either more or less significant, or even less difficult.

There are two important implications of Er's story at this juncture. The first is its suggestion that all of us come to the planet as souls who have come to the planet to learn some lesson in the life we are now living. That is the very first step in getting a soul perspective. The second step is found in the symbol of the spindle. The orbits of the spindle represent the imprint upon our lives that we associate with the position of the planets and stars at the time of our birth. The information found in that timing is the domain of astrology. The implications of Er's story, then, are that we need to see

ourselves as souls and that we can find hints as to our fate and destiny in our astrological charts.

The Soul Perspective

What does it mean to experience a soul perspective? It means that I *feel* myself first
and foremost to be a soul. As a soul, I *know* that *I am a soul*—a certainty different
than belief or faith that I am a soul. I know that I have come to the planet to learn a
lesson, live out a particularly unique possibility in the infinite realm of consciousness, and contribute to the evolution of consciousness in that way. There is a setup
that is beyond our understanding that has set this process in motion. The setup—
Hindu/Buddhist culture calls this *karma*—is paradoxical. Lessons are hidden in
experiences to which we are drawn without any hint of what the lesson is before the
experience is encountered. Struggle is not itself an inevitable circumstance of life.
Challenge is the circumstance of a life set up as an opportunity for learning. Struggle
is our unskilled response to challenge when it fills us with a sense of being overwhelmed. Suffering is the emotional face of struggle. Neither struggle nor suffering
is inherent or necessary to a human life. Challenge is both inherent *and* necessary.

From a soul perspective, challenge is the container holding a hidden gift that
will be revealed only when the challenge is embraced and the gift unwrapped. The
lessons hidden within our fate amass the wisdom that is the key to transcending the
perception of struggle. Challenges are the very substance of an invitation to seek the
source of the suffering in our misperception of who we truly are. We can accept the
invitation, or not. If we accept, we can evolve toward the person our souls destine us
to be. If we don't, both our challenges and our suffering will continue, and perhaps
increase. That is a central message of those many people who have transcended
unconscious states and fostered the journey of their souls along their respective individual paths. It is one thing to believe these notions. It is quite another to know this
as the truth of our own experience.

The Difference between Fate and Destiny

The notions of fate and destiny are often confused one with the other. There is little
more important in the understanding of the soul's journey on the earth than the difference between the notions of "fate," on the one hand, and "destiny," on the other,
and what it means that the web woven for the soul's earth life is "unalterable." These
three terms form a foundational construct for the soul perspective.

Fate represents the circumstances that have been programmed into our lives
from the moment of our birth. We are born into a particular family. We are born into
a particular gender. We are born into a particular culture at a particular time in
human history. We are born with particular genetic propensities and physical qualities. We are born with particular strengths, weaknesses and personalities, as will be
reflected in our astrological charts. It is fate that determines that you have been born
as a female into circumstances that result in your becoming sexually abused. It is fate
that determines that you have been born as a male in a family who presides over a

financial fortune accumulated over generations. Fate determines the color of your hair and the likely timber of your voice.

Fate is more than that. Within the setup orchestrated for souls will be an unfolding set of circumstances with which we are confronted. These circumstances will include relationships with particular kinds of people who embody the very qualities which we must confront in ourselves in order to overcome our fate and learn particular critical lessons. An adult who was a victim of childhood abuse will be confronted with other people who will perpetuate the abuse until the victim learns to choose into more functional relationships. An adult who is born into wealth will be confronted with continuing opportunities to learn how wealth fails to satisfy the soul's own yearnings.

What does it mean that Atropos has made this setup unalterable? It means that we will be confronted with the painful challenges not only of our original circumstances, but others that follow upon them. When we experience pain, we can be assured that fate is speaking to us. There is a lesson in the circumstance that gives rise to pain. The circumstance must be faced, and the lesson elicited in order for the pain to stop. The pain is programmed to push the soul to come forward to discover the lesson. If we evade one circumstance that fate has weaved into the fabric of our life without learning the lesson contained in that circumstance, another painful circumstance will take its place. There truly is no escape from fate's pain other than to face it, ferret out its lessons, and move on from there. Fate is the door through which we have to pass to enter into our destiny. Without learning the lesson embedded in the challenge which is our fate, we cannot gain access to the destiny that launches itself from that lesson. The energy that is embedded in the persistence of the fate needs to be released to fuel the launch of destiny.

Fate is a process that must be honored. We must dive into it experientially at every level. We must recover from our soul amnesia. We must embrace the challenge as the very source of the answer we seek. We must avoid the temptation to let our attention dissociate from the suffering and the very body that is the field of the soul's work. Souls must continue earthward, rather than escape to the soft arms of heaven whence they came. We must look inward to find the meaning of the outward, and downward, so to speak, to find the meaning of the upward. We must be willing to embrace the mystery—to participate in its working without any promise or hope of an ultimate understanding of the mystery. More than anything else, we must seek out and welcome our own soulness, whatever that may be. If we persist, the struggle will become a challenge, and the challenge will yield a gift.

Destiny is what follows our getting the gift of the lesson. Destiny is more open-ended than fate. A soul is a field encoded with information that is entirely unique to each soul. That information contains not only the fate to which the soul is magnetized, but the potential that the soul might achieve. The potential is defined not in terms of a fixed outcome to one's life, but in terms of how a particular soul's strengths, combined with the wisdom it has gleaned from its fate, can emerge as a creative force in the universe. The soul's destiny represents a combination of the soul's natural gifts and its acquired gifts, activated by a proactive choice to follow the passion that the now awakened soul ignites by its presence in the heart and partnership with the body.

Was it my destiny to become a lawyer? No. It was my fate, a pathway rich with challenges and lessons to be learned. I would have learned similar lessons from any other profession I might have chosen. Even within fate, we can make choices. The personality and soul always retain freedom of choice, and the fate will adapt challenges to meet those choices. You can't, it is often said, avoid your fate. Fate follows us until we turn to face it and embrace the lessons fate offers. It is fate's persistence that is unalterable.

Destiny is not unalterable, nor is it inevitable. Destiny is entirely a matter of the choices we make. If we choose to face the circumstances of our lives with the information gained by looking through the lens of the heart, we will be magnetized to the opportunities that contain the highest potential for the particular unique qualities that our souls have brought to this life. My destiny began to unfold as I focused my soul in the field of the heart and allowed my soul nature to use the heart's ability to connect with those opportunities that held the most resonance for that soul desire. For me, that desire has led to the experiences that yielded the idea of a soul perspective and a construct I have called the soul's critical path. There was nothing inevitable about this destiny, but it is the one to which my passion has called me—a passion that emerged from the marriage of the body and the soul in the field of my heart. Although the passion for that destiny spoke to me through my heart, I still had to choose it.

Without freedom of choice, the entire notion of lessons would be meaningless. Whether we make a choice from ignorance or wisdom, we are entitled to make it. And we have complete responsibility for the consequences of that choice. We can choose to evade our fate. We can choose to numb to the pain that carries the sleeping soul's message. American culture deeply encourages our numbing to the pain.

Do we have to attend the school of fate for a lifetime in order to discover what our fate was, in retrospect, as our fate gives way to the wisdom at life's end?

No. There are ways to do otherwise, the foremost of which is to learn to control our attention and learn to place it in the soul embodied within the heart-field. And Er's story contains the clue to another important aid, which is an understanding of the spinning orbs of the Spindle of Necessity. Plato regarded it as important, or he would not have repeated it in such detail.

The Spindle: How Destiny Is Hidden in Our Fate
(and How an Astrological Psychology Can Help Find It)

The souls passed under [Clotho's] hand, Er said, *and the orbits of the spindle, which wove the fabric of the life chosen by the soul.*

If Plato's story of Er's has any value at all, one of its central messages is that we can look to skilled astrologers for themes in own lives that comprise a story of how our fate may emerge into destiny. Over thousands of years, astrologers have associated particular habits, attitudes, passions, and behaviors with planetary positions calculated with mathematical precision in relation to the moment of birth. It is apparent that skilled and intuitive counselors are able to use the information produced in that way to explain unique themes that exist in the lives of individuals. Some astrologers observe in these themes an *evolutionary* potential in each of our lives—the opportunity to move from a posture of struggle to a position of strength. The passage from fate to destiny is such an evolution. One could say that penetrating the dark corners of our lives is the challenge presented by our fate, and that illuminating those corners brings us to a sense of our destiny.

The skillful interpretation of an accurate astrological chart is a mirror that reflects the personal issues that one is challenged to investigate and the personal strengths and gifts that cannot emerge into their destiny without exploration and resolution of those personal challenges. Looking in this mirror tells us something of how the Fates have woven *our* fate.

I have been careful, in the foregoing paragraphs, to sprinkle words of qualification about the interpretation of an astrological chart, such as *intuitive, gifted,* and *skilled.* The progress of the ancient art of astrology is not unlike any other human enterprise. In recent decades, astrology has become computerized and therefore easy to commercialize, just as air travel has made indigenous shamanism and Asian meditation more amenable to entrepreneurs who would market these other soul tools. Anyone can buy a computer program with canned interpretations that will sound familiar to the person who is the subject of the chart. However, the gift of an evolutionary astrology is not so easily elicited. In order for it to work, the astrologer who provides the reading also needs to employ a soul perspective, and to mirror that perspective back to the client skillfully in terms of the client's own life themes found in the birth chart.

Stephen Arroyo is a well-respected author of several books on astrology. He does not see himself primarily as an astrologer, but as a counselor who uses astrology as a tool for his clients. His books emphasize how astrology can bring a positive and cosmic perspective to the client's issues that the typical psychological perspective cannot.

Arroyo argues that astrology should be modernized into a more simple language that can be used as a tool to be employed in service of the soul's journey. His position is parallel to my own critical-path approach that would simplify and essentialize spiritual work that remains caught in the arcane language of cultures quite different than our own. In his 1989 book, *Chart Interpretation Handbook,* Arroyo essentially suggests that astrology offers the opportunity for an individual to see oneself as a unique individual, while at the same time seeing oneself in the large scheme of human existence that a soul perspective provides:

> By placing the human being in a cosmic frame of reference, astrology has a unique capacity for re-attuning a person's consciousness to his or her essential nature, and encouraging a depth of self-knowledge which is profound. No other theory or technique that I know of can illuminate human motivation or the quality of individual consciousness or experience so clearly, simply, and accurately. If astrology is utilized correctly, there need be no overlay of complex language or theory; it can just be a simple explanation of cosmic factors and life energies operating within and through the individual.

Arroyo argues that the soul counselor's job is not to give advice, but information. An individual must make his or her own choices regarding the wisdom of a subsequent action, because the opportunity for soul growth inheres in that very choice and its consequences. Following the advice of another person guts personal responsibility. The soul must choose its own way, but getting a big picture of the central themes in our lives—how our challenges and our strengths manifest in our personalities and behaviors—helps us to see the faint pathway that is the soul's first look forward.

For example, I have had a life-long tendency to hold attention in my mind and to identify with my thoughts. It is a common form of dissociation. A quick look at my own birth chart would reveal a propensity to over intellectualize. That would seem to be a problem. Yet that tendency is a reflection of a mental capacity that also serves me, underwriting both my professional life and my spiritual understandings. My own chart also illuminated the capacity, if not the early tendency, for expressing a heart-felt passion, although I did not know how to hold my attention there. In time, my discovery of the value of a heart-centered attention skill and a soul perspective placed my propensity to intellectualize into a different perspective. In time, I learned that when I let my heart lead my intellect—to look through the heart lens and the mental lens simultaneously—intellect became a primary strength that fostered rather than delayed the emergence of the soul. I did not have the ability to read that into a chart when I began to access one, but a skillful counselor might have done so—sparing me years of ambiguous feelings about a primary strength in my own nature. Discovery of heart and management of my literally headstrong nature have been central themes in my life, experienced first as struggle, then challenge, then gift.

So, we can take from Er's story the idea that our being on the planet means that a soul lies beneath the surface of our consciousness. We can take from the story the implication that clues to our soul nature are littered all about—like stars in a darkened sky. Even before we can experience ourselves as souls, we can begin to look for important clues to decoding the mystery of our lives within the major life themes in a skillfully interpreted astrological chart. We might learn that what troubles us are not weaknesses so much as challenges that a soul perspective may see as gifts of insight that illuminate pathways to our destiny.

CHAPTER THREE

Terrain	Stage of Consciousness	Perspective
Part Two: The dense body field and the earth	**Stage Two:** Attention is captured by the body, held in a provisional personality, and entrained outward by culture. The soul has lost control of the ability to control its own attention.	Life is a struggle. I (the personality) am a victim of circumstances. Things that happen to me are either good or bad. The bad is my fate. I can't control my fate or emotional reactions because those depend on what happens to me. Life is out of my control unless I outsmart it.

STAGE TWO CONSCIOUSNESS IS THE common state of humanity. At this Stage, we have forgotten that we are souls, where we came from, and why we came. The soul is present, but deeply buried and speaks to us only indirectly. The provisional personality senses that the world is threatening and that it is not truly in control. For many, that recognition is attended by a sense of struggle, suffering, and confusion. For others, this is a signal of the need to take control.

Our predominant approach to the confusion and suffering is presently the mix of conventional psychology, powerful pharmaceuticals, numbing agents, and preoccupation with work and entertainment that have largely taken the place of religion. In this world, those who can control do control—as far as possible. But control ultimately fails. Those who would heed the call of the soul amidst this chaos must recover the soul's attention and understand something of the terrain in which the forgetful soul has become enmeshed. That terrain is the body, and the body resides in a culture that seeks to control its behaviors.

Riding the Body

When I was eight years old, my father bought me a smallish sorrel mare. I had never been horseback before, and the mare was only slightly more experienced than I. My father introduced her to me in the middle of a flat pasture spotted with sagebrush and grama grass. I couldn't have been more excited.

He asked what I would like to name her. The mare had a white diamond shape on her forehead, bringing to my mind a star. I announced that Star would be her name.

My father lifted me onto the small pony saddle, put my feet in the stirrups, and handed me the reins. With no more than a single instruction—*pull back on the reins if you want to stop*—my father slapped Star on the rump.

Star lowered her ears and launched into a full run. The whole of my attention was jerked abruptly from any fantasy about what riding a horse would be like. Instead, my attention melded into the immediacy of an experience. All that was left to my control was the strength of my grip on the saddle horn. This new connection had brought me to an unskilled relationship with the powerful, startled, and very awake body beneath me. I managed to hold on, and Star eventually stopped.

For a few years after that, I managed to hold on while Star and I negotiated. She didn't want to hurt me, but she did not trust me not to hurt her. There were moments that were dangerous, particularly when she reacted in fear. Triggering Star's fear always seemed to result in lowering those ears and launching. I tried to get her to look at things through my perspective, and she did the same. Those years were rich, frequently challenging, and filled with lessons. Star was clearly a part of my fate. She was one in a long line of soul mates that delivered the challenges by which the soul learns.

When the soul joins the body in its first stage of development, the soul encounters its first soul mate, now carried in the womb of the soul's second soul mate—the mother. Little surprise that *mate* derives from the same linguistic root as matter and mother.

Quite beyond metaphor, my childhood experience of straddling Star and the experience of my nascent soul straddling the heart-saddle of my own infant body have a direct correspondence. In both cases, there was no doubt who was in control at the outset. A whiplash start is not unusual. Some degree of rough ride, at least, can be anticipated. To get beyond that rough ride and on to the next stage, the rider has to figure out how to evolve the *connection* with a powerful body into a collaborative *relationship*.

If a process of collaboration is to begin, it will start with a skillful invitation by the soul to the body. A skillful invitation is one without projection, expectation, or manipulation. The invitation is based in the recognition of an underlying connection that itself makes possible a relationship of mutual benefit. The invitation stands on a recognition of the dignity of the body, the mystery of its being, and the critical impor-tance of the body's role to the soul's work. The invitation is formed from heart-based attention skills such as patience, appreciation, love, respect, and presence. These skills are not automatic, but are the very substance of what souls must learn in order to progress on their own trajectories. Years may pass before a young rider can learn how to shift the dynamic of the relationship from a rough ride to a partnership. Before these skills are acquired, the relationship can be just the opposite—driven by projection, riddled with expectation, and dripping with manipulation. All too famil-iar in our human relationships, we see the same dynamic at work between the per-sonality dominated soul and body and with the same kinds of outcomes.

As the stories of horse whispering suggest, there is a point when the body will *want* to go where the relatively less powerful rider wants to go, because the body has sensed that the rider, the soul, knows where playfulness resides, and that love is found all along the way. And, the body has many appetites that the soul can learn to feed in healthful ways that benefit and stimulate the body while making it more ame-nable to the rider's agenda. There is a mutuality of interest between the body and the soul, and it is up to the soul to discover it.

When we left Er, the souls had drunk from the River of Forgetfulness—some more and some less. Overtaken by sleep, they were swept away to inhabit a body born into a common fate with the soul. In that way, the souls were stepping not only onto the backs of their bodies, but onto the backs of their fate as well. Like I fantasized my ride on Star's back, the souls might have fantasized that their choice of a life would be all light and love. There is a truth in that perception, but light and love take paradoxi-cal forms, and the ride will not be what we expect.

The Body Terrain: The Psychological Story

Stage Two Consciousness is in fact the state of soul *un*consciousness. The surface personality struggles in that state to make sense of a world made up of one challenge after another.

Those challenges often result in traumatic outcomes, starting in early child-hood. The challenges can take forms that are less apparent than outright neglect and violence or the more ubiquitous unskilled parenting. The challenge may be the sim-ple separation from earth's nurturing vibratory field, the loss of which is not compen-sated for by the bland flatness that increasingly characterizes a child's growing up in front of a screen within four walls filled with plastic playmates. It may take the form of hostile environments that challenge the body's health. The challenge will certainly include a rate of change more rapid than experienced in the latter half of the 20th century, except for the change that occurs in war and natural disaster. Perhaps the most fundamental challenge we all face is the sense of disconnection and isolation that is the very nature of our experience when we forget who we are.

In American culture, we typically look upon these traumas not from a soul perspective, but from the perspective of psychology. Like a soul perspective, psychol-ogy is both a construct (a way of thinking) and a perspective (a way of looking). Both perspectives create a story that forms the basis of an understanding of who we are. In the absence of a soul story, it is natural for those of us who grow up in postmodern American culture to form an understanding of life's challenges in terms of a classic psychological perspective.

I have a clear memory, as a three-year-old, of my mother screaming out her own frustration—an all-too-often event. As her primary audience, I can still remember the feeling of fear that overcame me. Somewhere in the consciousness of a three-year-old mind, the encounter with adult anger triggers a recognition that one is not protected and safe. Such an experience evokes no less than a fear of death. I made note, in my young consciousness, not to do anything to trigger such a display again—assuming, as a three-year-old typically would, that I might be the cause of her outburst. Objectively, and in the retrospective view of many decades, I can see that I was not in physical danger with this mother who in fact worked very hard to be a good and appropriate mother, but my toddler mind couldn't make such fine distinctions.

To survive a mother whose love seemed dangerously conditional to a child, I adopted a survival strategy. Most all of us do. The psychotherapeutic industry has labels for our adaptive strategies. In my case, it was *caretaking*. Caretakers make an unconscious trade of their own good behaviors (taking care of others, or making oth-ers feel good) in exchange for the good behaviors of others, including providing the caretaker with the approval that implies safety. We caretakers project upon others the expectation that they will do for us what we believe we cannot do for ourselves—that they will love us, particularly if we do what we think they want of us.

The assumption that an implicit trade is necessary is based in the belief that we are unworthy of the love that would otherwise nurture and protect us. It is, on our part, an unabridged manipulation, though we might be reluctant to recognize "nice" behaviors as manipulations. As time passes, we observe that the desired love is not forthcoming despite huge efforts on our part. We become frustrated and reactive because we do not experience the desired sense of security even though we have bent and reshaped ourselves for that very purpose. In the process, we have redefined our-selves into two people: one who is good, and one who is bad. It is our good behaviors that we offer up in trade, and the bad ones that we hide from our trading partner.

There are, of course, many strategies that children adapt to get love, or at least some sense of safety. Some children withdraw and try to disappear. Dissociation is the penultimate disappearance, and suicide is the ultimate. Some children become angry and aggressive to defend themselves. Some become overtly or more subtly controlling. All feel themselves to be victims, and their behaviors arise from that perception. These behaviors become unconscious patterns and persist into adult-hood, particularly if the behavior actually works at some level, as I discovered with my own strategy.

Over time, I honed to a science the practice of hiding my "bad" behaviors from my mother. I found—unconsciously more than consciously—that the same pattern held promise with teachers, then professors, and then clients. I worked—again unconsciously—to manipulate all of these people with good behaviors. Being the best student was my groove. I can remember catching on to the strategic benefit of that at about eight years of age when my fourth grade teacher—an alcoholic, I learned years later—praised my test performance and broke a yardstick over the head of one of my less fortunate friends. My goal was immediately clear. I needed to perform well for these authority figures in order to receive the approval that would reassure my need for safety. By age twelve or thirteen, I was safely in that groove. By high school, the groove had defined my identity. There were plenty of rebellious behaviors going on, but I kept them carefully out of sight. And I was completely unaware of the soul that lay just beneath those rebellious behaviors.

While it is natural and even appropriate for a young child to look to parents for a sense of safety and well being, there is a common tendency for Americans not to grow out of the belief that our sense of who we are is dependent upon the responses of others, and that approval of others is a necessary and good thing. An approval that indeed conveys a real sense of safety and love, however, is the grail that will never be found, so we find ourselves continually frustrated. That sets us up for a victim perspective—one that starts from the premise that we cannot control the world's tendency to disappoint.

The victim experience has another effect. With the advent of the notion of a "body/mind," psychology has opened itself to the notion that our minds create a reality that the body experiences. What is less apparent but equally true is that the body experience of fear reinforces the mental belief that we need to be fearful. Research has shown that we respond to the prospect of change with a process of filtering our perceptions through the memory bank of emotional responses held in the amygdala. That information colors how we proceed to think about the coming change. If the past was traumatic, we feel and then think that the future will be also. As long as we look at the future from our past experience, body/mind's hardwiring will incline us to see that our future will continue to be like our past.

We have observed that the body's experience of fear can be measured in a variety of ways—heart rate, hormonal response, nervous system activation, and so on. All of these contribute to a physiological picture that we call stress. We now know that chronic stress is an early marker for every one of the major diseases that define the American healthscape. Just like the old joke that death is God's way of telling us to slow down, the body's poor state of health becomes a clear voice for the soul that is trying to get through to the personality with the message that there is another way of looking at the world than through the stories told by psychology, science, and Wall Street. We have to learn to look at the future not solely through the lens of our past experience, but through another lens altogether. But the cultural support for looking at the world fearfully is pervasive.

Long after we are dropped on our heads by our parents, Americans suffer a common tendency to see themselves as victims, projecting blame for unhappy lives and negative reactions onto someone else. When parents are no longer around to blame, we shift the blame to spouses, children, and anyone else in whose presence we experience emotional distress. Don Umberto, an older Peruvian shaman (in Peru, he would be called a *paco*) with whom I spoke in Peru in 2004, told me that America is a culture of victims. He added that America was turning Peru into a culture of victims as well.

Embedded within this victim consciousness is an even more fundamental perspective. Our response to emotional distress is to see it as a *problem*. If we are willing to consult a therapist, it is often because we believe that we have a problem that the psychotherapist can help us to resolve. If we are unwilling to consult, we may simply view emotional distress as a problem to ignore, numb ourselves to, or to be gutted through. Any of these responses start from the premise that the distress is a problem. If we get ourselves to the therapist, the common response from America's psychotherapeutic culture includes an implicit agreement that the distress is a problem that needs to be fixed. The standard psychotherapeutic assistance would address the problem by various means, including helping us to re-engage with our childhood wounds, learn to establish boundaries, learn to respect ourselves more, learn to take more personal responsibility for creating the circumstances we feel to be painful, and learn to extract ourselves from distressful circumstances and relationships. Conventional psychology suggests that a psychological understanding and reframing of these childhood experiences will allow a maturation of personality—that we can develop and grow out of these early perceptions and compulsive behaviors. This approach of psychology presumes that if we are treated badly as children, we can get over it.

Applying a psychological problem-solving approach to my own story resulted in an explanation for my adult behaviors, and that understanding gave me a certain satisfaction and sense of hope that change would come into my life. However, what I found is that the mere understanding of apparent root causes and the dysfunctional strategies created to deal with those childhood issues did not solve the problem.

Conventional psychological perspectives allowed me to see myself as an adult, safe and far from the reach of an angry mother whom I had blamed for my unhappy connection with the world. I could adopt the perspective that my parents did the best they could; that I was an adult no longer in danger of maltreatment; that I could adopt appropriate boundaries relative to people who might make unreasonable demands upon me; and that I was free to make choices about the trajectory of my own life without the need for approval by others.

Learning from a psychological perspective that I was a caretaker simply gave a name to what my emotions continued to process as an internal and unexpressed disease that represented my paradoxical fear of being in the world—paradoxical because I operated with a relative sense of confidence and ease in my difficult, legal profession. Indeed, in that limited realm of life where I did have some sense of control, I did have a sense of confidence. Yet, none of that overcame a fundamental sense of being disconnected and isolated. It just gave me fewer people to blame. I was still a victim of a world that I could not control, and I was quite capable of reacting strongly when someone challenged my defensive perimeter. As I came into relationships, I continued to project my safety issues on those women, even after I understood the dynamic of projection.

It is not insignificant that psychology names an otherwise rambling sense of dysfunction in personalities. But naming is not the same as healing. We do not heal by giving symptoms a story line. There is an interesting slight of hand that occurs in conventional medicine and psychology. Both observe a pattern of *symptoms*, give those symptoms a name, then announce to the patient that the cause of their problem is the name given to the symptoms, whereupon the symptoms become the focus of treatment.

When the heart dysfunctions and deteriorates, both the dysfunction and deterioration are symptoms of some earlier cause. Yet, we label those symptoms as "heart disease," and treat it as though it was something we caught because we didn't wash our hands instead of looking at forty years of dissociation from the body and its needs. Psychology assembles the symptoms of chronic depression and then announces that we are chronically depressed, which is no longer a symptom but a condition to be treated. While this approach by psychology and medicine is not always obvious, it is pervasive, and it avoids the real necessity of locating early, root causes and understanding the means of prevention. In large part, the root cause of our body/mind dis-eases is soul repression. Soul repression doesn't cause heart disease tomorrow, but it will be a major contributor after a few decades of repression. In the same way, soul repression doesn't cause chronic depression in a day or so, but longtime repression will make that depression inevitable. The relationship between the soul and body is absolutely at the root of the body's health.

In an interesting evolution of the practice of psychology and medicine, the consciousness technology of meditation has been repackaged as a tool to address the symptom of stress itself, rather than as a tool to address and empower the presence of the soul in the body. As traditional meditation has become popular among alternative health practitioners, psychology and medicine have seen the camel's nose peeking beneath the tent flap. By sanitizing the deep tradition of meditation of its spiritual implications, psychology and medicine have now found a way for meditation to address symptoms called *stress* rather than explore the root cause of our most common dis-ease, which is a soul forgetfulness that gives rise to the symptom of stress in the body. Despite much effort given to a psychological approach, approaching our personal dilemmas as a problem to be solved doesn't often work. It doesn't happen because there is an underlying soul dynamic that conventional psychology does not account for. The soul dynamic implicates a different perspective about the challenges in our lives.

A soul perspective takes a radically different approach. It recognizes, for example, that we are continuously called by our souls and to be who we in fact are, and that the "bad" behaviors arise from the soul calling out—sometimes in paradoxical ways—for its own survival. Those behaviors inevitably surface, either out of sight of those whom we would manipulate with "good" behaviors, or in the form of illness from the dissipation of the extraordinary energy we devote to suppressing the "bad." Unconventional psychologists might view the "good" behaviors as soul denial, and the "bad" behaviors as the soul crying out for recognition. Rather than viewing the source of the distress as a problem to be fixed, the soul perspective regards the distress as a direct signal that the soul has a lesson to learn. That lesson is embedded in the circumstance in which we are having a distressful reaction, and that circumstance is a gift of fate offered for discovery and education of our souls.

How different it is to engage a challenging circumstance with the belief that it is a gift rather than a problem! Conventional American psychotherapy has worked very hard to help us adjust our attitudes toward our problems, and, having largely failed in that goal, has joined with the pharmaceutical industry to adjust those attitudes and disturbing behaviors by chemical force. If we were to see our distress as the indication that a gift is waiting to be opened rather than a problem to be solved, pharmaceutical intervention would be the exception instead of what has increasingly become the rule.

I have little doubt that my mother's personality was part of the setup of my soul's fate. My interaction with her as a young child and teenager dominated my reactions and behaviors well into my fourth decade. My initial encounters with her defined the fulcrum of my attitude toward life. Over time, as my three-year-old's adaptive strategy repeatedly brought more pain than contentment into my life, I was driven to make a choice. I chose, in some way, to go inward. I might have chosen to remain angry with her, and my life would have turned out quite differently.

Through the many steps of that inward journey narrated in the following chapters, I can say that I came to find the paradoxical gift in my mother's behavior—a result far different than "forgiving" her the sins of unintended parental incompetence. As I looked at my relationship with her from a soul perspective, I found that there was nothing to forgive. Her unconscious behaviors drove me inward. Those behaviors forced me to choose whether I would take responsibility for finding love and safety within myself. As I looked inward, over time, I found the soul awaiting me with the very means that would lead to a discovery of the inherent connection we share with everything. From that discovery, I could move forward to discover how to develop the relationships that would support the unfoldment of my soul's destiny.

Each of us has a fundamental need to experience unconditional love, which is the same as experiencing the inherent connection we share with everything. By denying me what I had naturally projected upon her, my mother threw me upon my own resources. What I eventually found through the variety of peak experiences that followed over the years was a means to experience that love and a means of experiencing myself—Self in a dimension larger than personality—as the very source of that love. That gift was embedded in the painful interaction with my mother that, by a natural psychological maladaptation, eventually led to a far deeper inner knowing—a smaller gift leading to larger gifts. The discovery and embrace of that love dissociated from any other human has been part of my destiny. Having embraced that destiny, I have become able to love another and to receive with delight the genuine love that is returned from another who is skillful enough to do the same. I have also come to sense that I am an inherent and conscious part of a universe that is inherently loving and conscious, and that the means of expression of that love includes the difficult challenges with which we are faced. This is a huge distance from seeing myself as a victim of problems that I can't control and did not cause.

One might ask whether I would have avoided distress had my mother been able to skillfully provide mother's love. If that were the case, my destiny would have been vastly different. Speculation is quite meaningless. It was my fate to encounter this mother. Her loving me more skillfully would have been about another life lesson, not the one that the Fates chose for me on this round on the planet. And I'm more than content to have this lesson revealed to me in a process of my soul's continuing unfolding. Preferring a different set of challenges because we are struggling with the ones we have falls squarely within the territory of "be careful what you ask for." Years later, my own soul has discovered a relationship with the soul that enacted the part of "raging mother" that is entirely transformed from the relationship that preceded her death. That footnote to my childhood story emerged in a ceremony recounted in a later chapter.

In time, I was able to heal that deep sense of separation and the maladaptive behaviors that the wounding implicated, but it was not because I had come to even an accurate or satisfying psychological perspective. It was because I found ways to wrest control of my attention back from a culture that sought to exploit my attention, and because I learned to place that attention within the frame of the soul and the soul's own experience. That perspective takes in a cosmos much larger than culture's worldview could possibly access. The cultural view of our emotional struggle is defined by a secular psychology that sees wounding, labels that wounding as a problem, and finally blames that problem on our unwillingness to get over it, instead of seeing challenges and celebrating them as the torch that lights the pathway inward— a pathway that guides our journeys beyond the limited perspective of personality. Only by bringing some preliminary attention inward to the soul's home in the heart can the soul begin the longer process of reclaiming the fullness of attention that is its inherent nature.

The scientific-cultural view literally sets the stage for the drama of our struggle, and psychology attempts to write the script in which we enact our stories by riding out the tragic outflow of wounded beginnings. But that play does not play. In our true stories, in our own plays, the three sisters of Fate have written that part of the script that takes us to a climactic second scene in a first act. As the play opens at the moment of our birth, Fate hands us the pen. We have to write our way to the end of our own play, and know that the curtain will fall by moonrise whether we grasp the pen or not.

The Body Terrain: The Soul Story

Even as we are handed the pen, American culture still paints the set that is the backdrop for this modern update of an older play. The off-migration from the farm has removed humans from a naturally nurturing and sustaining relationship with the earth, at least for those who were able to access it. We don't need to assume that lives in earlier times were easier just because they were more earth connected. We merely need to look at the pervasiveness of the disconnection from the earth at this point in time.

What we can see now is that the cultural embrace of a dogmatic scientific mind-set has shamed people away from their hearts and the experience of their souls, thereby increasing the degree of separation that humans experience. The technological domination of culture has increased the felt rate of change, placing more pressure on the ability of the human system to adapt. The recent bubble of prosperity has amounted to a siren song of materialism that tempts us to throw our pain into a consuming frenzy, only to drown in it. Traditional religion has been displaced to a large degree, even for those who ascribe to religious beliefs, by a secular psychology that assumes disconnection as the nature of the world, and that we must simply adjust to it. *Get over it,* behavioral psychology finally says in frustration. *Medicate it,* says psychiatry. This setting provides limitless drama for the soul story.

As the play begins, the soul has disappeared deep into the darkness of the body. For a soul whose immediate prior experience was the literal lightness of soul being— a timeless, weightless, boundless bliss—the contrast of entering the density of matter is not unlike being buried alive. Er delivers the prologue to our play and relates that this unexpected transition has been eased by a soul anesthesia—the merciful but fateful forgetting that comes from drinking at the River. So the soul sleeps its way into the body.

What is this body into which the soul enters? As I am speaking of body, it includes what we know as the body's physical parts, including the heart and the brain. It includes the emotions, the mind, and the ego/personality. All of those aspects of body rely entirely upon the soul's consciousness for their ability to become animated, to come alive. And the soul, technically speaking, does not enter the body, but comes into proximity to it by locating itself adjacent to the portal that is represented by the heart-field, which is itself something quite different than the physical heart. The body is just on the other side of this portal. As humans, we experience this coupling on either side of the heart portal as an event within the body, because we feel it in our chests, in the region of the physical heart.

What does it mean that the soul sleeps its way into the body? It is a centrally important question, and there is no objective way to answer the question. What I write here necessarily comes as an interpretation of my own subjective experience that is related throughout the book. My interpretation of my subjective experience corresponds to Plato's story of Er's vision, but Er's vision is not objective evidence of anything either.

Er's story suggests only that the sleeping soul is swept away into the body. If the soul awakens immediately in that new body, the clear message of Er's story is that the soul awakens into amnesia. It does not remember who it is. It does not remember that it is a soul. This is precisely consistent with my own subjective experience. It took over fifty years of my life for me to remember that I am a soul. Was my soul asleep during that time? That is a way of speaking about it. Drawing from our ordinary experience, we are aware that while our bodies sleep, our consciousness remains active, in dreams, in its awareness of the time that we need to arise, in its alert for the sound of the baby crying. It doesn't seem a stretch to analogize that the soul that is in a state that is not self-aware, like our ordinary sleeping state. We could say that, while the soul sleeps, its attention remains awake. Or we could say that the soul is not sleeping, but has awakened into an amnesia that prevents it from taking control of its own attention. I have referred elsewhere in the book to the "nascent" soul, and it is to this state of amnesia, whether induced by "sleep" or not, that I refer. In either event, the soul's consciousness and its attention animate the body. So long as the soul is not aware that it is a soul, however, the attention is like a fog, settling down in the hollow of the personality, in the cave of the sexual energies of the body, in the tight contractions of the fearful belly, and the other dimensional fields beyond time/space. There are no limitations on how the soul's attention can be divided in this state, or upon where it might go. That is the very lack of soul focus that must be addressed by the soul.

As the soul begins to awaken, it finds itself in a state of confusion, not unlike a hangover, struggling to remember who it is and where it came from, while the golden coin of the soul's attention has been taken by the body itself. This is the beginning of Stage Two Consciousness.

Now the dramatic tension is apparent, and the play continues.

Many people die without ever leaving this initial scene of Stage Two Consciousness. Failing to heed the soft whispers of the soul that seek the personality's attention, the personality may decline the pen and lose the opportunity to write the next act. It need not be this way. If the personality can listen to the soul's whispers, then the hung-over soul has a vehicle by which it can begin to search for what has been stolen. That search begins in this strange terrain where it has awakened.

The Soul Story: Getting Acquainted with the Body

Souls are not born in any sense that we understand. Bodies are born, and bodies die. Souls shift terrain by shifting dimensions. From that dimension that Er called the Plain of Oblivion, souls shift into proximity with the time/space dimension through the portal of the heart-field, where the body arises to meet it. The body is assembled from earth elements that are designed to respond to the life force that souls ignite. Souls enter into a fluid relationship with the body—sometimes more connected, sometimes less connected, with the degree of connection shifting with the attention's focus. The ego/personality that emerges in this circumstance is not the soul, but it functions with the consciousness that the sleeping soul has yielded to the body. With neither the soul nor the personality taking charge of attention and learning to focus it, the soul's attention can and often does drift away from the body, but it does not leave entirely until the body dies.

During the life span of the body, the soul can learn to call its attention back to itself, in which case it can call the body into resonant relationship. If the soul does not learn to regain and focus its own attention, the body is subject to the way in which personality manages attention, with the result that attention is often given over to television or other forms of dissociation. If the soul doesn't learn how to recapture and focus its attention, then its attention will remain dispersed. The soul's skill of attention comes to define the degree and quality of the connection with the body.

While we may think we understand what it means when we talk about a body *being born,* we really know little more about that process than we know about how souls originate. Scientific research has produced a prodigious amount of detail about the biology of birth and the physical developments that follow. We can get that process under the microscope, so to say. But there is no science that has penetrated the question of how and why earth, fire, air, and water come into being in the first place, or how those combine and emerge into a myriad of forms that become invested with the life force we sometimes call "consciousness" and sometimes narrow into the notion of "intelligence." Having discovered DNA and having "decoded" the genome doesn't mean we understand anything about its origin, how it has come to have the capacity for blueprinting and managing cellular response to the environment, or even how that coding is programmed to make both fingers and brain cells out of the generic cells that form the building blocks of the body.

The view of conventional science on this matter of human origin and the evolution of specific physical functions is still under the sway of the secular dogma commonly called Darwinism, even though Darwin cannot himself be blamed for how others have interpreted some of his observations into a position he would not likely embrace. This dogma assumes without the support of rigorous scientific proof that all life both emerges and evolves randomly, with the fittest forms of life surviving and overcoming the weaker. The dogma also assumes that consciousness arises from brain matter, instead of the other way around. However, it is clear that randomness fails as a theory to explain complex life forms, and the notion of survival of the fittest does not fit with the evidence of ecologies that include both the strong and the weak in interdependent systems.

On the other hand, a simplistic creationist view—for which there is similarly no scientific support– neither acknowledges nor accounts for the processes by which life forms or individual soul consciousness evolves and grows. This leaves the scientific theory of evolution in the realm of theory—struggling with questions such as how complex forms like eyes have formed, and it leaves the matter of soul evolution to the realm of personal, subjective experience. That subjective experience of consciousness suggests a middle ground for scientific hypothesis: evolution is a process by which creation proceeds.

I mention this debate over evolution to distinguish it from the notion of the evolution of consciousness to which I refer throughout this book. The body need not evolve *in general* in order to act as a platform for the evolution of soul consciousness that can occur within the life span of a particular body. I am concerned here with the evolution of consciousness from the perspective of a single soul. Whether the body evolves in general is largely irrelevant to the notion of the soul perspective. Sri Aurobindo suggests that soul evolution will ultimately result in evolution of the body as well, over time frames that extend beyond a single human life. I am not concerned with the latter question. In general, the present state of the body will work quite well for the soul's next steps within the space of a single lifetime—provided that we optimize its health and release from it the toxic holding that our earlier traumas and the environment have occasioned.

Nevertheless, within the space of a human life, there is a more narrow notion of how the body evolves that is very pertinent. Rather than use the term *evolve,* I would use the term *adapt* to describe changes within the body that occur within the frame of a single lifetime and over periods that range from minutes to months. *Adapting* and our notion of *healing* have much in common, since the failure to adapt is what creates the need for healing. Because the research from which this notion of adapting occurs has been described with reference to evolution in general, I'll return to that context.

A cutting-edge biological perspective has abandoned the dogma of evolution by randomness in favor of a view that DNA is programmed to evolve by a continuous process of adaptation within a single lifetime. Biologist Bruce Lipton was the first to explain for a popular audience that DNA has the capacity to sense changes in the environment and to write new programs that manufacture new proteins that will function in a changed environment. Of equal importance and perhaps startling significance, Lipton also pointed out how the body's own emotions are a critical part of the environment to which the DNA responds.

Fear, suggests Lipton, closes down the receptive mechanisms by which the cells sense the environment, thereby preventing the cell-based DNA from sensing what is happening in the environment external to the cells. From the perspective of our own autonomic nervous systems, fear literally causes a single cell to freeze up and close down, since it can neither flee nor fight. On the other hand, the presence of an emotional environment of love, suggests Lipton, invites the cells to open to a free informational exchange with the environment, so that the cellular DNA is again able to get the information it needs to adapt to external change.

What excites me most in Lipton's story is the point he makes about the emotional environment—because we can control that even if most of us don't yet know how. In Stage Two, we are not in control of our emotions because we are not in control of our attention. Studies conducted by the Institute of HeartMath have clearly established that a particular pattern of deep breathing and an intentional focus of attention upon the heart, together with an intentional heartfelt experience of appreciation, can shift the emotional environment of the body toward the positive, and create a state called coherence. These same studies show that this simple practice can measurably improve health markers, including lowered stress hormone production and blood pressure. Research by Richard Davidson at the University of Wisconsin-Madison shows that a heart-centered focus upon the experience of compassion is also followed by a cascade of positive emotions.

The direct significance of these studies is that, since we can control our own emotional response, we can optimize the adaptive response of our own DNA so that the body can adapt to changes in the external environment. Moreover, this research shows that we can find our way to positive emotions even in the midst of rapid change, if we simply learn to focus attention in our hearts. While good health *per se* is not a requirement for soul emergence into its destiny, there is little question that good health allows for an easier focus of attention upon the soul, with fewer distractions from poor health. Good health may also provide a longer time frame during which the body is available to support the soul's work on the planet. An unhealthy body simply cannot manifest the energy to power the soul's agenda over longer time frames. Not all souls need a long time frame for their work, however, and a particularly difficult health condition may be the very challenge that brings our focus to the soul. Why else would so many people say, for example, that the cancer was the best thing that ever happened to them? Whatever else cancer may do, it can teach us to focus attention, which is precisely why the Eastern meditation traditions use contemplation of death as a tool to teach attention skills.

A focus of attention upon the soul within the frame of the heart-field creates an environment of love in the body and allows us to move forward in a context of positive emotion. By controlling whether the body operates in an environment of love or fear, the soul that is in possession of the fullness of its own attention has the ability to create the optimal environment for the body's need to adapt to a changing environment. This research suggests that by coming to an experiential soul perspective, and directing the soul's attention through the lens of the heart, we can face challenge without the suffering that negative emotions represent. With this experience, our minds can open to the notion that challenge represents opportunity rather than struggle. Experiencing our challenges through the lens of the heart-field, and coming to an understanding of them as the containers of the gifts, ultimately leads us to the discovery of our own destiny. At a deeper level of skill, we don't have to feel *the fear and do it anyway*. The greater sophistication of a heart-centered attention skill is that the fear characteristic of the mind-based perception of a challenge diminishes as soon as we effectively connect attention in the heart-field.

By holding attention within the soul and the soul within the field of the heart, we flood the body with the soul's heaven vibration, a vibration we know as *unconditional love*. The body responds to the experience of this love with the release of long-held trauma and the hormonal flood that we experience in our bodies as positive emotions. When our attention is brought to our hearts by the heart-focused attention of another person, we call this experience *healing*. When we learn to do this for ourselves, we could call it healing, but I prefer to call it *skill*. Any such healing requires that we learn to control our attention and learn how to hold it in the soul within the heart-field.

An environment of love literally allows each cell of the body to open receptively to the soul's presence in the body. If we are going to end our own suffering, we must gather our attention, restore it to the soul, locate the soul in the heart, and share that presence with the body.

The Body as Field

Science has begun to provide important information that is relevant to the question of how the body works in relation to the soul. Quantum physics suggests that it is no longer reasonable to divide the world into matter (such as a body) on the one hand, and energy (such as what we have called "spirit") on the other. Instead, physics teaches that the entire universe and everything in it is made of light and energy vibrating at different speeds. In addition, the quantum physics notion of *quantum entanglement* suggests a connection operating at the atomic level beyond the limits of time/space. Two atoms, once in contact, continue to remain in communication and exhibit identical behaviors without the delay that we would assume is necessary for information to travel between the two. In this observation, we can see science's affirmation of a mechanism of connection of all that exists, even though physics has no theoretical basis for explaining how that happens. While this view is relatively new to science, more ancient spiritual insights have made the same observation. We can find these older views expressed, for example, in Kashmiri Shaivism, which taught the non-dual view that everything is made of one substance, which is consciousness, and that consciousness is vibratory—a quality it calls *spandas*.

Every-thing is energy in one form or another, vibrating at one frequency or another. My own way of speaking of the difference between the seemingly solid body levels of energy and those of the soul level is to say that the body is simply a more dense, higher amplitude field that vibrates more slowly than the soul. The soul is not of time/space, but it does make a kind of appearance in time by virtue of its relationship with a body that is in time/space. Whether there is a clear dividing line between time/space and the dimensions that are not so constrained is something that is not clear. I have suggested the notion of a heart-field that operates as an interdimensional portal to facilitate the connection between a soul and a body, but that is my attempt to language a subjective experience that occurs when I hold my attention in the soul in the center of my chest. More important than assuming that a dividing line exists between the two, perhaps, is the question of how the higher frequencies interact with the lower.

As molecular biology and quantum physics begin a mutual exploration—such as is found in the work of biophysicist Mae Wan Ho—we find that the body itself has the qualities that have been formerly attributed only to higher-frequency energy-transmission structures "discovered" or "invented" by science. For example, the body's connective tissue is made of a liquid crystalline structure that is sensitive to a single photon of light and transmits information-encoded energy at or exceeding the speed of light. Like the lower notes on the piano can resonate with the piano's higher notes, these tissues can resonate with the very high microwave frequencies (the high notes) that now fill our atmosphere, which is why there is much yet unknown about the short- and long-term health effects of our new technological environment.

Science is producing other bits and pieces of information that challenge its long-held assumptions. For example, the notion that the central nervous system is the primary or only form of communication in the body is now clearly outmoded. The central nervous system is only a part of a much faster and more complex system of information transmission that includes blood, hormones, connective tissue, and neurological tissue. Similarly, the idea that the brain is the primary center of consciousness and intelligence in the body has been challenged by research reflecting primary roles played by the heart and the gut in coordinating the body's responses to its environment.

Among the results of this heart-focused research is the interesting observation that the electromagnetic field of the heart is hugely larger than that of the brain. The heart sends far more information to the brain than the other way around. Heart-focused attention produces positive emotion. Holding attention away from the heart results in the production of negative emotion. Emotion is secondary to how we hold attention. Both the heart and the gut are constructed with much of the same neurological material that is so highly valued in the brain. It is clear from long extant and reputable research that the body produces and is sensitive to electromagnetic fields, although conventional science pays little attention to this fact outside of a few "practical" applications, such as ultrasound, magnetic resonance scanning, electrical stimulation therapy, and extracorporeal shock wave lithrotripsy (breaking up kidney stones with frequency waves). Practical applications are those we use because they work and that we hesitate to examine too closely lest they blow up our usual and comfortable assumptions about how the universe works.

For the purpose of describing a soul perspective, perhaps the most important point is that the body is itself a field—one comprised of a huge number of subfields.

It is itself an expression of consciousness—fields vibrating at various frequencies and encoded with information that define the manner of expression of the fields. With that recognition, the question from a soul perspective is how the field of the soul interacts with the field of the body in a way that serves the work of the soul and honors the very conscious nature of the body.

The answer has to do with resonance, entrainment and attention.

Resonance and Entrainment

My college roommate and I both played the guitar. There was an occasion when I stroked an *E* string on my guitar while his guitar was standing in a corner across the room. The corresponding string on his guitar began to vibrate and sound out an *E*, and then broke. My stroking the string on my guitar created a field of vibration which radiated out causing my roommate's guitar string to vibrate in response. That response is called *resonance*. Both strings were tuned, more or less, to vibrate at the same frequency, which is why one could resonate (*re-sound*) with the other. That my roommate's string broke indicates, at least, the strength of the resonance between these separate objects. The soprano whose voice breaks a glass is broadcasting a vibratory field that resonates with the glass in the same way.

Entrainment is a process that can occur in the presence of resonance. We all experience entrainment regularly. For example, you have listened to a band playing with a strong and rhythmic drumbeat. You may have noticed that your foot begins to tap quite on its own without your having intended it. This occurs because your body fields include the same frequency range as the drum creating its rhythms, which means that the body can resonate with the drum. If we could not, we would not hear or feel the drum. Our bodies are tuned—as a function of the complex fields from which they are created—to vibrate at many frequencies, including the frequency of the drum. If the drum frequency has a higher amplitude (meaning higher intensity, which we experience as loudness and possibly a direct physical sensation) than the same frequency that exists in your body, then the drum has the capacity not only to resonate with that same frequency in your body, but to wake it up and vibrate it, which is what happened with both my roommate's guitar string and your foot. This is called *entrainment*. Between two fields that resonate, the stronger field will control, or entrain, the other, unless the weaker field blocks the stronger field in some way (like walking away from the room where the band is playing, or just tuning it out by forcing our attention elsewhere).

Another familiar example of resonant entrainment is the experience of listening to the radio. Each station broadcasts a different frequency. Each radio station encodes its frequency with information. That information may be the announcer's voice, the rhythm and lyrics of a song, the content of the announcer's message, or an emergency signal. Our ears have *cilia*, located in the cochlea of the inner ear, that are tuned to particular frequencies, including those broadcast by radios. Our ears can receive the frequencies (resonate with the frequencies) and their encoded information. Our brains can decode the information. If we give our attention over to the radio, we become entrained to the sound of the radio.

When we dance, there is the possibility—not the inevitability—of giving our bodies over to the entraining rhythms of the music. Dancing provides an opportunity to discover the mechanism of relationship between the body and the soul. The body, if all hesitance and fear is released, can submit to the music and find itself entirely within the emotional field of the music—whatever feeling is encoded into the frequency field of the music. Getting that *feeling* is precisely why we dance. The entraining force of the music offers to take us out of the hopefully lesser-entraining force of our thoughts, our negative emotions, the nattering and brooding presence of the culture vulture, and the compromises our surface personality has wrought to make it through another day.

No surprise that college students—who report that stress is a primary problem—also say that they turn to music as a primary solution. But, it is not merely the music that creates the dance. The dance rhythm can be imposed by the music, from the outside. However, the dancer may respond to the music by contributing a form to the rhythm that is unique to the dancer. The combination of the resonance between music, the body, and the *design* or *form* brought by the soul of the dancer results in a collaboration of *creativity*. That forming field of information can come only from the soul itself—a soul that is in harmonic relationship with the body in the container of the dance. All creativity is of the same nature. It requires an entrainment of the body/mind to the rhythms of the soul's intelligence in some context within the world—painting, music, business, inventing. Learning to control our attention gives us the choice of what fields we will give our selves over to, and the choice to yield ultimately to the field of our own destiny—which may be the most challenging creative act of all.

This fundamental mechanism of resonant entrainment is how we interact with the world as a whole. Everything we experience is a vibration encoded with information, which we de-construct and interpret through our own vibratory nature, using the variety of interpretive lenses within our body. Our lenses are specialized: eyes are sensitive to and receive light frequencies; ears and bones respond to sound frequencies; the connective tissue receives light, touch, and sound; the mind is able to decode the information with which the sound of words is encoded. While that is an overly simple explanation of a complex process, it is enough to understand that the more we are able to move our attention through the range of external frequencies, the more information we can receive. Similarly to how we tune our own radio, we can scan our own internal frequencies across a range of informational possibilities infinitely more rich than a mere radio. We can scan with the eyes, ears, mind, and the felt senses of the body. We can scan with the heart and soul. Infinite amounts of information are standing by. We can attune to any of it. The skill comes in learning how to select what is supportive and resonant with our own soul fields.

The Central Importance of Attention

We scan with attention. Attention is how we tune ourselves to the universe and all the information that it contains for us to discover. Attention is how we tune ourselves to our own soul frequencies and the information encoded there as well, and how we avoid entrainment by those frequencies by which we do not want to be controlled. *Learning how to control our attention and where to place it are the most central of soul skills.*

Although we have the ultimate capacity to exert this control over attention, the nascent soul does not have control over attention early on, and the surface personality does not remember that its own source of attention is a soul that comes from those dimensions outside of time/space that we often call "heaven." How memory gets erased is only one of many mysteries about the origin of consciousness and souls that we can experience but can't understand. What was formerly a singular and rather simple perspective—*I am a soul in a process of learning*—has quickly become a different and more complex perspective. The soul has lost control of attention. The surface personality becomes the default gathering place where attention hangs out until its favorite television show comes on. The nascent soul is not yet ready to gather that attention back and is no more able to control the body and its personality than I could control my new mare.

If we can control our attention, then we can control our tuning. If we can focus and direct our attention, we can control what we tune to in both the external and internal worlds. If we cannot, then whatever has the highest amplitude (whatever is loudest) in the external environment will both resonate with and entrain our attention, which effectively controls our behaviors. If we don't tune ourselves to our own souls, we will be entrained to the frequencies of culture and to fear, upon which culture feeds.

When the forgetful soul enters that new body, there is an abrupt change in the soul's focus of attention, and in its perspective. In one moment, the soul knows that it is a soul and that it has chosen to take birth on the earth for a lesson yet to be revealed. In the next moment, the soul has grasped on to a powerful body that is speeding forward on its own. A new form of consolidated consciousness awakens. One is that of the forgetful soul that may identify more with the body than who it is, and the other is that of a very awake body carrying a confused passenger. It is though the center of the attention's gravity has shifted. The soul's consciousness has lost awareness of itself, and that same consciousness has animated the now wide-awake body, locating that new body consciousness in what we typically call the "personality," and to which I have occasionally referred in this book as the "surface personality," to distinguish it from the soul's distinct nature. The dominance of a body based personality and the passivity of a soul is no more or less than the entrainment of the soul to the high amplitude, low frequency rhythms of the body. The body based personality, in turn, has its attention pointed toward the loud noises of culture.

I've been asked whether it is not the surface personality which is forgetful, rather than the soul. One answer would be that Er's story is pretty clear on who drank from the river. My own answer comes from my interpretation of my own experience. It feels that my surface personality, while animated by the soul consciousness that enters the body at birth, is a combination of qualities. One set of those qualities arises from the astrological imprint on the soul itself, which is projected outward through the surface personality in a kind of default manner that does not necessitate any direct control of attention by the soul. Another set of those qualities depends on how culture has directed the sleeping soul's attention, such that the personality feels attracted to wearing shirts with logos of various retailers as a means (ironically) of defining an identity for itself. The surface personality is most certainly a result of both nature and nurture. That personality is not the repository, but the mirror reflection of the imprint of the soul's fate and destiny, which have come with a soul that knew who it was and then clearly forgot. If we do not make a distinction between the surface personality and the soul, there is no place to go with the resolution of our struggles, as modern psychology has clearly discovered.

Because of the soul's forgetting, the essential nature of Stage Two Consciousness is an involuntary, passive resonant entrainment of the surface personality by the world around us. The immature, unskilled, and undeveloped soul/body partnership can't focus its attention on the inner world of the body, which is where the soul and its own program for the soul journey is located. The attention of this immature partnership submits passively to the lower frequencies of the exterior world. Whatever can most skillfully gain the body/soul's attention in the moment controls this process of entrainment of the soul's attention. This is not to say that Stage Two Consciousness is not creative. To the contrary, this level of consciousness, *so* tuned to the external world, can be prolifically creative in that world. The key distinction of that creativity, however, is that the consciousness from which that creativity arises is not informed by the soul, the very point made by Sri Aurobindo in the quotation that was included in the book's introduction.

The collective wisdom of the world's spiritual traditions has a common comment to make about a singular effect of the body/soul's entrainment by the exterior world. What we read and hear time after time is that the exterior world is a *mirror* of our own interior world. That is quite different than saying that the exterior world is an illusion which does not exist except in our delusion. The exterior world exists, and exists quite without the presence of you or me as individuals, even though some of the form of the outer world is largely created by the collective perspective of individuals and certainly by some individuals alone. However, how each of us experiences that world—how we resonate with it—is quite different from person to person due to the particular perspective each of us brings to that encounter.

Fate, destiny, and *soul* compose the trilogy that expresses the collective of each person's individuality. *Fate* represents the tuning that navigates in the exterior world in the absence of the tuning guidance of the soul's own *destiny*. In other words, if we don't control our attention and direct it toward the resonances of our own soul field, fate will do it for us, since that is our default programming. So, we first resonate with the external world in a particular way fashioned for us by the mythical Sisters, like we resonate with the drum in the band. To do otherwise, we have to learn how to control attention, take it out of the place where the band is playing, and place it in the soul itself. Here the heart can lead the soul to resonate and entrain with the fields of information that tune the soul toward its destiny.

The Vulture Culture's Capture of Attention

The body has no capacity for attention before the soul enters into it, nor after the soul departs. Upon entering the body, the soul's attention is instantly entrained to the senses of the body, just like Star took my body for a ride I couldn't control. Like a ball that bounces from the soul to the body to the personality, culture sees attention as a loose ball up for grabs. The ability to control our attention and place it upon the information-encoded soul frequency is what must be won back from culture if we are to survive and thrive as distinct individual souls. This is precisely the circumstance and challenge of Stage Two Consciousness.

In many ways, America is not unique in challenging the individual soul, by turning the body into a field upon which the soul and culture battle for control of the focus of our attention. America is not the first nation to view itself as unique and superior, to have global and imperial ambitions, to overextend its economy by waging war in remote lands, to create a huge gap between a very small class of wealthy people and a large class of poor, to exhaust its natural resources, to experience and tolerate widespread discrimination, to suffer a resilient patriarchy, to sustain a huge gap between our best aspirations and our most common behaviors, to be blind to its own obvious hypocrisy, to develop a form of government that issues populist rhetoric while submitting to a behind-the-scenes control of powerful interests or a form of government that cannot competently navigate the changes that its society is experiencing. What is new is for these characteristics to get complicated and magnified by the ways in which America is unique.

The ways in which America is unique in human history are several, and that uniqueness is directly tied to the nature of the soul journey and the fate that has been woven for the souls who have become Americans at this particular time. I have already mentioned America's unique experiment of leaving a direct connection with the earth, punctuated by the off-migration from family farms. This has resulted in our being the first culture to move indoors where the primary relationship is with two-dimensional surfaces, the most attention grabbing of which are televisions, phones, and computer screens. The rate of change occasioned by the technology explosion is another. America is the first culture to face extinction at its own hands as a consequence of large-scale pollution occasioned by large-scale consumption. Pollution comes in many forms, including unwanted sound, invasive electromagnetic fields, toxic chemicals and metals that overwhelm the human capacity for adaptation and challenge our ability to control our own attention.

There is one other attribute of our culture that is critical to an understanding of the soul's challenge in recapturing its attention. I have already talked about the effects of the scientific mind-set, including its brain-centric notions of consciousness, that tend to isolate consciousness to such an extraordinary degree in the rational, left brain across the larger part of the culture. There is one feature of that isolation of consciousness that needs to be emphasized.

When we use the lens of our beautiful brains to do its critical work of separating everything into parts, and limit our attention to this separating process, we also inevitably see ourselves as separate and therefore isolated and vulnerable. The result of our relying primarily on our brains to connect with the world and each other is that we perceive ourselves as disconnected. There is an inherent emotional response to that perception, and that response is *fear*. Fear results inevitably from the brain's way of looking at the world, even if we engage in the mental offensive strategy of seeking to control the world with an accumulation of power. This fear, as biologist Bruce Lipton's work suggests, creates the environment of the body in which the cells cannot operate. This is precisely why power and wealth cannot create contentment.

It is for these reasons that America is the first culture to so psychologize itself with a treatment program focused on the brain. Critics of this psychological culture have emerged, such as the late psychotherapist James Hillman. Hillman argued that psychology has permeated our thinking and constituted a departure from the accumulated wisdom of the world that acknowledged souls.

The direct consequences of this American setting is that humans, while designed to adapt to change, are now faced with a rate of change to which they cannot adapt because their attention skills are weak. Our attention was stolen away by those very cultural circumstances that are destroying our health and our capacity for soul evolution. As a direct consequence, we see all around us signs of decompensation—the functional deterioration of a level of consciousness in humans that has worked for a time but is no longer adequate. Rates of chronic illness are rapidly rising among adults and children. Childhood rates of autism spectrum and learning disorders are now epidemic. Stress, now commonly recognized as a factor in the formation of every disease, already affects a majority of our population and is increasing in intensity. Life expectancy in America has declined significantly. Life expectancy for children is lower than that of adults. Mental illness is on the rise across the population. America has the largest per capita prison population in the world, and roughly half of that population suffers untreated mental illness. In the general population, mental illness could be said to be epidemic if we used the same measure as we use for the common flu.

How does the emergent soul respond to this circumstance?

From a soul perspective, the soul has the capacity to recover the memory of who it is and that it chose to take birth into this very circumstance. Is this culture challenging? Yes. That is its gift. Does the vulture culture pervade the entire world in which we live? Increasingly so. One cannot avoid challenge now. This challenge will remain the context for the weak attention that is the cause of the confusion that Stage Two Consciousness represents. There is no indication that things in the external will get any easier, for reasons that are beyond our understanding, except in our acknowledgement of a basic karmic scheme in which we are involved for the edification of our souls. Without a soul perspective, the personality of the unawakened soul will continue to be dominated by culture and will naturally feel that it is a victim of a fate that it cannot control. Its emotions will continue to tend toward the negative.

The Lens of the Heart

Like the brain-mind, the heart is also a lens of perception. Although conventional science would regard such a statement as fantasy, the research conducted by the Institute of HeartMath and others supports this view. Author Stephen Buhner's *The Secret Teachings of Plants* includes an excellent compilation of this view. Of course, all of the world's spiritual traditions acknowledge—at least at the highest levels of practice—that the heart is the seat of both wisdom and the soul.

While the mind lens navigates the world by separating it into parts, the heart does just the opposite. The heart lens navigates through connection. Its modality is not conceptual, as a thought is conceptual. It does not work first and foremost with language, which thoughts require. It works through the *experience* of connecting and, through that connection, by direct *knowing*. The heart gathers information in a sensory, felt fashion. This felt sense of direct knowing is not what we call emotion, which is a physiological response to what our mind perceives. The emotional response is indeed one means by which knowing can operate, if we are skilled enough to locate our attention in the heart and observe the information encoded in the emotional response. The heart is not by its nature emotional despite our common romantic assumptions to the contrary. The heart knows by participating with anything and everything.

The heart operates in a simple, binary *yes* or *no* process. What the soul is attracted to is determined by the soul's own vibratory nature, which resonates with those other fields that are relevant to its *nature*—the fields that are in some way important to the soul's fate and destiny. The soul provides the gyroscope for the heart's navigational capacity. The heart works by connection, and the soul field provides the magnetic energy that determines the strength of that connection. The strength of the connection determines whether it is attractive, just as a weak connection feels unattractive. We ultimately find our destiny by moving toward what powerfully attracts us when we have skillfully anchored our attention in the heart and merged it with the embodied soul. If we have not taken that step skillfully, we can still be attracted, but the attraction will lack clarity and may instead reflect a personality magnetized to the shiny objects dangled before it by culture or the fantasies of our own projections. Without that clarity, the soul is magnetized to its fate. With clarity, it is magnetized to its destiny.

As is true with the brain's perception by means of separation, the heart's use of connection is followed by a singular emotional reaction. As the body experiences connection through the heart's mode of seeing, it experiences itself as connected to everything, and feels neither isolated nor vulnerable. It does not experience fear. On the contrary, it experiences a sense of well-being that is associated with a sense of *wholeness*. Looking through the lens of the heart is followed by a cascade of positive emotion.

In this way, it is the heart-field that provides the doorway to emergence from Stage Two Consciousness into a growing soul awareness that I have called Stage Three Consciousness, even before we have developed the skill of locating our souls and attention in the heart.

Stage Three is the label I have given to the first steps taken by the soul in regaining its attention.

CHAPTER FOUR

PART THREE: THE BRIDGE
STAGE THREE: CAPTURING CONTROL OF ATTENTION
AND REMEMBERING WHO WE ARE

In Chapter Four . . .

A Knowing
An Awakening
Awakenings
Integrating the Awakenings
Reaching the Bridge
The 1990 Vision Quest
The Chiricahua Quest
The Awakenings Intensify Yet More
Building the Bridge With the Skill of Heart-Centered Attention
How Will I Know When I've Reached the Far Side of the Bridge?

Terrain	Stage of Consciousness	Perspective
Part Three: The terrain includes the body and the earth, but also includes the other dimensions beyond time/space. There is a move from the exclusively external to include the internal.	**Stage Three:** A battle for control of attention begins, with culture on one side, and the nascent soul on the other. The soul is now working, even below the level of conscious awareness, to capture control of the attention that has been taken by the personality and culture during the soul's forgetfulness.	Life remains confusing even as a sense of purpose has begun to form. I begin to shift from seeing everything as good or bad, to seeing what happens as *just is*. Reactivity begins to diminish as I learn to reclaim the projections that are the basis of my victim perspective.

STAGE THREE CONSCIOUSNESS IS THE rather long bridge we cross in order to leave the forgetful state that Stage Two represents. As we step foot on that long bridge, we are still more aware of what we left than what we will experience on the other side. The farther we go across the bridge, the more we are able to get a glimpse of what awaits us. But, while we are on the bridge, we still haven't completely left our past experience, and we still haven't arrived at the experience of what lies beyond the bridge. While a bridge represents an important step forward, it also represents the onset of a huge change, and change invites confusion as we have to leave things behind and open ourselves to something new. Stage Three is a time of awakenings from the forgetful slumber of Stage Two and the confusions that attend that transition. When we step off the bridge, we will have remembered who we are, even if we don't remember why we came. Why don't we remember why we came once we remember who we are? In the same way that more than one shaman has reminded me, I would say that the acquisition of a soul perspective *is a process.* The perspective is developed a step at a time. The first step is the recovery of the memory of who we are. Then we have to integrate that memory by adjusting the life that was based in a different identity. Ultimately, we *discover* why we came, which is itself a creative process. We came to create something that we can only discover through the heart's process of connecting the soul to its continually changing environment. Even if we have prophetic visions of that future, the unfoldment of that vision is a process of discovery.

A Knowing

In my early teen years, Ronnie was my best friend. He was a year younger, born on the same date in November.

Ronnie was a trout-fishing phenom. If his father caught three, Ronnie would catch a dozen. Nobody in his family, including his brothers, ever brought more home than Ronnie. He *owned* the small streams.

In the summer after my fifteenth birthday, I got my driver's license and an old Chevy truck. I had never fished a stream, and the parents were cool with our driving alone for the couple of hours it would take to get to where we could camp and fish. So the deal was hatched. I would drive; Ronnie would teach me how to fish.

Ronnie brought one of his father's old fly rods for me to use. A fly rod is longer and more flexible than the spinning rod that I had used in the lakes near our hometown. When we arrived at the stream, Ronnie put a small hook on the line and baited it with a red salmon egg—not the usual equipment for a fly rod, but this was not about style.

The width of the stream varied from about eight to twelve feet, running cold and clear from the steady summer snow melt in the high mountains of the Sangre de Christo range of the southern Rocky Mountains. On its way to the Rio Grande, the stream meandered down a narrow valley floor through rock outcrops and small meadows thick with fir, blue spruce and red willow. If you could see a trout, it had already seen you.

Ronnie handed me the pole and told me to drop the bait in the ripple that was gently cresting in the middle of the stream. "Let out some line," he said.

"How will I know if I get a bite?" I asked. I was feeling some performance anxiety and not wanting to screw this up.

"You'll know," Ronnie said. I remember feeling that Ronnie was being parsimonious in his guidance. He was parsimonious in general, including in his demeanor and in his speech. He reeked of common sense. If boys can have a Mona Lisa smile, Ronnie had it. In this moment, it felt stingy. I could use a little more how-to information on this important occasion, I thought. My mind, even at that age, liked a good understanding.

I let out some line. I could feel the pole trembling in my hands and see the tip bobbing as the bait rode the ripples in the center of the current. Was that a bite?

"How will I know if I get a bite?" I repeated. There was a greater sense of urgency now, perhaps a little demanding tone in my voice.

He didn't bite. "You'll know," he repeated. "Let out some more line." Whatever he knew, he was hiding it behind that Mona Lisa smile.

I let out the line. The ripples tugged. The tip of the pole bobbed. I turned my eyes toward Ronnie.

"You'll know," he said, voice still flat. Ronnie clearly knew, but he wasn't going to say more. "Let out more line," he said, pointing a bit downstream, "and let the bait drop over into that pool." There was a dark pool maybe fifteen or twenty feet downstream, shaded by a tall Douglas fir. If there were fish there, we couldn't see them, and they couldn't see us.

I let out more line. The bait slid down the smooth tongue of water darkening into the pool. Before I could think another thought, the pole bent sharply forward. It jerked in my hand. I had a bite.

And I knew.

More importantly, I knew that I knew, and that I knew without qualification. I just knew.

An Awakening

My question about how I would know was not helpful, as it turned out. The reason it was not helpful might help you to understand how we *know* the soul.

If I were to ask, "Is there a soul?" or "How will I know?", it would be the same as my question to Ronnie. While the question is literally a reaching out for assistance, and invites information, it doesn't invite a *knowing*.

Think of the word "soul" as a container, like a bucket. If I carry my bucket to someone with my question, "Is there a soul?", and they say, "Yes, there is a soul," what do I have to put in my bucket? I have someone else's opinion. If I ask, "What does it feel like?", and they tell me something, I can now carry their story in my bucket. When I took my bucket to Ronnie with my question, "How will I know," he refused to fill it. Instead, he told me how to fill my bucket with my own experience. I had to put that instruction into a different bucket, one that I might mark with different words such as "process" or "instructions for getting a bite" or "bite pathway." And that left my own "bite" bucket empty, and ready for filling with my own experience.

If I do not learn how to seek out and pay attention to my own experience, my "soul" bucket will never have anything in it but other people's stories. It does me little good to become an expert of other people's stories ("Bob says there is a soul, and he says it is blue. Jane says her soul is red. And I feel comfortable in my belief in souls and have faith that they exist because 80 percent of the people I have spoken to believe in souls."). Even those stories are a step removed from their experience, just as an understanding is not the same thing as the experience itself. I might as well collect bottle caps for all the good it will do my own soul work. In fact, carrying their stories retards my own soul work, because I have fooled myself into thinking I know something about my own soul, when just the opposite is true. The assumption that their experience of soul would be like my experience is not only incorrect, but might leave me looking for their experience in a way that I would overlook my own.

To speak of your own soul as though it were a concept that has meaning independent of your personal experience of it is . . . well . . . meaningless. If we give our attention over to culture and allow it to fill our buckets with the distractions of entertainment and the accumulation of consumer goods, there is no experience, and no meaning except in the eventual recognition that these pursuits don't satisfy. Only by bringing the attention to our own soul and its very unique response to that culture can we begin to sense the secrets that fill our bucket with something of worth. Ronnie's gift to me was an awakening to the *capacity for knowing* as a thing in itself, independent of what is known with that sense.

Awakenings

Among my acquaintances, I occasionally hear one say that they are *awakened*. I'm never sure what to make of that, except that these people seem to imply that they have arrived at a final destination. I can also see that at least some of these same people continue to struggle with life's challenges. I have also met or read about teachers who are called awakened, as though that is the final pinnacle, yet I also know that many of these teachers, despite their genuine engagement with deeper or higher states of consciousness, may continue to encounter very rough Part Two territory as their new powers and popularity also awaken in them an unbalanced sexual nature or bring them face to face with lots of credit cards.

Awakened is a term commonly used to describe an important spiritual event, particularly among practitioners of Asian meditation techniques. One is awakened, in this common usage, or one is not, implying in our own linguistic description of it a static state of being. That static state, if isolated, is sometimes called *presence*. It represents a certain state of consciousness in which the attention is under control. With that control, the consciousness is focused upon a continuously unfolding experience of the "now." The relationship with that unfolding now is non-attached, non-reactive, and non-judgmental. As those terms suggest, this state of consciousness is sometimes described in negative terms, such as what is left when the attention is withdrawn from what is external to it. The nature of this presence—what it is and what it isn't, and whether the notion of *soul* is contained within it—has been the subject of much debate over many centuries. The complexity of that debate is found in the perhaps impossible challenge of reducing to language the infinite nature of consciousness itself to the perspective held by a single human being. My smart buddy Ronnie couldn't even do that with instructions on how to catch a fish, so it's not surprising that we struggle to understand how to catch the nature of consciousness itself.

It is not necessary to come to a final understanding of what consciousness is, or what a soul represents within the frame of consciousness as a whole, in order to have a soul perspective. Humans probably do not have the capacity for such understandings. But we can understand that the static state of presence that simply watches without engagement is of a different nature than, and perhaps only preliminary to, a presence that steps forward and engages—and engages without attachment, judgment, or reaction. A soul that sees a relationship with the body as an opportunity for collaboration in service of the evolution of consciousness moves beyond a static into a dynamic state. Such a soul is continually moving, even if one has awakened before, toward another awakening. As a Sami shaman told me, "There is always more information." There is always more experience—more *engagements* between the soul and its planetary/cosmic environment—that will awaken us to deeper knowings. There is a paradox in these observations about the soul. The soul is, by its nature, a steady state that observes, experiences, tastes. And the soul is also a dynamic, if it chooses to engage.

A soul is presence on the move—attention with a mission that we call destiny. Attention is on the move even if our very skillful attention directs itself toward itself. In those moments of deep self reflection, in which we experience our own attention as the focus of an infinite consciousness, we may also experience the very *living presence* that attention represents. The soul is a living presence that engages. It can never be fully awakened, in the past tense to which that word implies. It is always awakening, engaging, present-ing, moving, living. A soul is consciousness focused for an appearance in time/space with a purpose it must discover in the frame of the density of matter. For that reason, I use instead a plural gerund form–*awakenings*–to signify a dynamic that characterizes a continuing process.

If our unskilled attention is hypnotized by a culture that has aggressively manipulated it to serve a consumer economy, then the event of slipping out of that hypnosis into an internal state in which we have brought attention back to ourselves most certainly feels like a waking up. When it occurs, an awakening is simply a momentary event that is repeated—hopefully more and more frequently—as the soul's ability to reclaim its own focus of attention increases. As I would define it, *awakening* never refers to a terminal, irrevocable arrival at a state of consciousness which is unlikely to revert to a less-awake state of consciousness. The control of attention is not an event that occurs once and only once. In the face of a culture that has a predatory relationship with the attention of its inhabitants, it is pretty clear that we need to pay attention to the process of paying attention on a continual basis. We have to be vigilant in our attention, lest it be stolen away. We have to learn how to hold our own attention against the onslaught of a chaotic environment that would distract anything other than the most skillful attention. And even the most skillful attention remains on the move within the frame of an ever-changing *now*.

It is possible that many people who feel they have arrived at a state of "awakened" have experienced the deep sense of presence they might describe as *I am that—I am that presence.* When that occurs, we experience such a radically different perspective—one that heightens our sensory experience to a state of awe—that we bookmark the experience as an awakening, as though we have in that moment risen from a sleep. And that seems to be a truth of my own experience. The light of consciousness in general has shined through the particularity of our individual soul consciousness to awaken us to the infinite nature of who we are just as the morning sun shining through the window awakens us from our slumber. Yet, even the constant state of feeling that deep presence to what is around me, including consciousness itself, is different than—I would say also *less than*—the next step of *engaging* by means of that presence, which is what souls do. When we engage, we embrace the further step of identification: *I am that presence focused upon a mission I will discover as my particular purpose, my destiny.* A soul has continual awakenings. It is the infinite consciousness getting to work in very finite ways.

The initial awakenings that occur as our souls grab at the attention hovering around the surface personality are only a beginning, a taste, a hint of the much deeper and deepening experience that comes from a sustained relationship between attention and the soul. Each awakening, then, is a knowing based in our own experience of our own soul nature. It is the experience and immediate apprehension of that experience—before we can think about it—that is centrally important.

When I experienced the fish on my hook, it took me out of both my mind (How will I know?) and my emotions (I'm afraid I won't know)—the common places for culture to fish for my attention. Realizing from my experience of catching the fish that I could know something without understanding it first—and without checking in to see what culture's understanding might be—was an awakening. Then I was immediately back into my mind and asleep again, but I didn't forget how it felt to come within myself and feel the direct knowing that arose from an experience that my mind, emotions, and culture did not intermediate.

It is in such moments that we may say our souls have been touched, or that our souls have touched the surface personality with which we have come to identify. Either way, the medium of that touch is our own attention. So long as our attention is dissociated from the soul and located in a surface personality that is itself not merged with the soul, the turning of the personality's attention to the soul makes the soul an *object* of our attention. When the attention eventually and skillfully re-merges with the soul, the soul is literally re-membering. The soul then becomes the *subject* and substance of our attention. Souls thusly re-membered subjectify the human body/mind/personality system and render us incapable of objectifying ourselves or others, because our attention becomes merged through the soul into the whole of consciousness of which souls are irrevocably a self-aware whole/part.

In this collaborative system of parallel lenses, the mind reaches for understanding through analysis, while the heart reaches for relationship through the direct knowing of connection. Neither can fully penetrate the ultimate mystery of the other, whether the other is a person, a plant, a process, or consciousness itself. What the tools of mind and heart provide are the means of skillful interaction with that to which we connect. We can understand and know how the something to which we relate *functions,* even if we cannot penetrate its ultimate and mysterious nature.

Even as our souls look out upon the world through the separating lens of the mind, the self-remembered soul embodied in the heart-field no longer objectifies, since it knows that the separation itself is no more than an aspect of the whole. Even as we then use the process of separation to view something or someone, we also necessarily see the something or someone in the selfsame wholeness from which the soul experiences itself. Separation, at this level of the merger of attention with the soul, simply becomes a process contained within the process of wholeness. Separation and wholeness are not static states, but dynamics of a beautifully polarized whole that dances within itself like *yin* and *yang,* feminine and masculine, light and dark. The identification with soul becomes the stage for the activism of consciousness. That is the threshold at which we are exploring, and such notions as *engaged Buddhism* are exploring that same threshold by reaching beyond the static state sometimes implied by the simple notion of presence.

Within the soul unconsciousness of Stage Two and before we form any intention to bring attention to the soul, there typically arise many awakenings—occasions of *soul shining through.* When I first met Eagle Sun, a Native American man who was to become a close friend, it felt as though we were already close friends. There was an instant recognition, a quickening of my emotions, and the arising of a desire to connect more deeply. He felt the same. We were talking excitedly and walking arm in arm minutes after we met. That moment was an awakening in which my soul leapt out and recognized his in the midst of a day in a week in a year in which my ordinary state remained predominately unconscious. The time that ensued with Eagle, over several years of doing ceremony together, were times that spoke to my soul, calling it out and creating pathway for it to emerge.

It is easier, of course, for me to see awakenings in retrospect than to recognize them when they occurred. In my late twenties, a friend asked me whether I would like to learn Transcendental Meditation. Even though I had no idea what meditation was, the offer so resonated with my repressed soul consciousness that the soul was evoked for that moment. "Yes!" was the answer my soul spoke before my mind had time to think. My soul response evoked an emotional response as well—a state of excitement that gave a joyful exclamation mark to that "yes." The awakening of that moment released enough soul level energy to allow me to persist through the daily one- or two-hour trainings for a week. Yet, in the moment of that awakening, I did not recognize the instant response to the offer as a soul response, or what I've later come to recognize as an awakening.

An awakening is a breaking through, whether or not the soul has progressed to the capacity to control attention or where it is placed. Awakenings come in different forms and in different degrees. Some may be an insight that leads to a new understanding. Some may be an experience that occurs while the attention of the soul is held in the body. Some may be an experience that occurs as the attention of the soul is held out of the body. Some may be subtle, while others may hit us like a speeding train. Some may involve all of these within a short span of time. Every awakening is a focusing and riveting of attention that propels the soul nature to the surface, if only for a moment, and every awakening is a shift for the moment to a deeper soul perspective. Each time the soul perspective surfaces, there is the opportunity to strengthen it and encourage its more frequent return.

My early practice of Transcendental Meditation brought other awakenings, including a sense of ease that came as my attention found a soft place to rest, and an equally important sense of distress as my attention was drawn to repressed emotions. I became aware that I was unwilling to contend with the great challenges those emotions implicated. I stopped meditating altogether rather than invite a deeper encounter with repressed emotions, but I could not forget the sense of awakening that had emerged in the meantime. It stood like a dog-eared page marking forward progress until other awakenings brought me back to that juncture, when I was ready once more to face my repressed experiences. I knew even as I stopped the meditation that I would return to it when I could. That knowing, too, was itself an awakening, one that re-cognized the connection between my attention and the inner. It required several more awakenings for me to re-cognize the connection between attention and the soul.

Integrating the Awakenings

By their nature, our early awakenings are precious but isolated events within the context of a relatively unconscious state characterized by a weak ability to control attention. If we are to get more value than a good story from them, it is important to learn how to integrate them into a more conscious process. Here are a few understandings that I would offer as helpful:

- A particular awakening may be far less important than the ability to control attention. An awakening is the indicator that attention has moved inward in the direction of the soul for the moment and invites us to cultivate that inward movement, which requires intention, commitment, and practice.
- Awakenings make energy available. When the attention is brought to the soul, the soul becomes more powerful, because attention is the very stuff of the soul. The more awakenings we have, the more fuel for the journey.
- We can cultivate awakenings by any practice that helps us to learn to control attention and, with that control, helps us to learn to bring the attention to the soul. We do that in the most simple and direct way by learning to focus attention within the field of the heart, where the soul field is most powerfully resonant.
- Sometimes it takes another awakening—another piece of the puzzle—to set up the necessary conditions for an integration of the earlier awakening into a larger understanding of our own engagement with the process of fate.
- Sometimes our awakenings appear as a response to something or someone who engages our outer in a way that provokes our inner. These might be said to be encounters with soul mates that appear in our lives perhaps only for moments, perhaps longer, to deliver a reminder of who we are.

It was almost eight years from the time that I first learned to meditate, and six years after I had stopped, that such an awakening as described in the last of these examples occurred.

My spouse and I had invited some friends over for a Christmas Eve gathering following an early midnight mass. At mass, we sat next to a couple that I had known since my teen years. After the gathering, the wife lingered until she was the last to leave. As I was saying goodnight to her at the door, she pushed a crumpled piece of paper into my hand, then left without another word.

I looked at the paper. There were five words: *chit, sat, ananda, lila, moshka*. I had no idea what they meant or from what language they originated.

The next morning, I called my friend to ask what this was about. She replied that she didn't know, but that these words were in my mind when we sat in church. I asked what they meant. She said that she didn't know. She could only say that she heard them clearly, and that she knew that they were in my mind. I had no idea that she was clairvoyant, or even what clairvoyancy was about. But it certainly caught my attention.

Those were pre-internet days. Now it would be easy to search for those words and get a full definition. Then, I didn't know where to look. The last of the words—*moskha*—sounded to me like it might be Russian. I had an elderly friend who was a Russian immigrant. I asked Maria whether she was familiar with the word. She wasn't.

Then my friend called. "I misspelled one of the words," she said. "It should have been *moksha*." I asked whether she had any further information or insight into what this was about. She didn't.

Days later, I found myself sitting with a friend from India while we watched our young children skiing at a nearby ski area. It occurred to me to ask him the question. I wrote them out on a napkin. He asked with evident interest where I had seen the words. I politely declined to say, not wishing to blow my other friend's cover. I simply asked him if he knew what the words meant. His translation was simple: *chit* meant absolute mind, or consciousness; *sat* meant absolute existence; *ananda* meant absolute joy; *lila* meant the play of consciousness; and *moksha* meant liberation. I thanked him then dropped the conversation pretty quickly.

In a few days, my Indian friend showed up at my home with a stack of books, all published by Himalayan Institute founded by his teacher Swami Rama. Rama, I learned, had some notoriety for unusual powers of consciousness documented by Elmer Green at the Menninger Clinic in Kansas. I dove in to reading those books. Within a few weeks, my friend asked me if I would be interested in hearing a lecture by one of Rama's primary students in Fort Worth, Texas. Again, it was an awakening moment. "Yes!" came out of my mouth before my mind could consider all of the ramifications. The desire to resume meditating had matured, and an integration was occurring. I flew to Ft. Worth. Before long, I received an invitation from my Indian friend to go to Rama's institute in Pennsylvania. The soul easily emerged this time to say yes!

Was I "awakened"? Hardly. I was still living in a challenging marriage. I was unconscious of the dysfunctional Stage Two patterns that were the substance of my fate and my own contribution to the difficulty of the marriage. I continued to project responsibility on my spouse for my unhappiness. I was still working in a profession in which, despite its success as measured by a financial yardstick, I felt unhappy and stressed. And my emotions continued to be repressed, while I continued to punish my body with long distance running in order to access—though I didn't understand it at the time—the rush of endorphins that helped me to repress the emotions through which the voice of my soul was screaming to be heard. My mind was still caught in my own perspective of victimization—projecting blame onto the people and events around me for the struggles of my life.

Was I experiencing awakenings? Absolutely. I was beginning to move toward that critical moment of stepping onto the bridge of Part Three even while my predominate state of consciousness was hanging out in Stage Two.

Did I understand what was going on within my consciousness? Not at all.

Was my soul making itself heard? Yes.

Reaching the Bridge

Even as the awakenings accelerate, our attention can remain the captive of culture. The awakenings are like bubbles rising up from a soul boiling just beneath a surface personality caught in a struggle with fate.

There is a juncture where the critical mass of awakenings is such that we begin to form a clear intention to leave Stage Two behind us. We are no longer willing simply to drift, to suffer, to be the victim. We form a new attitude. That new attitude, even if it contemplates the existence of a soul, is not the same as a soul perspective. It might take the form of a commitment, such as a new determination to do something that changes the status quo. Though not a soul perspective, it is most definitely a new perspective. While the ultimate object of this commitment might be the recapture of our attention and the placement of that attention firmly into the field of the soul, the step onto the bridge of Stage Three is seldom understood in such direct terms. We might feel that we simply need to pay more attention to ourselves. We might engage a new practice like yoga or *chi gong*. We might hear ourselves say that we are not going to live our lives in the way that we have done before. Something shifts.

That commitment marks the beginning of momentum that has the potential to carry us forward. When we make that commitment, the bridge appears before us. On the near end of the bridge is Stage Two. On the other end is the very critical and singular awakening that marks the culmination of Stage Three and the beginning of Stage Four Consciousness. For me, the end of Stage Three was the near death experience I recounted in chapter one. Only in retrospect could I see how various awakenings illuminated for me the path across the bridge of Stage Three that arrived at a climax with the death experience. Critical to starting that crossing was the commitment to do a vision quest.

The 1990 Vision Quest

My awakenings began only slowly in my teen years, continued to emerge in small spurts in my twenties, then began to accelerate in my thirties—all and each alerting me to the need to change something central in my life. There came one awakening that—standing on all that has gone before—became a tipping point. By "tipping point" I mean an experience that leads to the recognition that I could no longer continue my life as before. A change had to occur. It is as though the awakenings that had gone before were about to go critical, and just one more would do the job. The awakening that set my foot on the bridge finally and firmly occurred in 1990.

During the five years prior to 1990, Eagle Sun and I were doing our periodic sweatlodge ceremonies. In those ceremonies, I felt safe to express my emotions and found a place of acceptance. That sense of safety was itself an awakening—one that allowed a simple being present to the impulse of the moment and breathing out into the warm and gentle space of the group environment Eagle had created. These experiences stretched the frame of my conventional perspective. That was an awakening. My friend's cryptic Christmas gift spawned an awakening that led to my meditating daily after my visits to Ft. Worth and the Himalayan Institute. The continuing challenge of my marriage and professional work were providing an increasing motivation for opening myself to significant change in my life. My renewed practice of meditation was increasing my control over my attention.

In 1990, Eagle Sun introduced me to John Milton.

Milton was teaching "vision questing" in Crestone, a small mountain community in southern Colorado. The program was simple. After an orientation that included a couple of days of introduction to Buddhist and Taoist notions of "pristine awareness," he had us take our tents and bedrolls out to the side of a steep hill at the foot of a 14,000-foot peak in the Sangre de Christo range of the Rocky Mountains. A small stream ran along the bottom of the hill.

Milton told each of the five people involved in this venture to pick a separate campsite, draw a figurative circle of not more than 100 paces in diameter, and not to leave it for six days. As part of our preparation, Milton instructed us in simple qi gong exercises intended to help us maintain energy during the fasting that he encouraged while on our quest. Milton suggested various ways of connecting with the earth and nature spirits, a process that would be familiar to the indigenous traditions of virtually any culture. The basic strategy of the exercise was to "be" on the earth and "do" as little as possible, and to cultivate a state of awareness not mediated by our ordinary minds.

For a busy American mind, the prospect of doing nothing for six days—and not eating for most of that time—sounds beyond strange, as well boring and frightening. I came prepared to fill my time with my own meditation practice, and soon found that there was way too much time to fill with that. I began going through the motions of connecting with the earth despite my then inability to embrace them with any supporting belief. I practiced the qi gong exercises. I fretted about food and walked back to my car to get more. I stared at the 100-mile long western horizon that I could see from my mountainside vantage point. My mind drifted across an internal horizon that felt like as many miles of memories and fantasies.

As I sat or paced, I began to see that my boredom was a failure to pay attention to what was right in front of me. I tried just paying attention. As there was less and less to distract my attention into the external, I found myself paying attention both to more subtle levels of what was occurring around me and to my internal reactions to those events.

Then I noticed the flies.

There were lots of flies in the warmish fall days that made this quest more pleasant than not. As I sat on the ground in my running shorts, a fly would frequently land on my leg. When it did, I brushed it off. At one point, the act of holding my attention upon my inner response to whatever was happening in the external allowed me to recognize that my brushing was a conditioned response. I stopped the movement of my hand in mid-brush, allowing a fly to stay on my upper thigh. For a few moments, I simply watched the fly. I paid attention to the sensation of the fly walking amidst the hairs on my leg to graze on the dead skin. Then another fly landed, and then more. All told, eleven flies clustered on my leg.

Okay, I thought, *that was fun*, at least for a certain value of fun in the absence of ordinary distractions. I could not hold attention, finally, and became bored again. I stood up to walk down to the creek, literally in hope of being distracted by a different scene. The flies lifted off, swarmed around my leg as I moved down the hill, then alighted again on the same leg, in the same place, as I sat by the stream. *One, two . . . yup, all eleven had come.*

This scenario was unfolding late in the afternoon of my fifth day on the mountain. While I was looking forward to being with the others around noon on the next day, I also realized that my consciousness and body had calmed down from the more agitated state that I had brought into the small circle of wilderness several days before. That calmer state allowed the flies to sit with me, and me with them.

In that moment, a dragonfly landed on the boulder inches away from where I was leaning my shoulder. The dragonfly held a grub in its mouth, dropped it on the rock just in front of my face, then flew away. I paid little attention and only later wondered whether I should have paid more. Was that grub for me? It was a nonsensical question from the perspective of our conventional perspectives. But I didn't take time to explore the alternative. Something else had captured my attention.

I heard tinkling bells. It wasn't immediately apparent where the sound was coming from. I was at a distance from all my questing companions, and far enough out in the mountainous woods that bells would certainly be an unusual sound. Then I sensed that the sound was coming from the stream just a few feet away, as though it were floating on the ripples that sparkled with late afternoon sunlight.

Before I could think more about what was transpiring, the sound changed. *Voices singing . . . no . . . a choir . . . wait . . . Celtic music.* Was a Celtic choir ringing down the stream? How clear and beautiful this sound was. It lasted perhaps a minute, perhaps two, certainly long enough for me sit still, in rapt attention, afraid to disturb the moment. As soon as it stopped, my head was turned by another sound arising behind me, from over my left shoulder. Two male voices, clearly distinguishable as such, were singing in duet. This sound quickly faded—more than a few seconds, less than a minute in duration.

Then the soundings stopped. Evening breeze rose gently up, pulling me from this reverie. I stood to return up the slope to my tent. As I walked, I began to hear drumming. The drums seemed to be carried in the wind itself, with my attention drawn to the tops of trees moving with the breeze. For several minutes I stood, listening to these wind drums.

On the following day, I joined my questing companions. There was a shared euphoria, which I took to be the response to arriving at the end of a week endured alone. We shared our stories, laughing playfully with one another. In a private conversation, I spoke to one of my companions about my not wanting to return to my home, complaining to her of the painful relationship that awaited me there. She gently but bluntly told me her assessment of my story, saying that I had no insight. I didn't understand what she meant, although she suggested that I see a counselor.

No insight. Those words were ringing in my ears as I began the three-hour drive home. In retrospect, I can easily understand that the absence of insight was the result of my attention being fully captured in the external and my projection of responsibility for my unhappiness onto the people and events in my life. This recognition formed the basis of an understanding that would unfold as I integrated the experience of the vision quest over the years that followed. But there was another awakening unfolding in that very moment.

As I drove, it felt as though I was driving through a metaphor. The farther I drove, the darker the clouds became. In the literal, I was driving down from the mountain, but I felt as though I was driving into a deeper and deeper depression. The next morning, I meditated, and cried. The tears came from a realization that, during the week of my quest, I had so gradually emerged into a state of euphoria that I had not recognized the transition. Coming down rather quickly from that state into my normal consciousness brought me to the realization that my busy family and professional life was being lived in a state of depression that was so normal in me and in the community in which I lived as to be invisible. Only my week on the earth was able to pull me out of it for a long enough moment to see where I lived. The fish had come out of the water, and seen water for the first time.

What pulled me out?

The honest answer is that I don't know. And the answer may be irrelevant, since the important thing was the awakening. But my mind wanted to have an understanding of how the awakening occurred, because such an understanding helps replicate and stimulate these critically important awakenings.

In time I came to understand that the earth has an electromagnetic field called the Shumann Resonance. This field is located between the surface of the earth upon which we stand and the ionosphere. The field's frequency hovers around 7.86 Hz. That frequency, as it turns out, is the approximate frequency that our human central nervous systems generate when we have stopped thinking and have moved into a state of relaxation. In humans, we call it the *alpha* wave. In that state, our attention may be pleasantly active or passive. The frequency is also associated with the state of consciousness through which we pass when we have stopped thinking and are on our way to sleeping and dreaming. Thinking and other waking activity evokes what is commonly known as a *beta* brain wave. It is faster than the *alpha* wave. Dream sleep is associated with a slower wave we call *theta,* and dreamless sleep is associated with *delta* waves.

Understanding the nature of the Shumann Resonance suggested to me that my uninterrupted sitting upon the earth resulted in a resonant experience between my own body fields and the earth field. The earth field, being far stronger than my own, entrained me to its own rhythm. I had come back to the earth, and it had embraced me. The earth's field had blessedly overpowered my own. I came to the sense that I had been held in an unconditional love by a being much more powerful than myself.

Our off-migration from the farm has most probably cut our culture off from a relatively common experience of the Shumann Resonance. Without this grounding, calming effect, human consciousness is cut loose—a condition that requires more skillful management if attention is not going to move helter-skelter in response to the plethora of attentional distractions that are increasingly present in our culture.

On the morning after I returned home and felt the emotional response to this awakening, I called a counselor. After a few visits, she said my issue was more spiritual than otherwise, and referred me to her own spiritual teachers. For two years after that, I commuted once a month to Santa Fe to work with those teachers. The counseling might have explored the issue of projection and the nature of my adaptive pattern, but it did not. In retrospect, it seems an opportunity missed. On the other hand, the counselor was correct. My issue *was* spiritual, even if it was also psychological. These were simply alternate lenses through which to look at my experience of myself and my perspective on the world.

From the details of that two-year teaching, a single shining teaching occurred, and it was a version of the one repeated later to me in my own near death experience: say the truth about yourself. I began to practice that, with much fear and trembling, with my own spouse. There were consequences. The consequences were rigorous, difficult, and emotionally draining. And all of them were positive—from a soul perspective, at least—absolutely positive.

By 1995, I felt that I was ready to bring more change into my life. Truth telling was getting easier, even as I was yet unable to do it skillfully. I was learning that each time I told my truth, consequences ensued, but I always felt better, and felt more energized.

That increasing energy allowed me to do five more of the six-day vision quests over the years from 1995 to 2000. This was a way of ratcheting up the soul pressure that would break up my cultural mind-set while practicing and deepening the skill of controlling attention. During these quests, my experiences became more specifically clairaudient, and the nature of the awakenings deepened. In 1995, the nature of the awakening was startling.

The Chiricahua Quest

In April of 1995, I met John Milton and two other questers in the Chiricahua Mountains east of Tucson, Arizona. Again, we sat at Milton's knee for a couple of days as he prepared us for the six days of the "solo" that would follow. Even before I arrived, I felt better prepared. I had learned more about fasting, and had brought some seeds, dried fruits and teas from which I could make sun teas and juices to support the fast. Having spent considerably more time doing solo nights or weekends outdoors, I felt more comfortable with the idea of spending this time alone in unfamiliar woods. It was easier now to embrace the practice of making offerings to nature spirits, even though I still felt unable to connect. I had now experienced a deeply mysterious "unseen," so I could easily contemplate that others might exist. I could now invite the unseen into my circle—if not with expectation, at least with a sense of possibility.

By the time I put my tent up and marked out the 100-paces diameter of the circle within which I would stay, I could feel my attention returning quickly from its normal preoccupation with daily routines of family and work. I soon experienced something that I recalled from the 1990 quest without having paid attention to it before—a basal, droning sound that I could both hear and feel in my ears. The sound itself was unremarkable. What was remarkable was its strong presence. In retrospect, I know that it was a prelude to a richer experience of sound. In the moment, it gave rise only to a suspicion that it might be significant because my 1990 experience had included extraordinary sounds. And, though it was fairly loud, I was skeptical. Could the sound be coming from the truck tires on the interstate? No, I thought. The interstate was perhaps forty or fifty miles to the north. And I couldn't really tell whether the sound originated in or out of my head.

Within a day, my preoccupation with the drone sound was shifted by another sound. A faint rhythm began to resound in my ears—one that danced, as it were, upon the drone sound. The drone sound remained without diminishment in volume, but there was something now layered over it that I couldn't pin down. Again, my skepticism declined to accept any source of this new sound other than some unknown cause in ordinary reality. I found myself down by the small stream that intersected my circle, holding my ear close to a small waterfall and listening to the movement of rocks that might account for the faint rhythm. I could hear rocks bumping each other, but there was no rhythm there.

Within another day's time, my skepticism gave way to a sharp focus of attention as the new sound not only evidenced an increasingly clear rhythm, but began to manifest word-like sounds. These came and went, as though teasing my attention, causing me to listen even more closely as these new sounds receded. As I was able to capture them, words began to emerge into clarity, though they were unfamiliar to me. I pulled out my pen and notebook and tried to write down what was I was hearing.

As I did so, a kind of interactive process emerged. As I notated the music, or tried to write a word that seemed to capture the word-like sound, there would often arise an intensification of the sound, both in volume and clarity. I say "capture the sound," since the sounds seemed to form words, but the words were not in English or otherwise familiar to me. It became apparent before long that if I wrote down something incorrectly, the sound would get louder. On one night, the sound was so insistent that I found myself lying in my bedroll with my knit hat and pillow pulled over my ears. I smile as I write this, thinking how often I have worked to open a door that, when it actually opened, I promptly slammed it shut.

But the sound persisted, and so did I. By the fifth day, I had managed to notate the music and lyrics of what I confirmed years later to be a *sanskrit* mantra consisting of three words repeated over four stanzas. I had never heard either the music or words before. Then, after five days of an increasing insistence of this rhythmic sound, there was a moment in which it was done. The sound—or its source—seemed satisfied, and it stopped. I laid my pen down, as if in acknowledgement that the work was completed. Then, within just a moment, the sound started up again.

With jaw dropping clarity, the music began to repeat the words of the mantra in another musical form than its original expression in what I now know to be a classical Indian chant. No longer was it the raga rising up from the tambour drone. Now it was one musical genre after another, changing quickly from country western to jazz to blues to Western to classical to pop to orchestral to soprano solos, and so on. I felt that it was trying to communicate something. What was it trying to say? My mind said: *The infinite variety that makes up the cosmos arises from a single, first sound. And each form of expression of this primordial sound has its own distinct beauty.*

There was another and even more obvious effect. These sounds and this natural setting had again rendered me into a state of bliss, this one tangibly more intense than the blissful experience of 1990. Perhaps it was a little different than that. Perhaps, in the state of bliss that nature had rendered, these extraordinary sounds were available to my now differently tuned inner ear. Either way, the habits of my personality and its habitual surrender of attention to culture had now surrendered attention instead to what had existed in abundance at some former time in the background of culture—to what is now buried deeply beneath and beyond the hustle bustle and chaotic disharmony in which we live day to day.

For the rest of my time alone, perhaps another twenty-four hours, I continued to experience the state of bliss that I now associated with a sense of unconditional love that was the hallmark of my 1990 experience. I was in that state at noon on the sixth day as my two questing companions picked me up on their way down the stream to return to our base camp with Milton. Walking away from my circle, I continued to hear the drone sound. Even carrying my backpack, I felt my feet wanting to dance down the road. I felt elated, and a sense of playfulness underscored the rest of my day.

That night, my companions and I threw our bedrolls together by the stream. As a gentle snow began to fall, more complex sounds began to arise again above the sound of the drone. It seemed that I was now receiving several channels at once in a cacophony of sounds distinguishable but unintelligible. I heard myself think: "This is what schizophrenia must be like." It startled me. I reached out into the air and turned it off, as one would turn the knob on an old radio. The sounds stopped, leaving only the drone sound behind. Again, I had closed a door that I had worked so hard to open. I had touched another reality and didn't know how to engage it. The next day, I started the engine of my pickup to start the drive home, and the drone sound stopped.

The drive home was significantly different from my experience of five years before. This time, there was no sense of an impending return to depression. Moving down the highway, I could see the pavement and metal fence posts sparkling with life. The inherent vibratory nature of these formerly inert objects was now visually striking and alive for me. Years later, in reading about Kashmiri Shaivism, I found descriptions of this precise experience. Shaivism describes this experience of all reality as alive with the same energy as a recognition of the *non-dual* nature of reality—including both what is ordinary regarded as living and what is typically regarded as inert or dead. Quantum physics has come to a similar view that everything is made of the same energy, but scientific observation cannot convey the subjective experience. I began to understand that everything is conscious in different ways. More awakenings.

My returning home to a relationship that remained challenging did not knock me out of this emergent state of non-dual recognition and experience, which declined slowly more into a memory and intermittent direct experience after a couple of months. Years later, and with increasingly intense repetitions of that experience, I began describing that 1990 vision quest experience as my first conscious encounter with unconditional love. I didn't know of any other way to describe the depth of the experience of feeling *held* by this resonate relationship with the earth. I have reflected upon my time as a child—the time of wandering in the hills, the time horseback, the time *away*—and came to understand the similarity of these times to my intense questing experience. I have not overlooked the deep irony occasioned by a cultural separation from the earth that resulted in my paying money to a teacher for the experience of re-introducing me to an experience that is the birthright of every human being. I have sensed the tragedy of our cultural evolution into a lifestyle in which high-amplitude frequencies and attention-sucking technologies have overcome the subtle and quiet earth frequencies that have held us to the Earth Mother's breast, and that formerly helped us cope with the challenges within which Fate had hidden our destinies.

The Awakenings Intensify Yet More

The vision quests of the next several years were each unique to themselves. I weaned myself from Milton, and found partners with whom I could share this solo experience at a mutually supportive distance. Each of the next four quests occasioned a return of the drone sound. Each contained some particular experience that led to an insight that led to a new understanding. Each sent me home with a reminder of the sense of unconditional love that seemed to flow so easily out of nature when I let my attention focus there. I noticed that the experience was softer if I was near water, and perhaps more mental if not. I began to regard the water quests as feminine, and the more desert experiences as masculine. In 1998, a masculine quest produced a template of information— a particularly detailed form of a medicine wheel that spiraled upwards in a form that revealed a way of looking at how change comes and is integrated into our lives.

In late spring of 2000, I did another quest alongside the Chama River in northern New Mexico. There was a full return of the clairaudience, complete with another and different *mantra* and its ultimate explosion into the genres of musical expression. It left me in a joyful, tearful, surrendered state of bliss that has become the hallmark for me of the experience of unconditional love that has been a central gift of these earth excursions. Yet, even with the grace of these blessings, I found myself still struggling in Stage Three Consciousness—moving on the bridge, but not yet seeing the other end. I had definitely left Stage Two, but hadn't managed to get across the bridge that only a retrospective view allowed me to see. I didn't know I was on a bridge, even as I was crossing. I only knew there was movement trying to happen, and that—despite the felt hugeness of these questing experiences—my sense of forward movement was feeling blocked.

Later that summer, my vision-questing partner of many years called. "There's a shaman coming to Santa Fe for a presentation tomorrow," she said. "You need to come and meet him."

I don't think I had heard the word *shaman* before. He would be speaking at an educational institution, my friend said. Again, my soul said "Yes!" before any thought could arise, and I was in my pickup on the way to Santa Fe on the next day. The shaman was from Peru. Although I had no frame of reference for shamans at that time, I could later easily say that he was not traditional. He held a PhD, and had retired from the position of president of a small college—the Peruvian equivalent of a combination of high school and trade school. He spoke Spanish and was of Spanish heritage. He was in the United States to tell the story of *ayahuasca*, and to encourage people to join him in Peru for ceremony with this plant medicine. It was a compelling story. And something in it spoke to my soul. I *knew*, without understanding, that I needed to experience directly whatever this shaman could share. In a few months, I traveled to northeastern Peru to be with this man.

Ayahuasca is a thick, bitter, reddish-brown concoction made from two or more plants that include the ayahuasca vine. The word *ayahuasca* is frequently translated as "vine of the soul" or "vine of death." There is a good deal now written about the plant, which is primary among the plants used for healing along the Amazon. The plant routinely stimulates visions—what we would call *hallucinations* in our culture, a term that many people might use to imply a dreamlike state that is simply unreal. The *ayahuascaros,* the shamans who conduct the ayahuasca ceremonies, have consistently told visiting anthropologists that the plant directly conveys information that helps the people heal, grow food, hunt, and survive. Only slowly has the anthropological community begun to listen to this story.

There were five ceremonies in the course of ten days. In the first ceremony, I initially saw something that appeared like Ping Pong balls shot at high speed across my field of vision. That was followed by the appearance of an extremely complex three-dimensional matrix that I initially took to be a wrought iron fence but eventually saw simply as a matrix. More compelling, however, was the throwing up. This seemed to last for two straight hours, rendering me more and more exhausted and increasingly fearful that I would die from this uncontrolled purging. At some point in the purging, I felt something enter me. I was on my hands and knees, and I felt the something occupy my arms and legs, as well as the trunk of my body. Whatever had come in seemed very powerful. With that power, my purging became more powerful and intentional, as though I was now collaborating in the effort to get something out of me. After the ceremony, the man who was on the mat next to mine told me that I had been growling throughout the ceremony. His comment confirmed my felt sense. The spirit of a large cat, perhaps a jaguar, had entered into me. As the ceremony ended, I felt fully calm, awake, and balanced, with a sense of wellbeing that continued throughout the next day.

At the beginning of the next ceremony two nights later, I found my awareness literally traveling out of my body. I could see the dirt street that fronted the shaman's retreat center; then it moved down the street to a corner. I turned the corner, found myself beneath a streetlight that illuminated a clinic that I had not previously seen, and then realized that I had left the ceremonial room and needed to be there. My awareness returned immediately to the room. On the next day, I walked down the street and turned the corner. The clinic was there, as I had seen it on the night before.

In four of the five ceremonies, I threw up within an hour of ingesting the aya-huasca. On each of those occasions, the purging was followed by remarkable visions that I won't detail here, except to say that they involved, among other things, many snakes and a figure that seemed to be made of leaves. I felt none of the fear that seems to be common among people who encounter visions induced by this plant. Central among the visions was the experience of being impregnated, giving birth to a light being that quickly expanded to adult human size, and watching that light being move back into my chest. Within about four or so hours after the beginning of each cere-mony, I would rise to my feet and dance to the rhythm of the shaman's drumming, and continue dancing for perhaps a couple of hours. Despite the purging, and prob-ably because of it, I slept well and felt quite centered, calm, and strong during the mornings that followed each ceremony.

Whatever else might have happened as a consequence of this brief sequence of ceremonies, my life took another turn—similar to what I experienced after the bliss states induced by the vision quests, but now more so. The experience broke the hyp-notic hold of culture on my attention and the content of my consciousness. I felt as though my head had been blown off and that I had, for the first time in my life, had an experience that was completely unmediated by my rational mind. Within weeks of my return to the States, I realized that all of my longstanding allergies had disap-peared. I realized that the rather loose worldview that sustained my conventional life could no longer contain or explain what I had just experienced. These experiences contained information that answered questions that my former state of mind couldn't even conceive.

Within weeks after my return, I found an American teacher who taught a ver-sion of Peruvian shamanism. His approach was based on a loose marriage between American psychology and the traditions of the shamans of the mountains of south-ern Peru. The mountain tradition does not involve the use of ayahuasca. I returned to Peru twice with that teacher. In the next year, I returned with another teacher. After that, I returned on my own. For several years, I worked to deepen my under-standing of how shamans look at the world. I found many teachers. I practiced what I learned. I applied it in my life. I began to see the cosmos in terms of energy, rather than seeing it solely in its very partial expression as dense matter in a time/space mode. In time, my attention became more and more my own. It was in the context of these teachings that I had the near death experience of 2003—the awakening that became for me the end of the bridge that led to Stage Four Consciousness.

Ayahuasca is illegal in the United States except for use by churches that can make the case that the ayahuasca is a sacrament central to the practice of their reli-gion. Peru's government, perhaps in partial response to this criminalization by the United States, has granted ayahuasca the status of "national treasure." My own expe-rience with the ayahuasca and America suggests to me that America suffers from a deep cultural fear of anything beyond the day-to-day reality that is literally formed by the way in which attention is glued by culture to itself. Inner exploration—the freeing of the soul—is held suspect by America on all fronts: governmental, religious, aca-demic, social, economic, and scientific. The work in the shamanic context helped to free my mind from the judgmental presumption that our scientific culture is necessarily superior in its view of "reality" to the view held by indigenous shamans. Anthropology has had to make a similar transition. Current readings in that field would suggest a deepening respect for the beneficial and powerful effects of the plant medicines, including ayahuasca.

There would be more encounters with ayahuasca in the future. For the time being, it had freed my attention from its captivity in my rational mind. This freedom gave me the opportunity to develop the skill of intentionally placing my attention elsewhere.

Building the Bridge with the Skill of Heart-Centered Attention

The bridge metaphor implies the development of a skill—something that inherently takes time to build. The skill consists of the ability to control attention with intention alone, combined with a growing knowledge of where to place attention. I use the word *knowledge* instructively here, to distinguish skills based upon personal experience from those that rely upon mere information. By *knowledge,* I mean the direct knowings that arise from our own experience (feeling the fish bite), instead of the beliefs we form from the understandings created by the experience, beliefs, or faith of others. All of these latter categories I would call *information.*

As we gradually build that bridge, we also gradually leave behind the experiences of having our attention controlled by culture and move toward the point where we can return that attention to the soul.

Meditation is the familiar name of the primary practice by which we learn how to control attention. Meditation is not the bridge but the tool to build the bridge. It is an important distinction because there is a time when we tend to drop the form of meditation that builds the bridge of Stage Three and use an entirely different form of meditation that is useful as we proceed into Stages Four and Five. There is an old Asian metaphor for this same notion, which is that we may use a boat to cross the river, but we don't carry the boat on our heads as we climb the mountain that is on the other side. In the same way, the forms of meditation that we use to build the bridge can be different from the forms we later use to cross the terrain that is beyond the bridge.

Confusion easily arises when we begin to use the word *meditation* to describe a particular process and fail to make distinctions about the different kinds and uses of meditation, since a trip to the bookstore or internet will quickly yield hundreds of books re-languaging many traditional forms of meditation, which is what I'm also doing here. My own purpose in re-languaging is to define very narrowly the particular form and function of the larger notion of meditation that is critical to building the bridge. There are other and more advanced forms of meditation that follow crossing the bridge, but all of them depend upon learning the *preliminary and primary attention skills* that I am calling the *bridge.*

All of the myriad forms of meditation, whatever else they do, involve just two processes: (1) learning to control attention, and (2) learning where to put it.

To address the first step, the rather generic forms that we know as mindfulness meditation or transcendental meditation would work fine, since both help the student to get control of attention by taking it away from mind and emotion. For the second step, I would suggest the use of the technique developed by the Institute of HeartMath, for several reasons. First, it places attention in the region of the physical heart, which is also the center of the heart-field. Second, learning to place the attention in the region of the heart teaches you to learn the first step of controlling attention while it also takes care of learning where to put the attention. Third, while there are definitely other places to put the attention, my own experience suggests—as I suggest throughout this book—that attention belongs to the soul. The embodied soul is held in resonant entrainment with the heart-field. Once we have returned attention to the soul, the soul can then explore infinitely by placing the attention anywhere revealed by the heart lens while remaining grounded in the body. HeartMath's approach seems to me to be the most efficient way of dealing with the preliminary steps of attention skill development that create the platform for more skillful soul work.

Many have walked over that bridge before us, and their stories are often instructive. But, like Ronnie's insistence on not telling me about how it felt for him to catch a fish and limiting his teaching solely to how one catches a fish, it is important to focus first on the essentials of *learning how to control attention and where first to put it,* before we explore more broadly the limitless places where attention can explore.

Learning control of attention is a primary focus of Stage Three Consciousness. Learning to place that attention in the soul within the heart-field is more the object of Stage Four. Exploring more deeply in the body, into matter in general, and into the other dimensional fields with that soul attention from its base in the heart-field is the focus of Stage Five.

How Will I Know When I've Reached the Far Side of the Bridge?

You'll know.

The far side of the bridge will look different for every soul that arrives at that other side. The singular experience that marks the arrival at the far side will be unique to each. But that particular experience will be a turning point, and it will have a single import.

Whatever the experience may be, it will telegraph the knowing that *I am a soul. Before all else, and regardless of what is happening in my life, I am a soul.* The experience will not be a mere understanding. It is certainly not a mere belief—one adopted without the benefit of personal experience. Nor is it an act of faith. It is an experience in which the *knowing that I am a soul* arises without doubt and without thought. The knowing arises so suddenly and forcibly that it precedes the opportunity for thought. It precedes the capacity of the body for emotion, even though both emotion and thought come crashing in almost immediately thereafter. It may happen as quickly as the surprise of being hit by a bus, and perhaps with as much force. Or the force of the impact may present itself in the subtlety of a meditation. It may arise as a scream of *I AM* from the soul itself. Whatever the means by which the recognition presents itself, there is no room for doubt. My near death experience left no doubt.

So Stage Three has a beginning and an end. The beginning is the determination to change and open ourselves. The end is the experience of remembering who we are.

There is, of course, the question of what follows that remembrance. The next step is yet another beginning. We have just remembered that we came on purpose. It is an exciting time, but we need to get past the excitement of that, get past telling everybody about it, and move on to figuring out what that purpose is. A new stage of work is about to begin and, along with it, a new act in the play that we have undertaken to write.

CHAPTER FIVE

In Chapter Five . . .

The Janus-Faced Soul
Projections
Reclaiming Our Projections
The Vision of the Inner Marriage
Engaging the Vision

Terrain	Stage of Consciousness	Perspective
Part Four: Anywhere that the empowered soul now directs its attention, including the body field, the other dimensions, or the soul itself	**Stage Four:** The soul has now captured control of attention and is able to direct attention, with some effort, to itself, to the body, and to other dimensions that contain information for the soul's further journey, setting the stage for learning how to engage more deeply with each of those destinations.	Life and its challenges are neither good nor bad, nor "just is." Life's challenges are now a gift of opportunity for soul development. "I" is now characterized increasingly by my identification with soul rather than with the early personality. The soul now assumes responsibility for creating a partnership with the body in the service of the emergence of soul destiny. I no longer project responsibility for my fate or destiny on everything and everyone else. I am no longer a victim.

The Janus-Faced Soul

AS WE LEFT ER'S STORY, the souls were on their way to earth. Er tells us that the souls elected to come, that they would forget their choice to do so, and that a fate and destiny were embedded in the life to come for each soul. It was left to the soul to awaken to the true purpose and nature of the journey and to move forward on its own, aided by the guardian that walked along with the soul.

The singular event that marks the end of Stage Three and the beginning of Stage Four is the experience of knowing ourselves as souls in a new and undeniable way—a knowing grounded in an experience that irrevocably shakes and begins to reshape our former identity. Our former identities were built from a naive view of childhood traumas, career choices, gender, marriages with or without children, and the variety of unpredictable life circumstances subtly formed by the vicissitudes of fate that became the narratives of wounding and triumph that we tell over and over again. These events, choices, and stories came together to form the identity that we know as *personality*, which we also call *ego* when the personality feels so fragile that it also feels the need to defend that identity against any and all judgments, including our own.

The new and clear recognition of our inherent soul nature—*I am a soul*—shakes this personality formation loose. Our astrological charts might have provided hints, but nothing could predict or prepare us for the sheer force of coming face to face with our souls and seeing ourselves as souls clearly for the first time. *This is who I am. I am this. I am.* In a single moment, as we realize that we are the soul, we become aware that we are looking through new eyes—soul eyes. This soul awareness is far more expansive in its view than the tiny vision afforded by the eyes of the body/mind that has contained our former personality. These newly opened soul eyes can look back at our past through the window of the now-shaken personality, and forward with soul eyes toward a path unfolding in the direction of the soul's destiny. Yet, as bright as the soul eyes are in this startling moment of awakening, they look forth from a sense of identity that is still just emerging—a sense of identity that is itself still immature. For most of us, this is a moment fraught both with confusion and a deep sense of liberation. The sense of liberation arises in the exhilaration of the moment of recognition, and the confusion arises in the fact that the identity connected with the surface personality is now shaken but not gone, while the identity has yet to resolve and integrate in the now self-aware soul. The remembrance comes, as it were, in an instant, but the shift of identity now requires time and the work of integration. Both soul and personality may co-exist in a state of mutual confusion as the matter of identity gets worked out while the skill of holding attention in the heart-field is developed.

The Roman god Janus was said to preside over such beginnings and transitions. Often depicted as having one head with two faces, one face is turned toward the past and one toward the future. At the outset of Stage Four Consciousness, the soul is Janus-natured, facing the past and looking simultaneously into the future. As the soul emerges into clear view at the end of Stage Three, it is literally beginning its journey in the body in a self-aware state for the first time. It cannot move forward without resolving the attachments of its former identity. Yet, it looks into a future that is already sweeping the soul into a stream of change that cannot be avoided or postponed. In this way, the recapitulation of the past is inevitably mixed with momentum of the future. There is no clean break between the two. It is the Janus nature that represents the imperative to drop one vision amidst the arising of another. We can see that if the past is not addressed, its weight will drag the soul down, perhaps to drown in the current of changes that now pull the soul forward. Even with the insight that *I am a soul,* it is both necessary, and now possible, to sort past from future, fate from destiny. Even with that insight, because of the very need for that sorting, there are no guarantees of the soul's forward progress on the path that destiny has laid before it.

Janus has also been portrayed as the gatekeeper. Just as the end of Stage Three was a bridge, the end of Stage Four is a gate. When we pass through the gate, we leave the victim story of the past, and move into the deeper reaches of our own soul story, which is the beginning of Stage Five Consciousness.

The essence of Stage Two Consciousness is a forgetting that we are souls and a tendency to struggle with life's circumstances. The essence of Stage Three Consciousness is awakening from that forgetfulness by the remembrance that we are souls rather than isolated human beings. The essence of Stage Four is the work that leads to the development of a soul perspective that is itself far more expansive than the simple remembrance that we are souls. This new soul perspective includes the formation of a new identity and the consolidation of new understandings around that identity.

Bringing this new perspective—*I am a soul*—to my own victim consciousness, I could now look back upon the "facts" of my victim story with some measure of detachment that could not exist in the pain that the perspective of my loosely knit personality had engendered. My mother, the story went, failed to love me. I felt unsafe and unworthy of love. I had to find a way to survive, so I began to hide myself and create a surface personality that someone could love. I used this presumably more attractive self to manipulate love, and ultimately did so with everyone that I encountered. This story did not have a happy ending, bringing me only to the realization that my strategy had denied me the very love that I so ardently sought. Over time, my new soul perspective would deepen into an understanding of how this old story had arisen and an understanding of the same events from the perspective of a soul who had chosen these experiences.

This old story and victim perspective is also the story and perspective of modern psychology. Psychology accepts the premise that we are victimized as children and that we are left to heal those woundings by the adoption of an adult perspective, one in which we can form better self images, stronger boundaries, better understandings of the shortcomings of the wounding adults, and lower expectations of the people upon which we have projected our hopes. Because psychology has so captured the narrative of healing in our culture, psychology is itself one story by which culture also holds us in its story, away from the experience of our soul natures. Culture is happy to keep us in the old story, which makes us easier to manipulate and available as a consumer of pain remedies of all sorts. In order to drop my story, I also had to drop culture's psychological paradigm. In order to drop that psychological perspective, I had to understand it *and* gain the new soul perspective, which took some time beyond the simple remembrance that I am a soul. I had to look backward skillfully in order to move forward effectively.

Now, looking about with the soul's own eyes, a new story begins to emerge. I am a soul, this story says. I was born into a family that represented the face of my fate. My family helped to define the struggle that was my fate, but did not cause it. Now, the soul's eyes see that my fate caused the family. Without the projection that my struggle is caused by family, there is now room to see fate as the container of something else, and my struggle with fate begins to diminish. By seeing my fate as the golden container of the destiny to come, I am released from the perception that challenge requires struggle, and that perception releases me from a tar baby relationship with my fate, which I have sought to avoid by cursing and striking out at it. Destiny will not necessarily be less challenging, but I *choose* and *embrace* the challenges of destiny, because the passion that is now arising in my heart calls me there.

As the soul story continues to emerge, the soul that was hidden is no longer hidden and speaks in its own voice—first through the old personality and then without regard for it. The soul looks back at its struggle with fate, both with compassion and with gratitude. That fate, the soul recognizes, has gifted the personality with the deep and poignant struggle, which was the means of the personality's discovery of the very tools that brought attention itself back to the soul, and allowed the soul to transcend its fate and cultivate the destiny that lay before it. The substance of this transition is evidenced in the growing joy of my soul presence within this body, and the increasing ability to function in relationship with the people in my life. Love—the deep sense of our inherent connection with everything—has emerged. And that very love is the substance of the increasing momentum of the soul along the path of its destiny as well as the means of the soul's navigation upon that path. As the soul story finds its full narrative strength, it tells of love that emerges from the soul to join with the love by which destiny calls to the soul.

Just as the first work of Stage Three Consciousness has been to wrest attention back from culture and finally replace it in the soul, the first work of Stage Four is to wrest our soul story back from the victim story of Stage Two and Three. The second work of Stage Four is the further development of soul skills. In Stage Three, we learn how to control attention. In Stage Four, we learn where to put it.

My near death experience not only brought me to the undeniable awareness of my soul, but also scrambled my too-small worldview once more, just as the ayahuasca experiences of three years before had scrambled the even smaller worldview that held me before that experience. The difference was that the death experience brought me firmly to a remembrance that *I am a soul.* All of my other understandings immediately became subordinate to that. Just as the story of the personality had to give way to the story of the soul, so did the old understandings have to stand down to permit new understandings to rise up. This transition took several years.

While the ayahausca had broken the cultural hypnosis by which my soul and the consciousness mechanisms of the body were trapped, that only opened the door for my attention to redirect itself elsewhere, to new experience, and thereby to new understandings. What emerged as the next truly significant step was the soul remembrance of the near death experience. It would take longer yet for new understandings to emerge.

The soul remembrance is not simply a return to the meadow of Er's story. In the meadow, before the forgetting, there is a naïveté that characterized the soul's self-aware nature. It does not anticipate what lies ahead for its soul journey on the earth. It cannot anticipate how the Sisters of Fate have shaped the fate the soul has yet to encounter. This Stage Three remembrance—*I am a soul*—that follows the forgetting is far different. The new soul remembrance arises directly into the soul's own battle to reclaim its consciousness from the resilient grip of the provisional personality that has formed in the absence of the soul identity. That provisional personality carries the painful memories of the experiences of that personality in the body following birth. Decades of painful experiences have imprinted them-selves upon this estranged consciousness following the soul's entry into a new body. This is how the soul evolves within the frame of a single life. The larger con-text of that evolution, of course, is the longer journey the soul takes through many painful lives that preceded the current life. Taken together, these lives create an arc that represents a grander process of learning and deeper exploration of the soul's engagement with matter.

If the forgetful soul has left heaven trailing clouds of glory, as the poet Blake saw it, the remembering soul now trails clouds of painful experience. Emerging self-aware in the body, it remembers its home in heaven but now within the frame of a body/mind emotionally battered. The new self-awareness triggers a paradoxical poignancy—one filled with both the exhilaration of homecoming and the sober realization that the road ahead remains frighteningly unknown.

Even as I remembered my own soul nature, it became necessary to address anew the big picture, the worldview, the ultimate understandings that underlie—con-sciously or unconsciously—all of my behaviors in the body and the world. No longer could I passively be carried along by the dominant culture's secular assumption that ultimate meaning could be found in the American dream. That dream was a projec-tion, and it was dead. And I was not yet able to dream the dream of my own soul. That was still ahead for me. There was other work before me before the soul's own dream could emerge. I needed to understand how my victim story was itself a projection.

And I did not understand even that much. What I did understand was that I wanted to understand more about the dying experience I had just had. Without understanding how to go forward, provisional knowings arising from the heart/soul began to guide me—amplifying and speaking the voice of my soul through the din of the chaos that had overtaken the momentum of my mind's former understandings. Within weeks of my death experience, I found a conference at Naropa University in Boulder, Colorado that focused on the subject of death and dying. I signed up.

Projections

Roshi Joan Halifax was among the speakers. I had heard of Joan Halifax, having crossed her trail in Colorado. Now at Naropa, I sat at the back of the room, watching this smallish, bald woman in her black Zen robe. She delivered a speech that reminded me, more than anything, of a polished politician stepping off the plane and delivering yet one more time the same speech that had been delivered many times before. Yet I found myself crying several times as I listened, and a little frustrated at having no insight into why those tears were forcing themselves on me in the midst of some old and familiar cynicism.

When she finished, I walked to the front of the room and waited while others asked their questions or related some personal story to her. When they had left, I asked her simply whether I could come to see her. She gave me a very direct look and told me to e-mail her.

Within a few weeks, I met with Roshi in Santa Fe. We shared our interest in shamanism, the subject of her doctoral work. I told her of my experience with the ayahuasca and of my near death experience, along with some narrative of my spiritual history. I told her of the difficulty of my now second marriage, the first having ended six years before. At the end of our conversations, Roshi said bluntly, "You need to reclaim your projections."

I didn't understand what she meant by projections, though I rather assumed I did. I had read about them. But I didn't have any myself, I thought.

What is projection?

Projection comes in a variety of forms. In its essence, it is a story we make up about someone else. The story originates in our own unconscious desire for someone else to do for us what we think we cannot do for ourselves. We make someone else responsible for something for which we fail to take responsibility. We say to others "love me," when we have failed to love ourselves. When we fail to feel love, we blame others upon whom we have projected this power. We ask others to change how we feel, rather than taking responsibility for managing our own feelings. When we unconsciously project that responsibility, we follow it with an expectation that the person will perform the projected role. When they fail to meet our expectations, we react—with disappointment, anger, and other forms of manipulation.

I returned home. The "truth telling" with my spouse that had ensued from the impetus of the near death experience had brought conflict, and had now reached an impasse. We were stuck in an angry exchange of blame for the apparent failure of what was now my second marriage. I discovered that my spouse was keeping things from me. I e-mailed Roshi to tell her that I had indeed reclaimed my projections and was going to get a divorce.

Roshi's quick e-mail response was to the effect of *get down here.*

We made another appointment to speak on the way to my doing some business in that part of the state. When we spoke, I told Roshi that I had caught my spouse in several deceptions. In my own lawyer-like way, I made the case that superbly justified to my mind why a divorce was necessary, and why my spouse was at fault.

As I was speaking, I watched Roshi's hand rise up from her chest to her neck, as though she were holding back something. By the time I finished my self-justifying speech and sat back awaiting validation from her, her hand was gripping her own throat. She stood and erupted at me in anger, saying that I had violated my spouse. Her anger shocked me. The conversation ended abruptly, with some sputtering on my part as I tried to understand why she had not aligned with me in my battle.

That night in my hotel, I had a dream in which Roshi and I walked through a double door into a room where we both prayed. I awoke from the dream with a clear understanding of what she meant by projections. As I arrived home, I found an e-mail from her apologizing for her reaction and expressing compassion for the challenge of the situation my spouse and I found ourselves in. I wrote back that no apology was necessary, and that I was grateful for the insight she had awakened in me with the grace of her anger. The teacher had slapped the student, and an awakening had occurred.

What had awakened was a rather simple and big picture view of the nature of my pattern in relationships. I saw that I had routinely projected on a partner the responsibility for providing me with a love that I did not know how to provide for myself. On the other hand, I now understood that I had unconsciously so devalued myself that I could not imagine how someone else could love me. So, I had reasoned in some unreasonable and unconscious way that I would need to manipulate a partner to love me and give me what I could not give myself. I had seen this pattern even in my earlier marriage and called it "caretaking," but I had not really understood the depth of projection that this pattern entailed. Nor did I understand that a mere understanding and naming of the projection dynamic would not take it out of play. I was not ready to understand that an understanding has no power on its own to change a pattern.

I also hadn't realized how my projections inherently violated another living being and had brought forward a deeply controlling behavior on my part. If I examined my behaviors on the surface, my taking care of my spouse financially and attentively seemed gentle and benign. Like one of Bonnie Raitt's lyrics goes, "On paper it looked pretty good." Now I was getting a deeper glimpse of that picture, and I realized how hard it would be for someone else to live with me and deal with the force of my intelligence and lawyerly skills put to the task of controlling their behaviors, particularly when they didn't understand any better than I the dynamics that brought and held us together. I felt deeply ashamed. But I could also see the genesis of this strategy in a three-year-old child's mind that had calculated the necessity of manipulating love from a mother I had perceived as both dangerous and critical to my safety.

During the weeks that had preceded this second exchange with Roshi, my spouse and I had agreed upon a technique for calling brief truces in which the volume of our arguments could be toned down. It consisted of our going into a room that we shared for meditation and sitting face to face on our pillows with the agreement that one of us could talk and the other would listen without interruption. We called it a "check-in." The evening I returned home from my second visit with Roshi, which was the night following the night of my dream, I asked my spouse if we could have a check-in.

She agreed, and we sat on our cushions. I began to describe my shallow and fresh understanding of the notion of projection as a preface to making an apology for my controlling behaviors. I could see that she was puzzled, both that I would be apologizing and because she didn't really understand the notion of projection either.

Before I could get more than a few sentences of my planned speech out of my mouth, I saw some movement over her right shoulder—something as subtle as the distortion of light that rising heat creates in the distance on a hot highway. In the moment of that sensation, I had a clear but brief vision of men and women facing each other over thousands of years. In the vision, women sat below men in a posture that implied an inherent imbalance of power and in which women were forced to compromise themselves in exchange for some form of security and safety. That vision transformed into an image of a woman dying painfully, crushed under a landslide of rock. Within just another instant, the movement that I saw behind my spouse's shoulder surged forward and hit me in the chest with such force that I was literally knocked off my cushion.

I was overcome, unable to speak. I could not convey my experience or understanding in any meaningful way, other than to sit back up and attempt an apology to my spouse for the projections that I had brought to the relationship. I don't believe she grasped what I was saying. I sensed that she thought that I was accepting blame for the conflict in our relationship. In my own mind, I was beginning to take responsibility for my part in creating the unconscious dynamic of our relationship. And I was beginning to understand that she had an equal responsibility for creating the relationship through her own projections. Although the act of taking responsibility was important, it had been punctuated and anchored in my being by the grace of an archetypal vision that delivered a direct taste of the violence of projection. It was a deeper awakening, one step beyond the awaking of the dream of the night before.

For a child, a parent is a natural source of affection, protection, and love. When a parent demands particular behavior as a condition of providing the love and affection that parents often treat as commodities, a child naturally adjusts its behavior in order to manipulate that sense of affection and love. The repetition of this transaction between child and parent gives rise in the child to a habitual way of looking at relationships in particular and the child's relationship with the world in general. The child's habit of adjusting behavior to manipulate positive response in another persists in the child as it matures into an adult. As an adult, the habitual behavior—like all habit—resides in the unconscious and controls the adult's behavior while the adult remains unconscious of the source of the behavior. Yet, as adults, we invariably find that we are unable to manipulate the love we ultimately want from another, and find ourselves angry, resentful, or disappointed that our expectations of those others have not been met. This is a consequence of our having *projected* our own natural capacity for loving ourselves. We have the capacity to access the experience of unconditional love that is the nature of the very whole of consciousness of which we are also made.

When we feel that our own capacity to make a decision is unreliable, and we look to others to make decisions for us, we have *projected* upon others our capacity for decision-making and given away that power. We have failed to explore our own capacity to make decisions. When we feel that we cannot experience love except through the love of another person, we have projected upon another person our power to experience love without another person. We have failed to explore our own capacity to experience love in the frame of our own consciousness or that of consciousness as a whole. When we feel that our lives lack sweetness and we give way to an addictive craving for sugar, we have projected upon food our power to self-generate sweetness and have failed to explore that capacity within ourselves. Because all of these projections fail to get us what we want, these and similar failures become the foundation of a victim perspective.

One might respond to this description of projection with a protest. We can—one might argue—experience the love of another person offered generously. That is absolutely true. The difference is that we cannot enjoy what by nature can only be freely given if we feel that love can only be earned or manipulated. It seems that we cannot truly enjoy the love of another unless we reclaim the projection that it is the only way we can be loved.

Do we need love from others? The answer is both yes and no, depending upon the perspective from which you ask. When we experience our "human" natures, it seems inevitable to acknowledge that each of us needs the love of others. On the other hand, when we directly experience our soul natures, we are so filled with love that it seems unnecessary for us to have the love of any other human being. On the third hand, when the soul emerges into a collaborative relationship with the body, both are true. Our human nature is itself the nature of the body. Because the body experiences itself as isolated and vulnerable, the body has an inherent need to feel safe and loved. The soul nature *is* love, which both provides and constellates the very love the body so deeply desires. The skillful soul can share its experience of unconditional love with the body, but the body also wants to be touched and loved by another. The love we need from another is first and foremost a love that our human bodies require, even when the soul has infused that body.

Before the emergent soul can seduce the body into a collaborative dance, the emerging soul must reclaim the projections the fearful surface personality has made.

Reclaiming Our Projections

How do we reclaim what we have projected of our own capacities onto others? It is easy to say, hard to do, for the reason that the projections are unconscious. They become visible, however, in the people to whom we react. Any reaction to another person is the telling clue that we have projected an expectation upon them. How often do we think that we have made an error, for example, in choosing a partner for a relationship? "I was so infatuated," we might say, "that I overlooked obvious character traits that I should have known would make it impossible to live with him (or her)." On the other hand, it is possible to see through the more clear lens of a soul perspective that we unconsciously choose (as fate would choose for us) those very partners who in some way accept our projections and expectations until the whole unconscious arrangement becomes apparent. This is the dynamic of fate, and relationship becomes one of its most powerful means.

In the shamanic traditions of indigenous cultures, there is also a recognition of projections, but they may be seen as dysfunctional and disabling energetic connections rather than psychological constructs. From a shamanic view, projections are constructed of subtle energy formations by which we suck and are sucked of energy. When I have projected upon another human the responsibility to love me, I have also connected to their energy field, and my expectation of love acts like a rather predatory pump—like a vampiring mosquito that has taken up permanent residence on my arm.

In the American version of indigenous shamanic teachings, these connections are called *cords*. To effect a cure, the shaman approaches the cord directly, cutting it loose. In my own experience, the act of cutting a cord creates a window of opportunity for the person being treated to experience the absence of projection. That experience is an awakening, which must then be integrated by the reclamation of the projection, absent which the cord will reform out of the old perspective that created it in the first place. Because the American psyche is distinctly different than the psyche of the earth-connected indigenous peoples, that integration is at least in part a psychological process and then a soul process, which brings us back to the necessity of learning how to capture and control attention. In other words, there is no ultimate "cure" for the disease of projection or the presence of cords. American pharmaceuticals are helpless in the face of this unconscious disability. Only the development of attention skills will move us beyond this level of unconsciousness, because the attention skill allows us to focus attention back in the soul, obviating the felt need for the projection in the first place.

When there is an absence of projection, the potential arises for two strongly connected souls to partner skillfully and intentionally, *beyond* suffering. This is a potential of Stage Five Consciousness that can only be met by the reclaiming of projections in Stage Four.

Following my exchange with Roshi and the visionary insights that so impacted me during the "check-in" with my spouse, there was a respite in my marriage during which we made a deeper effort to sort through our issues and revisit the possibilities for relationship. In the meantime, I attended a training conducted by Roshi that is a centerpiece of her work—being with the dying. During the workshop, she mentioned several times an emerging technology for learning meditation she referred to as heart-centered meditation developed by the Institute of HeartMath. I felt drawn to checking it out.

What I found was a body of research that established without question a number of direct health benefits from adopting a heart focus of attention combined with a pattern of deep breathing and an experience of appreciation felt directly in the heart. It was clear from the research that this "coherent" heart state had the ability to entrain the myriad rhythms of the body in a way that helped to dispel depression and negative emotions. Of equal importance, the Institute of HeartMath had developed a mechanism, "emotional self-regulation," grounded in heart rate variability that allowed a meditator to sit in front of her own computer and see in real time whether the heart focus was having the desired immediate effects in the physiological heart. From a meditator's perspective, this was nothing short of revolutionary. It was an important answer, if not a complete answer, to the age-old question meditators always ask: "Am I doing it?"

I traveled to the Institute of HeartMath in California. Within a few months, I was bringing attention to my own heart and quickly learning—with the benefit of the computer—how to hold my attention there. It was not hard to *feel* the difference. I began coaching clients in the technique, and began using the technique and the technology in combination with shamanic work as well. This took place in late 2003 and early 2004, during which time I also trained as a cranial-sacral practitioner. It was easy to combine all three approaches. The cranial work helped me to help clients reach a deep state of relaxation quickly. The Institute's technique helped me to focus in my own heart while working with clients, and gave me an easy way to help clients achieve a heart focus while I was working with them. In turn, my clients' heart focus helped them become more energetically open to the benefits of the shamanic work. It was a time of exciting discovery for me.

As I began to open to the significance of the remembrance of my soul identity, it became a natural step for me to understand that the doorway to an exploration of my own soul nature was the heart itself. I was beginning to connect to a central theme found in the spiritual and religious literature over the ages: *The heart is the seat of the soul.*

It became obvious that to explore my soul, I had to engage the heart. My meditation shifted to a heart focus. It meant that I had to remove my attention from its habitual orientation to my thoughts. My mind is strong, and it does not release its hold on attention easily. By this time, however, the ayahuasca had done its important initial work, which was to help the mind understand that its prior understanding of the world was far, far too small. The mind, humbled by the ayahuasca, did its best to yield to this new focus, and began to open to new understandings.

It was in this shifting context that the next awakening came in the form of a vision. It was this vision that, over a period of several years, led me to a far deeper insight about the nature and feel of projection than I suspect a mere psychological understanding can provide.

The Vision of the Inner Marriage

I was in a shamanism workshop in California near Joshua Tree with about ten or so people. We were seated on the floor. The teacher was performing a Peruvian shamanic initiation called the *kawak* on each of us, one at a time. This took place about a year after my near death experience.

To do the *kawak,* the shaman uses one or more stones. These stones are called *kuyas.* These names originate in the Quechua language of the indigenous peoples of southern Peru. The stones had previously undergone their own form of energetic initiation by the shaman prior to our initiation. The shaman uses the kuyas to trace lines from the bottom of the occiput at the rear of the skull to the center between the eyebrows. The lines traced extend from the occipital lobe vertically over the center of the top of the head and laterally around both sides, above the ears. Within the cranium, there is a structure that mirrors the pathway of the stone, called the *tentorium.* When I noticed the correspondence between the tentorium and the pathway the shamans scribed with the stone, I wondered whether the shamans knew of this.

After the shaman uses the stones to trace over the head in this way, she traces a line from the occipital vision center to the heart, moving down the back and sides of the neck, forming the shape of a necklace. Again, I thought of the pathway of the tenth cranial nerve—the vagus, so called because it wanders vagabond-like from the head to the heart and other organs. Like the underlying tentorium, this centrally important vagus nerve laid beneath the path of the shaman's stone.

The shaman's intention in this ritualized initiation is to connect the vision center of the physical brain with the eye of spirit and the heart itself, in the understanding that inner vision must be guided by the knowings of the heart. The ultimate purpose is to empower the physical capacity for sight with our capacity for mystical sight and to ground that visionary tool in the body. During the time of these awakenings, the sense that the heart is the central and most powerful field of the body arose strongly in me. I came to feel that *grounding* inevitably involves a heart-centered attention.

At this moment, I was expecting nothing from this exercise. I had received this initiation from indigenous shamans in the mountains of southern Peru several times. Receiving the initiation one more time from an American teacher who was working her way through copious notes didn't suggest to my continuing skepticism a more fruitful outcome. Nevertheless, I sat quietly with eyes closed, paying attention to the feel of the stone.

Within a moment of her putting the stone to my head, a distinct vision flashed into view. Although it startled me, I kept my eyes closed.

Two eyes appeared before mine. A woman's eyes. There was a transmission from her left eye to my left eye. I could both see and feel the transmission.

The vision disappeared. There was nothing objective that would indicate the eyes were those of a woman; I simply knew it. My breath was taken by the literal shock of such a clear vision appearing before me. My attention was riveted to the darkness that remained after the eyes disappeared. Then, before another thought, the eyes reappeared. There was another transmission from her left eye to my left eye.

Again, the vision disappeared. I remained breathlessly alert, eyes tightly shut, searching the darkness. The teacher finished the initiation and went on to the next person. A few seconds, at most, passed. The vision resumed, now in full screen mode and as clear, if not as bright, as a television.

I am in a shallow valley.

Everything is gray, covered in ashes. There is a small stream to my right, but it is also covered in ashes. There is no water that I can see. There are a few very tall trees standing, but they are denuded of foliage and most of their limbs. No other vegetation is apparent. The sky is gray. The place has the feel of death, and I feel alone here.

I walk up the center of the valley. I am drawn to my left, where I see a small lump beneath the ashes. Walking to this place, I kneel and brush off the ashes. There is a woman there, her skin pallid. I know that she is not dead, even though she appears so.

I feel panicked, not knowing what to do. I think to run for help. Leaving the woman, I run down the valley and arrive quickly at Ausangate.

Ausangate is a mountain held sacred by the shamans of southern Peru. It is the home of the Q'ero Nation, a small fragment Andean peoples regarded to have descended directly from the Inca culture. Much of what comes to America as the form and substance of Peruvian shamanism comes from the Q'ero.

The teachers with whom I have traveled to Peru say that Ausangate manifests a masculine energy. Upon the occasions of my pilgrimages to Ausangate and subsequent meditative visitations, I encountered a feminine energy in addition to a masculine energy. In the vision space of prior meditative encounters, I had discovered and entered into the mountain's feminine opening at the base of the mountain.

I enter the mountain through the vaginal cave, but help is not available. The mountain is silent and will not help me. It feels that I am being left to my own resources.

Whatever is going on, the next step seems my responsibility alone. I return to the valley, feeling completely helpless. I sense great grief and sadness there. What happened here has occurred at the hands of the masculine. The violence was devastating.

I kneel by the woman and touch her gently. I see again that she is not dead, but she is deeply wounded. The words, "a timeless time passed," come clearly into my mind. I leave my hand on her.

In this timeless time, the valley floor greens. The stream runs with clear water. The trees spout limbs and foliage. Animals appear, and I can hear bird song. Rain falls. Wind blows in the trees. The sun shines brightly and clouds disappear. This all happens in a kind of reverse order, as though an unwinding of earlier events is occurring.

I look at the woman. Her natural skin color is restored. With my help, she stands. I take her hand, and she mine. We walk out of the valley together, taking the same path I had raced before to Ausangate. Arriving at Ausangate, I understand that this is not the place we are to come, and we continue on to Salkantay.

Salkantay is another of the sacred mountains of southern Peru to which I had pilgrimaged prior to the time of this vision. The shamanic teacher with whom I traveled there says that the mountain manifests the energy of the "wild feminine."

Arriving at Salkantay, a cave opening presents itself and we enter together. We are met by women who inhabit the mountain. I am able to see the beautiful and regal nature of a great cavern within the heart of the mountain. Although I have been allowed this far, the women do not allow me to enter further. The woman with whom I have come is taken by the women of Salkantay into the cavern. I have the sense that this is the heart space of the mountain.

From where I wait, I can see that the woman is cleansed, nurtured, and healed. This being done, she is brought back to me.

She and I join hands again and walk, returning now to the feminine cave that gives access to Ausangate. There, in similar fashion, I am taken in and given the same ministrations as the woman has received within the heart of Salkantay. When I emerge, I find that the woman awaits me. Again, we join hands.

Throughout this vision as I am sitting on the floor in the midst of my workshop companions, tears are streaming from my eyes. At first, the tears express the deep sadness and grief for the pain of the earth, the feminine, my own feminine, for women, and for myself. These distinctions disappear in the moment of grief. As the vision proceeds, the tears express the joy that I experience in the presence of the healing that is being offered in ways that feel relevant to all of this pain.

The vision ends with a deep felt sense that a story is begun, not finished, in this moment. I sense that a marriage has been arranged, and that a wedding is to follow.

For those unfamiliar with the traditions of shamanic work, this is a classic shamanic vision, unique for me because of its import, its clarity, and the spontaneous way in which it arrived. Often, we intend our journeys. As is often the case, we try to shape those journeys. This one intended me. It was undertaking to shape me.

The immediate personal context for the arrival of this vision was pretty straight-forward. I had practiced law for over thirty years. I was not happy there. I wanted to leave, but was struggling to let go, because it felt as though I would be risking my security. It really made no rational sense to leave. Over time, the continuing success and relative ease of the practice had made it easier to find a comfortable place within it. I knew the drill. I knew my strengths. It was not taking a great deal of time. Yet, I *knew* that this was not how my life was meant to be spent. My relationship with women was troubled. My second marriage was ending. A few months before, I had had nine teeth removed because they were dead—a result of old amalgam fillings that had poisoned the teeth, the bone in my jaws, and the rest of my body. I was quickly recovering from a toxicity placed in my body as a child by a medical culture itself so disconnected from the body that it was insensitive to the dynamic of mercury poisoning. By the time of the vision, my body was already making good progress toward recovering from the symptoms of this poison. It was only some months later that I recalled speaking with a friend about the removal of her teeth, as she was encouraging me about the prospect of getting the mercury out. "You'll find that your [internal] visions will increase," she said. I had paid little attention to her comment at the time.

A day or so before the vision had arrived in the shamanism class, while working with a divination process in the same class, I made notes in my journal that presaged this vision. A later look at my journal suggested that I had realized that I did not trust my own feminine to participate in the process of supporting me in the world. Even though I recognized, in some way, that the nature of the feminine archetype was about giving birth—about creating and manifesting in the world—I didn't trust that my feminine could do it. I felt that my masculine self would have to schlock it out on its (my) own, which meant working from the analytical intelligence that had been providing financially for a long time. In the same way, my experience with women had suggested to me that I did not trust them to show up, to partner, or to love me. And yet these understandings hadn't occurred to my analytical mind before the opening that was occurring in the space of this class.

So it wasn't a surprise, even if it was a shock, to find a suffocating, almost dead female figure in the vision. My relationship with my own feminine energy had now been revealed to me in the form of a scene tantamount to nuclear winter. It wasn't hard to extrapolate that relationship to the level of world culture. Many others have written about it. Our Newtonian, materialistic, scientific, and analytical worldview stands at a distance from the earth and from our own bodies, both of which have become dangerously polluted as a direct result of that equally toxic mind-set. In my own reactive and unconscious arrangement of the intelligences of my body, I had become conditioned to see and experience the world through this Newtonian perspective of separation. It was not simply an abstract understanding. It was an absolutely visceral, body-level experience. Newton's vision was exacting a toll from me, one that I could not much longer pay.

In the context of this old and habitual mind-set, the arrival of this vision scrambled my thinking yet once more. I threw myself back into my analytical mind to get an understanding, which was my default and habitual way of trying to deal with new experience.

Several days passed from the classroom vision before I was able to leave the analytical mind's efforts, which felt like a dog chained to a stake, wearing the ground to nothing without being able to get beyond the length of the chain. Sitting in meditation, I finally resorted to the simple strategy of asking to be shown the next step in working with the vision.

The thought appears in my mind that the feminine will receive two teachers, as will my masculine. Nothing else was said.

The following morning, I again asked to be shown the next step.

The thought arises that the two teachers will be Ausangate and Salkantay, that both will teach both the feminine and the masculine, and that the feminine and masculine will be taught separately.

Tears accompany this communication. It has been two years since I had first visited Ausangate in Peru. There, I had been given two stones by shaman Don Francisco, the head of the Q'ero Nation, whose home is high on Ausangate, above 12,000 feet in elevation. In the moment of the communication that came in this morning's meditation, I know that the two stones have been given to facilitate this teaching process, in the way that the shamans of the mountain tradition of Peru use stones as crystalline transistors that receive, transmit, and amplify the transmission of information through directly connected lines of subtle energy. Like the plant medicines, these physical supports are not ultimately necessary, but nevertheless seem to offer some assistance until one learns to make the connections directly and efficiently. The Peruvian shamanic tradition incorporates those activated stones into a portable altar called a *mesa*—a Spanish word for table—that contains the connective amplifiers for all of the spirit level helpers with which the shaman makes regular connection.

On the next day, I ask again for the next step.

During this meditation, I understand that I have identified myself with the masculine figure through whose eyes the vision is seen. This has caused me to see the feminine as separate—a projection of my own feminine outside of the frame that I feel as "me." Within the space of this insight, the feminine in the vision is reclaimed, brought back into my own sense of who I am. She is no longer "she," but a feature of "I." I am both the masculine and the feminine seen in the vision. In the meditative space of this new perspective, the vision resumes.

The feminine part is called forward to begin the teaching she is to receive in preparation for the marriage. She presents herself at the mouth of the cave at the base of Salkantay.

I am aware of watching this scene as an intimate observer, detached from the feminine as though she is again projected away from my sense of "I-ness." I consciously shift my perspective to enter the feminine, and my perspective thereafter seems to shift back and forth, between one of looking through the eyes of the feminine, and another of seeing the feminine projected.

Upon arrival within the mouth of the cave, I [the feminine] am met by three women. Two of them take me by the arms, one on each side. I am led into a cavern by the third, who walks before us. Each of the women is clothed in a luminosity that appears as a robe but is not of any material substance. I am naked, feeling neither frail nor robust. The cave is brightly illuminated, but with no apparent source of that light.

In the cavern is a large pool of luminous water. I am conducted into the pool. The pool is lined with crystals. I am surrounded in the pool by women who hold me supine in the water. One holds my head, others my feet and hands, while others support my torso, allowing me to float and be held with absolutely no effort on my part. Within the frame of the experience itself—as distinct from a mental interpretation of what is happening in my vision—I hear the thought that being held in the water is an initiation that consists of both cleansing and the experience of being held. It feels that I am floating in gentle undulations of love, and held in the hands of the Mother.

After a time, three single-terminated crystals are touched to my body. These crystals, like all the other crystals in the pool, are not solid, but vibrating luminous shapes, like rather dense and intense holograms. The first is touched to my perineal area, the second to my sacrum and the third to the base of my skull. Then the crystals are inserted into my body in these three places.

Three more crystals are brought by the women. These three are faceted and round. These are placed in my lower three chakras, in order.

Two animals now appear. The first is a small dragon, or serpent, swimming in the water. I have seen this dragon in a dream several weeks prior. With great force, the dragon swims into my body through the vagina and positions itself so that its head is at the top of my spine and its tail at my sacrum.

The other animal is a female black jaguar, one who is already familiar to me from past archetypal encounters. She has walked with me for over a year now, but comes to me again here in the archetypal water pool. Her eyes, I see now, are also crystalline and shine in turn in various colors—red, gold, green, and black.

More crystals are brought. Two are inserted into my eyes, and others are inserted into my ears, tongue, and nostrils. Others are blown into the whole of my skin, like crystal vapor. The thought occurs in my mind that these crystals are tuning my capacity to sense vibrations of various frequencies through out my body and to decode the information carried on these frequencies.

Crystalline vapor is now applied to my hair, which is long and hangs down below my shoulders. The thought occurs in my mind that each fiber of my hair is a luminous thread connecting my capacity to know to the luminous threads and matrix of the universe which infuses and underlies all creation.

Now I am lifted from the water and laid gently upon a stone platform where again I am surrounded by women. The thought occurs in my mind that I am to be imbued with and tuned to the four elements. My womb is filled with the rich dark soil of the Mother. My body is filled with blood rivers. In my heart is placed a bowl—a half sphere. The thought occurs that is only half, and that the other half will follow in subsequent ceremony. The bowl is filled with fire, and fire is also placed in the tips of my fingers, my palms, the bottoms of my feet, and in my eyes. In my mind, the thought comes that this is not the fire of the sun but of the molten center of the Earth Mother. It is not the fire of illumination but the fire of healing touch.

Finally, I am lifted above the stone table and into the air, which infuses my body and surrounds me in some tangible manner. A necklace is placed about my neck with a pendant forming a spiral. The thought appears in my mind that the spiral is the symbol that, when invoked, will permit me to fly, not only through the air, but through the earth, water, and fire, and through the three worlds of the shamanic cosmos.

I am now floating above the table. The women move me, using intention alone, from this position to a standing position.

By the same means, I am clothed in a luminous field of the same kind worn by the women of this cave. The thought arises that it is both a protective shield and a connecting and nurturing field.

I find myself now floating above the floor, sitting in a meditative posture, amidst a circle of women. The thought arises that these women form a counsel of guides, ancestors, and lineage, available to me as I need them.

There is smiling, laughter, celebration. This ceremony is complete, and there is more to come.

I continue my daily meditation. The vision has taken a rest. Within a few days, it resumes.

The masculine returns to Ausangate. The entrance to the feminine cave appears below a stone altar. I [the masculine part] enter the cave and am met by three women who conduct me to the central cavern. There, I am laid out on a stone platform where seven women disconnect my chakras—by unscrewing them in a counterclockwise fashion—and remove a more subtle energy body. This body is taken to a small pool that is filled with bubbling and circulating water, and the body is immersed there.

My perspective comes in and out of this subtle body, as I can in one instant see the process from a short distance, and in another instant feel the water. The thought that I am being cleansed comes to mind, and that the water contains the vibratory resonance that will allow the masculine to resonate with the water energy of the feminine.

After a time in the water, the subtle body is removed from the small pool to the other side of the stone platform, where there is a large fire in the center of several concentric stone circles. There, the subtle body is placed standing in the fire. Again, the thought arises that there is a cleansing, and a tuning that creates a capacity for resonating with and knowing the feminine fire. This fire seems to come directly from the molten fire of the Earth Mother's core.

The subtle body is then returned and reintegrated into the more substantial body—which has remained on the stone platform—by the seven women who screw in the chakras in a clockwise fashion. The subtle body appears as a luminous garment or field around the more substantial body.

The ceremony is complete.

The vision continues.

The knowing arises that the feminine and masculine will have work to do in the respective mountains. The feminine will visit seven chakras that reside within the energy field of Salkantay, starting at the bottom. The masculine will do the same with Ausangate, but from the top down. The feminine will enter from the bottom, and the masculine will enter from the top of the mountain.

At the heart level of each mountain, there is a luminous bridge connecting the two mountains. In my mind, I hear words distinctly, as though spoken to me, simultaneously with seeing the bridge: "the arc of the covenant."

Although we often associate the word "arc" with a curved line, like a rainbow, an arc can also be straight, as is the case when there is an energy connection between two objects.

Over the next days of meditation, the feminine and masculine are conducted through the mountains. In each mountain appear two figures—a masculine and a feminine, both ancient and human-like. There is really no narrative to these experiences apart from the sequential exposure of my own masculine and feminine parts to each of the distinct chakra energies of each of the mountains. Each of my parts visits each of the two mountains. No mental information is imparted.

On the last day of the vision, thirty days from its commencement, the vision is crystal clear.

I am an observer of the scene.

Both my masculine and feminine parts are kneeling before an altar. The altar is at the center of the luminous bridge—the arc of the covenant—between the mountains. Behind the altar stand the four teachers—two women and two men. It is apparent that the marriage is about to take place.

The vision ends. The marriage has not occurred. It is quite apparent, as days ensue without the return of the vision, that there is work to be done before the marriage ceremony can be completed and the marriage consummated.

While I have referred to the vision as "mine," I can't know this to be the truth. It is not a story that I shaped, but one that clearly has been shaping me. It feels that the vision has sought to be told, and that I have been the avenue for the telling at the same time that the vision story has undertaken to shape me in its form.

Engaging the Vision

After the vision ended, I gradually began to understand that the vision had set the stage for an aspect of the destiny that I was invited to live. I could see in time that a central theme of my own emergence from fate into my destiny was to find the way to bring my own feminine nature to a state of vibrancy. This process, in turn, required that my own masculine nature become almost completely reformed as well, in response to the rehabilitated feminine. In the course of this process, both the masculine and feminine that operate separately within me would have to learn how to come together into a potentiated partnership. There is little question that this partnership is not an end in itself, but a means for new work to ensue. In retrospect, I can see that part of this work has been accomplished in the plant medicine journeys narrated in the following chapters. And I can see in the notion of soul and body a way of looking at the masculine and feminine that has nothing to do with either sex or gender.

It was also apparent to me that this vision mirrored the central and obvious pathology of American culture. I sensed that the vision pictured Stage Two consciousness at the level of culture—the struggle in which our own culture is also now unconsciously engaged. The masculine has so long waged war upon the feminine that the feminine is at the edge of death without an inevitable rebirth. The masculine hegemony and patriarchy has left the world at an impending risk of literal nuclear winter or its environmental equivalent.

As with culture, so with individuals in that culture, and with both men and women. Women have embraced the masculine and the patriarchy in themselves to compete with and survive among men, with the consequence that their feminine may atrophy in the same way the feminine in the men has atrophied. And yet, it seems to be that it is women who will lead the way back to the emergence of the feminine. It seems to be women in whom the feminine speaks most clearly and directly, even though I feel that my emergent feminine is stronger than the feminine I see in many women. Even if the feminine is more available to women, it is just as important for women to listen deeply, at the level of the soul, as it is for men, and as easy for them as men to be caught in the thought and emotion from which our attention must be skillfully extracted and returned to the soul.

As dreams go, the vision has both a nightmarish quality (the cultural circumstance of the consequences of thousands of years of suppression of the feminine and the female) and a quality of redemption (a way out and forward). In the same way, the vision portrays the unconscious struggle within the frame of our own fate, the bridge that takes us from that unconscious engagement to the remembrance of ourselves as souls, and the relationship within us that forms the gateway to our own destiny.

At the end of Stage Three Consciousness, the soul has awakened to the memory of who it is and recognizes that it has taken up residence in a temporary body on the planet. Emerging for the first time from the domination of the cultural consciousness, it is as though the soul takes its first full and free breath, and—just as quickly—is swept into the challenge of the next transition. Yet, the soul that faces this next transition has come into a soul level awareness that also immediately provides a new level of connection. No longer stuck in the cultural perspective of a secular psychological identity, the new self-aware soul can tap into the larger, other dimensional realms beyond time and space, where myths and stories are encoded into fields that stand available to inform the individual soul journey.

As the soul looks forward now, it feels the pull of the story contained in a new vision of itself, one that defines an arc of movement so much larger than the small vision held by culture. As the soul looks forward through the lens of this new and powerful vision, the past—its habits, patterns, and stories of victimization—holds little allure. The release of patterns that was such a struggle before now becomes quick and relatively more painless. In the indigenous perspective, there is the possibility that we drop the patterns all at once, like a snake sheds its skin. And, like the snake, we do it on the move. As we begin then to embody afresh the vision that has appeared to the new soul consciousness, everything begins to accelerate. How do we support this new change and integrate it?

We do that in precisely the same way that the movement along our journey has accelerated before. We learn to control our attention. We learn where to place the attention.

We remember that all of what we think of as our personal awareness and consciousness must be returned to its immediate source, which is the soul. So we bring our focus of attention to the heart-field, and within the heart-field to the soul itself. We hold this attention in this central field of the body with breath, and we tune it to its most powerful form by bringing it into a state of awe and pristine awareness, to non-judgmental and unconditional awareness. And we anchor that awareness there, in the soul, as a concentration of *soul* focus and *soul* presence in the center of the heart-field. Then we connect the soul's own attention to the earth, to our earth-body and to the other dimensional spaces. These connections define the fields within which the embodied soul operates during this sojourn on the planet. From this posture, the sparks of a new and passionate connection begin to fly. The occurrence of awakenings, synchronicities, and peak experiences accelerates.

In Stage Four, our soul attention travels in an increasingly intentional manner. Instead of being the passive beneficiary of awakenings that occur without our intention, we now purposely direct our awareness wherever we choose, while keeping it anchored in the soul held squarely in the heart-field. The soul uses the lens of perception provided by the heart, which facilitates a movement toward the object of the soul's desire. The heart operates by attraction, and it moves toward that with which the soul feels the strong resonance we know as attraction. The heart voyages out upon the oceans of interconnected realities—body, earth, the other dimensional fields—carrying the exploring, curious, and now self-aware soul.

In this state of openness, the vision will find us. The vision serves, perhaps, many functions. In the soul journey, there is a very specific function that such visions perform. The soul cannot progress on its path without the body. The body cannot respond without the engagement of the body in the rather singular function that has been variously labeled as *healings, tunings, activations,* and *initiations.* All of these distinct notions describe a singular process that occurs at every level of soul work, including the initial steps that lead from the unconscious forgetfulness of Stage Two to the preliminary awakenings of Stage Three to the more elaborate kind of vision that might occur in Stage Four in preparation for Stage Five. A healing is always a tuning. A tuning is always an activation. An activation is always an initiation. These are the doorways that lead toward the upward movement of soul consciousness toward expansion and individuation. We expand beyond our fate and individuate into our destiny. We can only open for the eventual arrival of our vision. We open increasingly as we drop our projections, our expectations, our manipulations, our identity of victimization, and so on. In doing so, we also automatically transcend our fate and find our destiny opening before us. When we have journeyed to the horizon from which we see into the face that is our destiny, we are at the threshold of Stage Five Consciousness.

CHAPTER SIX

In Chapter Six...

Moving On
Back to the Amazon
Taste, But Don't Let It Control You
Soul to Soul Now
The Arc of the Covenant
Going Deeper
The Column that Connects Heaven to Earth
The Arc Experienced
Stage Five Consciousness

Terrain	Stage of Consciousness	Perspective
Part Five: The body is now the temporary home base of the soul as it explores the density of time/space in the context of its connection with the other dimensional fields that provide constant support for the soul journey.	**Stage Five:** The soul's ability to focus attention grows as it goes increasingly into the other dimensions, and as it explores the density of matter. The soul's control of attention is no longer simply conscious and intentional, but increasingly automatic and, one might say, becoming more *skilled*.	Life is often joyful and full of energy, yet even more challenging in new ways. The soul's work is at the edge of the evolution of consciousness through the expression of its own purpose through the power of the body and the passion of the heart. I identify both with the whole of consciousness and with my particular soul role as a co-creator of the play of consciousness.

Moving On

THE VISION OF THE INNER marriage came early in 2004. My father passed away at the end of that year. The relationship with him had been challenging for several years as his health slowly continued to fail and his projections became more and more demanding on all of the family. The gift of my relationship with him came in my gradually learning to recognize and resist the manipulations that attended his projections and finding my way from a defensive reactivity to a place of compassion for his struggle. Watching him also allowed me to see *the him in me*, which helped me to root out some of my own unconscious patterning and projections. In that way, I came to see him as a powerful, if paradoxical, teacher. That acknowledgement allowed me to embrace and honor the many deeply positive qualities his life evidenced. The heaviness that attended the challenge of that process hung on after his death, and it felt like it was time for me to clear that.

My second marriage had also ended that year. At the time of my father's death, I was still in the process of trying to get at the mutual projections that attended that relationship. And I knew my law practice was no longer compatible with the changes that were coming forward in me, but I couldn't get myself to close it. With all of that on my plate, I started looking for a place where I could spend some time shifting gears. A friend suggested a shamanic retreat in Costa Rica she knew about from an internet ad. The trip promised another encounter with the ayahuasca, along with the opportunity to listen to Jeremy Narby, author of *The Cosmic Serpent,* and David Abram, author of *The Spell of the Sensuous.* They were the daytime program. I booked the trip.

It was a nice break. The weather was lovely and warm, a comforting contrast to the January winter of northern New Mexico. The ocean was inviting. I rode fast horses and talked with slow people. I felt fortunate to be part of a very small audience for Narby and Abram, with ample opportunities for questions and conversation. I played my Native American flute. Abram did card tricks. There was some drama with the Ecuadorian shaman. I declined to do a second ceremony with him after the first seemed unskillful on his part. Our host—a young man who had himself spent four years with the Shuar tribe of Amazonian Ecuador—stepped in to conduct the remaining ceremony. I declined to participate and had dinner with Narby and his companion instead.

Our host interrupted my dinner with a request that I assist by watching over the other participants during the ceremony. I was happy to do that, and finished assisting a little before midnight. Then our host—the last-minute shaman—approached me. "Now it's you and me," he said. It felt like both an invitation and a challenge. My rational mind balked and quickly chalked up a short list of reasons to decline. I checked in with my own guidance. My heart said yes. I accepted his invitation and internally declined any challenge.

The ceremony that followed was singular and distinct, seeming to cap the experiences with the plant medicine that had occurred almost four years earlier. I did not throw up in response to the medicine. The visions were clear, and the experience was soft and sensuous. Toward the end of a vision that included crystal-clear forms made of brightly lit serpents highlighted with beautiful patterning, I saw a fairy godmother-like figure standing across a room. She wore a tiara and a bustled, floor-length evening gown. Smiling, she spoke directly to me. With only minor exceptions, there had been no verbal communication in the several earlier journeys that took place in Peru. The prior journeys had been deeply experiential and visual, but there was relatively little communication that the linear rational brain could recognize as language. Now, this direct communication conveyed a grand sense of unconditional love in both the message and the feeling that accompanied it. The feeling was similar to the bliss of the vision quests, but deeper, as though the very chemistry of my body was being changed. "Let *me* take care of you," the she-vision intoned softly. Whatever I had carried to Costa Rica dislodged and let go in that moment. The physical shift and release were palpable.

The ceremony was brief, ending a couple of hours after it began. I walked to the beach. The sky was clear. Stars shined across the vast canopy of darkness. Standing barefoot in the sand and close to the breaking waves, I heard another voice speaking in my head. "*This* is your home," it said. The meaning was clear. Not this beach, not Costa Rica, not the jungle, but the cosmos—*the cosmos is your home,* the voice was telling me. And it felt as though I *had* come home again, and seen it for the first time. I felt I had received the gift of the plant medicine. I felt grateful. And I felt relieved, as though a marathon had been run and I had crossed the finish line. It had been hard work. In my mind, I left the plant behind, firm in the conviction that this plant was an intelligent being in devoted service to the evolution of human consciousness, and that I had received its gift. Now I felt that I could move on.

As I made the trip back to the States, I was beginning to see the sweep of my life in a simple metaphor. I had been driving down the road in my old pickup, the story went. The brain had been behind the wheel most of that time. The brain would scan the horizon ahead, straining to see what was coming down the road so that it could avoid disaster by controlling whatever appeared ahead. The brain was pretty sure that disaster lay ahead, since life had already presented one struggle after another. The brain thought that if it could just get a little smarter, a little better at anticipating, it could prevent bad stuff from happening. Of course, it never could really see what was coming, and it could never control it when it arrived anyway— except in the very conventional way of working hard, planning for the future, and hoping for the best.

And my crotch—my head's companion—had been riding shotgun all this time. Occasionally, it would grab the wheel and try to steer the truck. There were crashes that followed. Each time, the head would take the wheel back and say something to the effect of "haven't we learned our little lesson now?"

In the timeless time that stories span, it became apparent that this very masculine duo was neither avoiding the crashes nor controlling the future. During this timeless time, as the heart waited patiently for its turn at the wheel, the head finally relented, perhaps in a temporary retreat caused by the plant medicines and the outrageous nature of the visions that were getting past its vigilant skepticism—perhaps in some acknowledgement of the failure of its own way of doing things.

As the heart took the wheel, it also scanned the horizon. But it wasn't trying to avoid disaster or even difficulty, and its motive was not to control. To the contrary, it drove toward whatever attracted it. It followed its own vision, seeing the horizon as connected to itself, and moving with the grace and ease of an internal sense to which the horizon itself responded by yielding up its secret gifts. The heart did not understand where it was going or what it might find when the truck arrived, but that's not the heart's job, after all. It just points the way.

In the meantime, the head had moved to the back of the pickup and looked backward down the road that we had just traveled. Occasionally, the head would say "Oh, now I get it." And sometimes it did get it, and many times it didn't. But the head could make arrangements for dinner and hotel when the heart parked the truck. The head was very good at planning when it knew the short-range objective. The crotch found itself in the back, too, leaning on the side rail, waiting to find out when the play might include it. Things started working better.

In that timeless time, the crotch and the head had not only acquiesced to the heart's grip on the wheel, but responded to the possibility of collaborating with the heart. The body's intelligent head and sexuality had seemed to have discovered themselves in a larger way when taking their lead from the heart. Everything was on board, and everyone was breathing again, but the heart gently insisted on the wheel, even as the head in particular made the occasional grab. The journey continued, and laughter was often heard from the front seat shared by these three as they leaned with excitement toward the horizon.

It was almost a year and half after the arrival of the vision before I could get the law practice closed. Another trip to Peru and another brief relationship came and went. I took a year off to remodel my law office into a wellness center that offered the healing modalities that I had accumulated on the journey. I backed away from the search for relationship for a time. My writing began to occupy more time. I was finding myself in a new mode. I had quit saying, "I am a lawyer," years before when asked what I did for a living, and had shifted to saying that I made my living as a lawyer. I was slowly recasting my identity, seeing myself more and more as a soul, and less and less in terms of the activities of the personality through which my soul was experiencing its fate. I was identifying less with my mind's effort at speculating about the future. My daily meditation started and ended with holding my attention in my heart. This was an exciting time, full of energy and optimism, and still attended by the confusion that the mind experiences when it attempts to reduce unknown into known. Confusion may be the mind's most starkly honest posture. The heart was moving me forward, and the mind was in a continual game of catch-up.

Within a couple of years, it was clear that the small community where I had been born, raised my children, and practiced law was not large enough to support the wellness center. I closed that down and moved to Crestone, a small and very spiritually geared community in southern Colorado, intending to re-gather myself. I was feeling my way, moving forward in the direction that my heart was drawn, and working on not having to understand what the heart was pulling me toward. I assumed that whatever story my mind would make up about this transition would be fiction, even though I didn't discourage the mind from trying. So I practiced feeling my way and not getting invested in whatever understanding came up. My mind continued to cast about to find ways of packaging my work, to put a name on it, and get some writing done that would put a foundation under it. I wrote, got stuck, and threw out volumes that seemed promising until I descended into the recognition that I hadn't found either the message or my voice. The soul was still sitting below the surface, but just below. There were pieces of writing that were as clear and genuine as my soul, just as there were pieces of the soul that were clearly emerging into my surface personality.

At some point, the notion of this book came into view, and I wrote several chapters while holding the end generally in mind. The rest of my life was hectic, as I began again to give way to my penchant for learning through relationship. This took time away from the writing, but it also continued to bring the gifts of insight that illuminated more subtle levels of projection than I had previously reclaimed in their more obvious dimensions. In time, I was able to approach the book and sit with it. It was feeling somewhat stale—close, but not in the center.

The choice of Er's story still seemed a helpful metaphor for the message of the book, but I gradually realized that I wasn't seeing the connection between the story and Stages Four and Five. The first three stages seemed to flow from the story easily enough. But it seems that the only message from Er was that the destiny was out there somewhere beyond the fate, and that our astrological chart—our inherent nature—contained the texture of the gifts that could emerge from our potential.

My new partner and I mused about Peru, and about the plant medicines. Responding in part to her interest, I began to ask myself, and my guidance, whether it might not be time to "check in" with the plant again. The simple answer was—yes. It was an *awakening*—now my code name for a clear heart choice made in the midst of the head's confusion in the face of big decision. We chose a destination in Peru and booked a trip. Six years had intervened since the last experience with the plant in Costa Rica.

In those intervening years, I felt that I had not taken on the big tools, like the plants or the vision quests. There had been journeying, and daily heart meditation. I could feel the sense of heart guidance growing in me. I was practicing my qi gong, and doing yoga. Crestone, true to its reputation in spiritual circles, was providing a background of supportive, clear, and intense energies. And I was also aware of some lethargy in me. I knew that a larger push might help, but it just wasn't getting on the calendar. It felt sometimes that I had come again to living more in my mind than my body, and only the scent of the book and the yearning of my heart were pulling me forward. The soul was willing, but there was a kind of holding back, as though the soul's orbit had stalled its slow descent toward the planet of my body. Now, I felt almost relieved that I was going to challenge myself once more.

Back to the Amazon

We traveled in late March of 2011 to an ayahuasca center near Iquitos in northeastern Peru. The program provided for four ceremonies to be followed by a *huachuma* ceremony, all within the space of ten days. *Huachuma* is the local name given to the San Pedro cactus which, when prepared as a medicine, is regarded as a master teaching plant—just as the ayahuasca is regarded. I had encountered the huachuma in the earlier years of working with the ayahuasca, but had not connected deeply with it, and I was a little disappointed that our week would end with this plant.

Our shamans were both indigenous, but with an interesting twist. Sara, the senior of the two, is about forty years of age, and has eight or nine children. She is small, less than one hundred pounds and about five feet tall. Her husband Luis was not present. I was told that they partnered in this work. She is of the Sawa tribe that lives along the Amazon some distance from Iquitos. Our other presiding shaman was Jungle—an Anglo man who appeared to me to be about thirty and who had a reserved demeanor. Because of my presumption that indigenous peoples are people of color—and forgetting that we all descend from indigenous tribes—I was surprised to learn that Jungle was Sami. The Sami tribe traditionally occupied the region between Norway and Russia. They herd reindeer, a practice that continues despite a long conflict between Norway and Russia for the traditional Sami lands. Jungle told me that his grandfather was a shaman, and that shamans were executed by Protestants for practicing their work not all that long ago.

Our ceremonies took place in a *maloka*, a round ceremonial room with a wooden floor raised above the jungle floor. The room was screened around the whole of its perimeter to give light and air and to prevent as many insects as possible from coming in. Geckos patrolled the area above the walls and would occasionally hit the floor with an unceremonious *plop*. The room's pitched roof rose over twenty feet in its center and was made of leaves. Several altars were arranged in the room, with the shamans seated before the largest one opposite the entry. Sleeping mats had been laid out for all of us, although sleeping was not our purpose. Lying down was likely, since it was hard to sit up once the plant took over the body despite the shamans' encouragement for us to sit up. There were about a dozen participants in each of the ceremonies.

The ceremonies began after dark. The first ceremony took place the evening of the day of our arrival. Jungle dispensed about a measuring cup of ayahuasca to each of us. That was more than I had received in earlier ceremonies, and that alarmed me a bit. The ayahuasca decoction is uniformly bitter, regardless of the various herbs that particular shamans may add to amplify its medicinal effect or blunt the taste. I had to overcome a gag reflex, and quickly washed my mouth out with water. Nausea came fairly quickly. I think I was the first in the maloka to throw up, but I looked forward to the visions I expected to ensue after the purging, as had been my prior experience.

No visions followed. I was disappointed. Then I realized that there was a dialogue clearly occurring in my mind, and that my internal vision was held in a kind of grey, soft light. I kept my eyes closed and concentrated.

I heard, "*Do not confuse the field with the plant.*" The meaning seemed immediately clear to me. Since my prior experience with the ayahuasca, I had adopted an understanding that the plant itself was an intelligent being devoted to the education and healing of humans. I had personified this understanding with the name *Mother Ayahuasca*, a common way of referring to the plant among those who encounter its deeply feminine nature. I had assumed that whatever information and healing came during the ceremony came from the plant itself. I was apparently wrong.

The new understanding that emerged in the moment of this ceremonial dialogue was that there is an other-dimensional field (a frequency encoded with information) extant outside of time and space that works alongside the plant itself. This field, while connected to the plant, is not limited to the plant's dense nature. In a very real sense, the field is more powerful than the plant, and equally *real*, although conventional consciousness would assume the contrary. Rather, the plant is the means by which the field gains access to the human consciousness. My sense is that the ayahuasca tunes humans to the frequency of the field itself so that the field can work with and inform the human soul field.

Much has been written already about the N, N-dimethyltryptamine (DMT) that occurs naturally in ayahuasca. What had dawned upon me was that the chemical change and the common visions were not what the field sought to accomplish, but merely the way in which the field used the plant to facilitate communication. New possibilities presented themselves. Perhaps, I thought, there are visions that are common to the plant itself, and there are visions that are facilitated by the plant. The former could come *from* the plant, and the other might come *because* of the plant. So, while the role of the plant is important, it is the communication of the information from the field to the soul that might be the ultimate objective of this encounter with the plant. The nature of the plant is to take control of the human system so powerfully that it is difficult for the human personality to resist—and ultimately difficult for the human to resist the information that the field seeks to communicate when the plant has wrested the attention away from its habitual orbit of mind, emotions and culture. That wrestling might be greatly resisted, and the rigor of the experience may flow from that exchange.

What was also becoming apparent is that the plant worked in at least two phases, where before I had only experienced one. The first is to "heal" the body, but perhaps not in the way of which we ordinarily think. That healing might come from the plant, or the field, or both. The healing is not necessarily an end in itself, but also a means of raising the capacity of the body system to tune to and resonate with those higher frequencies that inhere in the field or the plant or both. Many may argue that the healing is an end in itself, and for individuals whose consciousness is focused on physical survival and improvement of emotional states that is certainly a valid perspective. But, when consciousness becomes focused through a soul perspective, survival itself is only a means to the further evolution of consciousness in general, to which the individual soul is itself a means. In either event, healing requires a human cooperation—surrender to the process, and a willingness to integrate and foster the changes—without which the first stage cannot do its work. This surrender requires some skill in itself. If we cannot control our attention enough to come to the place of surrender and attend to what the plant is attempting to do, then we cannot receive what the plant offers.

There is collaboration afoot here. The soul leads our surface personality level consciousness to an encounter with the plant, if it can. And if it can, the plant shifts the body's capacity for receiving information by loosening the hold that the personality's worldview has on the ability of the soul to come forward. As the body's capacity is transformed, the soul can come forward relative to the personality, more and more. As the soul comes forward, there is a greater opportunity for the soul to connect with the guidance of the other dimensional fields that seek to inform the individual soul in the purpose of the soul's work, which pushes forward the connection between body and soul as a means to foster the dance between heaven and earth. So, what begins with a body/mind upgrade is truly a collaboration—one might say a conspiracy—between the nascent soul and the ayahausca field that leads the body to the plant. In this process, healing cancer—for example—is not so important in itself as ending the body's preoccupation with a condition that does not allow the focus of energy and attention on the soul's agenda. The ultimate purpose is to create a physical vehicle that can vibrate at higher and higher frequencies in order to communicate with the ayahuasca field and—as became apparent in these ceremonies before long—other fields also encoded with information for the soul's edification.

So, the first phase of working with the plant medicine is the healing. The second is the communication that begins as the body becomes able to receive and record it. In this first ceremony, the door had opened to this communication, as it had in the last ceremony I had done in 2005.

As this first ceremony moved later into the night, I heard another pointed and simple communication: *the notion of the plant as Mother is a projection, as is the notion of Earth as Mother.* The idea wasn't entirely new to my thinking. I had had some sense of this in my meditation just a month or so earlier. But now the message was more direct. My mind was immediately excited with the many implications that might flow from this simple message, but this was not the time for the mind to engage, either in the moment of the ceremony or in the days that followed. I did not want to re-engage the mind too powerfully, since my purpose in being in the jungle was to do the opposite.

Two evenings later, I approached the ceremony with more confidence, without really understanding why. I felt on task, purposeful. Jungle gave me the same amount again. This time, my body accepted it without tightening up. I sat up on my cushion and began to feel that I might not throw up. After about twenty minutes, however, the nausea quickly arose and overtook me. I threw up strongly, as before.

What followed was familiar from the ceremonies of years before. The memory, once evoked, was clear and strong. I had been here before. The visions were crystal clear. A pattern flashed onto the screen, moving in a serpentine fashion. I saw small colored dots that allowed for a transparency—like a pointillist painting in motion seen at almost microscopic range, in which the space between the dots was much larger than the dots themselves. These formed shapes that looked like complex plumbing, but morphed into humanoid forms that seemed to be leaning outward to look at me. The scene was brightly lit, sometimes from the front and receding into a dark background, and sometimes the opposite. My attention was drawn hypnotically into these scenes. The difference from prior years was that I now felt stronger and more focused. I remembered what the ayahuasca field had said just two nights before. *Do not confuse the plant with the field.* I began to work with the assumption that the vision that I was seeing in this moment was a vision of the plant itself, and was not the field where I would seek a communication and connection.

This time, I worked with my breath to focus my attention in order to get past the plant. I tried to open the main energy channel in my body. I could feel that energy that was getting stuck in my pelvic area, and it felt as though it was trying to push up, and that it was important to help it. This was not easy, and required lots of breathing and sheer will. The stuckness of this energy was reflected in the way my pelvis would rise from the mat while I laid on my back. In the air, my pelvis would vibrate or pulse in an almost sexual way. It did not feel sexual, although that was not always the case in the ceremonies of earlier years. The sound of my breathing was evidently loud. Jungle spoke through the darkness quietly but firmly to "be quiet." I had not heard anyone else, so I assumed he was talking to me. What I did hear felt like it was coming through a tunnel, and that I was hearing it from deep down in that tunnel. During this time, my attention would move in and out of the plant vision itself. I could feel myself losing control, giving into the hypnotic movement of the vision, then getting it back. Jungle's songs—the *icaros*—would reach out and bring me back to a focused state.

As I gathered and regathered myself, I would hear myself say "OK," as though coaching myself through the process and acknowledging with that "OK" that I had recaptured my attention from the plant vision. In particular, I used my breath to focus the energy of my body with the intention to connect to the higher frequency dimensions in which the fields reside. In other words, I was working on the assumption that the work here was not to get lost in the plant itself, but to use it as a tuning, clearing, or healing that would give me direct access to fields of information beyond the plant experience itself.

After some of this back and forth, the ayahuasca field began to communicate and talk again, and to coach me itself. It seemed to cycle. There would be work, then rest, then work again. Never did I feel completely overwhelmed. At some point, the common plant visions shortened in their duration as my attention would move back and forth from the plant to the field. In these intervals, the field began to give me the language—an understanding through which to look at this experience and to answer the unarticulated question I did not know I had brought to the plant with this return to the jungle.

The field was speaking clearly. It had my attention.

Taste, But Don't Let It Control You

Now, there was a seeming cascade of information.

Taste the plant, the field said, *but don't let it control you.*

The field continued. *Feel the animal, but don't let it control you. Ride the plant, ride the earth, but don't try to tame them. They are wild. It is their wildness that you want. You need to call them to you, to a partnership. They need to want to work with you. That is not their natural state. Sing your soul song. Connect your soul field and the higher fields to them through your heart. The heart is like a saddle. Use it until you can ride bareback. Then, invite them to the dance. All and each of the earth fields can be invited to the dance.*

All of this came in just a few minutes. These words are not an exact repetition of what the field was pushing into my mind, but it was what my mind could gather and hold in the moment. It was challenging to distinguish my own thinking from what I was hearing. The thoughts simply formed in my mind. My curious mind has a tendency to move quickly from the midst of experience to interpretation of the experience—the means by which we develop understandings, including the lesser understandings that arise from interpretations that are premature or simply inaccurate. But these were thoughts that were entirely unfamiliar to me. I was not thinking them. It felt that they were thinking me.

The field was giving me instructions about how to use the plant to get to the field, but it was showing me that the very way of dealing with the plant had a much larger application. The field spoke of plant, animal, and earth, but it felt as thought it were speaking of the density of matter in general, including my own body. The medicine could only be talking to my soul. These were operating instructions for the soul arriving on the planet.

The field was telling the soul that it had to taste and feel into the density of matter while resisting the hypnotic, seductive nature of matter, starting with the plant that was, in that very moment, seducing me into an experience that was horribly difficult to transcend. Only a little reflection on the day that followed the ceremony would suggest that my soul experience of the body itself is of the same nature. The first work of the soul is to enter the body, taste its nature, feel its wildness, and call it to a collaboration that is not the body's first inclination anymore than it is the forgetful soul's first inclination to dance with density. Only as the soul gains the skills of attention that allow it to focus on the threshold of density does the potential of partnership arise. Only when a partnership begins to form can the body be invited to the dance that serves the soul's destiny in particular and the evolution of consciousness in general. In the cascade of words that flowed from the field in the darkness of this jungle ceremony, there was a huge emphasis on the notion of *partnership.*

Nothing in my engagement with the ayahuasca field suggested that the plant, the body, the earth, or the density of matter in general are in any way *less than* the soul or the heaven consciousness from which the soul is distilled. The density seems simply the other pole of a duality formed out of the mystery of the cosmos for the very purpose of this dance that can occur between the mind of heaven and the dense body of earth. Heaven provides, it seems, the design for innovation, and density provides the materials. But neither is static. Both are dynamic. Neither heaven nor earth controls, and the lead in their dance may be passed back and forth. Each influences and inspires the other. The plant makes it possible for the soul to access heaven in a way that washes away the forgetfulness first occurring because of the merger of soul with density. My experience made sense of that translation of the word *ayahuasca* as the vine of soul. It served the same function as my near death experience. It helped to emphasize that I am a soul, because it communicated to me in that way.

A soul relationship with the body in particular and matter in general has to be developed. It is as though matter is available to work with the soul, but not yet so willing that it does not need to be courted, seduced, coaxed. Horse whispering comes to mind. The horse is amenable to falling in love with a human, but may not know it until the particular relationship begins to develop. It starts with the invitation made by the human and develops with a gradual warming to a relationship, all coaxed by the human's non-threatening and curious presence. Like the horse, all of matter responds to the soul's invitation to relate in just this way. And that relationship between the soul and the density of matter is in the nature of all relationship, including the complex dance between two humans. There is a process of getting acquainted, of experiencing each other, of feeling into their connection to determine the strength of the mutual attraction, of sensing into the depth of intimacy that is the potential of the meeting of the two, and the beginning of the dance. The *you* that calls to matter is the soul, just as the you that calls to another human is, ultimately, the soul.

Putting just two of these communications together—*Mother is a projection* and *the soul invites matter into partnership*—I found myself feeling into the emergence of a new construct, one that was previously outside my consciousness. It is far larger than the current popular notion of a *body/mind,* both of which I sense are on the body side of the body/soul polarity. It is the flip of the notion that the body is sinful, and that we need to attend to our true home in heaven. It holds a far different tone than the arrogant notion that the body is the mere ass upon which the mind rides. Of course, it is light years away from atheistic postures that are energized by poor science and disdain for subjective experience as a foundation for epistemology. Agnostics, at least, honor their subjectivity and limited experience as a foundation for the epistemological position of neutrality. Conversely, the emerging construct is quite different than the psychodynamic spiritual Western fusion of dropping our anger, not taking things personally, and coming to a skill of compassionate awareness. As important as these latter steps are, they remain steps toward something beyond that. The soul demands its own construct, and that construct demands a more expansive view.

What is emerging, not only in my consciousness I'm sure, is a sensibility to a post-Mother relationship with earth that partners from a sense of equality and seeks a co-creative collaboration based in greater skills of human consciousness. I felt as though I was receiving instructions for creating a relationship with earth that does not exist now and has not existed in the past. It felt strangely appropriate that these instructions should come at a point in time in which the prior human relationship with earth was failing. That very failure is opening humans to a new level of relationship. Yet, the deep and apparent failure of humans to live in balance with the earth made the suggestion of a new relationship seem futile in this moment. If we couldn't succeed as children of a loving mother, how could we possibly move to a relationship that required a higher level of skill? And perhaps the notion of skill is precisely the difference. A child's naiveté, even in the face of a loving mother, does not support an ultimate goal of the evolution of consciousness.

At our cultural best, we hold the earth within the frame of a relationship in which "Mother" says it all. We have been her children. And in this jungle ceremony, I was beginning to hear that this time-honored perception, now in the dangerous stages of an ignorant, arrogant, and rebellious dishonoring, is a projection. Our dependency on the earth has already given way to an unbalanced and unconsciousness human perspective that is dominated by an angry masculine. That immature and unbalanced *puer* has wrapped itself unconsciously and increasingly in a patriarchy that seeks to control and dominate the earth, the body, women, and the feminine in both men and women. The dysfunction of this projection and an immature, arrogant teen-like rebellion against it is mirrored in the anger and hatred that I carried for my own mother through much of my early life.

Yet, it is through that mother-child relationship that we have had access to the earth's nurture and a sense of connection and love and being held on the breast of the Mother. But that experience has become increasingly unavailable to our unskilled consciousness as we have left an agrarian lifestyle. In the myriad ways in which the human relationship with earth has changed, it is clear that the notion of Earth as Mother is also changing, and that the old relationship is no longer true. *Mother* is a projection that no longer serves a human population that desperately needs to mature into a capability for responsibility that transcends its dangerous teen years. Now, the agrarian experience that naturally coincided with that projection has been lost, albeit unconsciously, by conventional culture. It is being lost rather than being transcended, as we depart from family farming for the first time of any culture in human history.

As we leave the farm, we leave also the possibility of the direct experience of that nurturing relationship without having replaced that connection with anything else. It is apparent that we have not transcended the field and forest as a form of relationship. We have abandoned it, and it was the only one we knew. That relationship is still alive now only in underdeveloped countries where traditional farming survives, but it is dying there as well in the face of the greed of globalization and its rendering of land into one more commodity to be sold and "developed."

So, as the old projection of Earth as Mother falls away unconsciously in our own cultural experience, we are being called in the fecund darkness of a jungle ceremony to look upon the relationship anew—to embrace a different way of connecting that is perhaps our only way of surviving our own present inability either to connect with matter as mother or surrender to the vision that invites a more skillful and mature connection. We are being called in what feels like the last moment. It is a unique moment in time. In this moment, human consciousness has bumbled beyond the hypnosis of an unconscious agrarian connection to the breathtaking, dangerous, and very necessary awakening that is the potential of having left that connection. Severing that connection provides a very brief opportunity to reform the connection skillfully from our own hearts before the chaos of transition carries it all away.

It requires a new vision—perhaps one that calls us to connect with the heart of the earth rather than the nipple on her breast. It is time for the masculine to wean and grow up. It is time for our souls to speak directly to her soul.

Soul to Soul Now

There was an interesting twist in this second ceremony that underlined the field's injunction to drop the story of our projection. Months before I knew I was headed to Peru for this ceremony, my partner, a clairvoyant, told me that my birth mother wanted to speak to me. My mother had died years before. Just a few months before my partner spoke of her, I had felt my mother's presence on the occasion of her birthday. I jokingly replied to my partner to tell her to "come on." But I felt unable to connect on my own. Then, in Peru, as I prepared for the second ceremony, I got a massage. While working on me, the therapist said, "You know, John, your mother wants to talk to you." Obviously, something was up.

As the dialogue with the field regarding projection came to a close in this second ceremony, the voice of my birth mother formed up in my mind. *Now you can drop the projection with me, too,* she said. No more carrying the memory of her as birth mother, as angry mother, as struggling mother, as the soft mother whose hand I held through the last days of her life as she very consciously and purposely set her mind on dying.

Soul to soul now, she said. I was invited to release my own mother projection both at the level of personal mother and earth mother. Personal and universal were merging into their own dance. I could feel my personal mother revert in my own field to a soul with whom I had this primary working connection. I could sense the strength of her soul stripped now of its earth form and fate. I smiled and laughed at her presence, remembering that just before her death she blew kisses to people she had not liked during her life. I blew her a kiss. No emotion other than a joyful recognition, and, now, a second goodbye, and a thanks for her paradoxical help. As I could now see her in a different way, I knew that I could see the human relationship with matter—the body, the earth—in a different way. *Soul to soul.*

Something was truly up. There was room now for a new vision.

The Arc of the Covenant

In the ayahuasca ceremony in which this dialogue with the field continued, another seemingly unrelated thought formed in my mind. The vision of the inner marriage related in the previous chapter returned to mind without any apparent antecedent in this particular ceremony. The words *arc of the covenant* blazed across my mind. The arc that had been so prominent in that earlier vision as a horizontal bridge of light between the sacred mountains was now emerging also as a vertical column stretching from heaven to earth. I found myself standing in the column, between heaven and earth, with the column running through my heart. The column of which Er spoke was coming alive in me, and the words I heard described that column as an arc.

When I had first heard the words "arc of the covenant," I simply assumed they referred to an energy connection. I had heard, of course, of the Ark of the Covenant, but was unaware of the differences in the spelling and meaning until I did some research. The Ark refers to the *container* of the tablets of stone upon which the Ten Commandments were written. That particular usage held no significance for me, until I realized that an energy connection is also a container of information. The information encoded into a frequency that represents a field of energy is also a set of instructions, which is precisely what the Ten Commandments are. At the time of my first hearing these words, however, I had no inkling that these arcs were the containers of information, much less of the information they might convey.

Dots of smaller understandings that had populated my consciousness from the series of earlier awakenings were now magically connecting. Now there were two arcs, not one. And it would only be months later that I could see the two not as alternative understandings of the same phrase—*arc of the covenant*—but as a singular combination of the two. The horizontal and vertical formed in my mind's eye, only later, as a *cross*. This visual joining implied the necessity of merging the two in a conceptual understanding. The horizontal arc now clearly referred to the juncture of the masculine and feminine in me, while the vertical arc was the joinder of the masculine of heaven with the feminine of earth, through me. And more was to reveal itself of these joinings in the *huachuma* ceremony that was to follow later in the week.

But on that evening of the second ayahuasca ceremony, days before the *huachuma* would play a role in the unfolding of this mystery, I saw the vertical arc as a distinct and singular bond of energy. In the moment that followed, the word *responsibility* came strongly to mind. I heard that my inbreath informed action—as though the inbreath drew down the frequencies of heaven—and that my outbreath manifested in accordance with the information brought down in that way. As the dots continued to connect quickly in this moment, I heard that the vision of the inner marriage called on me to make a promise to assume responsibility for what I would manifest. This was a larger conceptual unfolding of the joinder of the masculine and feminine represented by the horizontal arc of the covenant. I could see now that the anticipated but unconsummated marriage of the feminine and the masculine of my earlier vision predicted a marriage that could now be understood in another, deeper way. The forthcoming marriage was indeed a joining of masculine and feminine, but now the bride and groom appeared in more clear focus. The masculine was indeed my own soul, and the feminine my own body.

The marriage of masculine and feminine—soul and body—must occur in order to facilitate a second marriage between heaven and earth. And these marriages have no purpose other than to bring the soul into relationship with the body so that heaven may join earth in an ultimate purpose of evolving by co-creating—for transforming humans and earth by their own voluntary, willful, loving connection as means to the further creation of consciousness in the evolving fullness of manifesting in the density of matter. Can heaven join earth only through an energetically activated human, one in which soul has joined with body in a conscious, collaborative, and loving marriage? It seemed so in my emerging understanding. In the process, the soul has to take the lead in the courtship of the body, just as heaven has taken the lead in sending the soul as its emissary to the earth plane. Through the soul, heaven courts the earth by the soul's preliminary courting of the body. What I was being shown would become an irresistible experience in just a few days to follow, although I had no hint of what was coming in the moment of this ceremony.

Like the Ark of the Covenant, my arcs were containers of information and instructions by which the soul and body communicated with each other and by which heaven and earth also communicated with the body/soul and with each other.

The third ayahuasca ceremony loomed large now.

Going Deeper

After the richness of the information that had flowed from the first two ceremonies, I hesitated. I found myself feeling that I had received what I came for, and incredibly more than I had expected. I thought of cutting my stay short.

I talked to the retreat facilitator a bit about this, who suggested that I talk to Jungle. Before talking to him, I felt into myself and realized that I was also dealing with a little fear about doing another ceremony. Perhaps my resistance was simply a result of some fear about ingesting the medicine, which always seems so rigorous. Perhaps my personality level identity was resisting the huge change that the soul level information of the ceremonies implicated. Perhaps I was feeling relieved that I had gotten by so far with so little difficulty in the ceremonies and feared "tempting fate," as one might say in the ordinary usage of that phrase.

I talked to Jungle. He said simply that there is always more information. End of conversation. Talking to Jungle, I quickly came to the feeling that I simply needed to let the process go forward.

In preparation for the third ceremony, I had a session with the massage thera- pist again. I asked him to do what he was skilled at doing, which was to work with my energy. I was beginning to feel like a fighter working with a trainer just before step- ping into the ring. With that work done, in the afternoon that preceded the third journey, I again felt confident, calm, focused, receptive, prepared. I took a full cup, which settled well again. It took longer for me to purge, and there was less purging this time. I also became aware before long that Sara was in charge of the ceremony, although Jungle had dispensed the ayahuasca. We learned later that Jungle had some- thing of his own to deal with—some sorcery directed at him by a jealous shaman outside our circle. He could not hold the energy of the space for himself and all of us as well. It was a good reminder that the Western romance with indigenous shaman- ism is not a casual fling.

As the ayahuasca overtook me, it was apparent that the ceremony would be gentler. Jungle sang some, but Sara sang most of the icaros. After I purged, the matrix of colored dots came alive in full color and action, and I realized that I was again see- ing the same level and manner of detail that I had seen more than once in years past. The matrix was serpentine, constructed of small patterns that encased openness, so that the figures were transparent, and the structure open. The scene was completely and deeply three dimensional, not only in a strand of the matrix but in the layering of strands above and behind others. The scene was internally lit, but sometimes shifted such that it appeared to be lit from my eyes, with shadows cast behind the matrix. Again, the serpentine shape would morph into a human shape with the same transparency, and the shape would seem to crane over to look down on me, as I was lying on my back during this time.

This was surprisingly boring to me, since I felt I had been there before and that there was no more information to be gleaned. However, it was still mesmerizing, and I found myself intoxicated enough that my attention seemed too attached to the movement. I have no idea how long this lasted, but awakened to the touch of Sara's hand holding mine, and the sounds of her singing and the leaf rattle, the *chakapa*, that she shook over my face. She had seen that I had been caught by the plant and had come to help me pull my attention back.

Over the several minutes that Sara worked with me, I could feel myself coming back to a plateau somewhere above the depth of the plant. After the ceremony, I thanked Sara and Jungle for my experience and asked whether I had gone too deeply into the plant. She said yes. I recalled the advice of field from the prior ceremony, that I should taste but not allow the plant control. I had tasted, then lost focus and lost control of my attention.

After Sara brought my awareness back from the seductive abyss of the plant experience, more information began to come. Much of the information was initially visual, which then became the subject of some dialogue and understanding. I continued to work hard to manage my energy. I used some energy-balancing techniques the massage therapist had suggested. I visualized the energy channel that rises vertically in the core of my body, and found it open now. I knew this to be what is commonly called the *kundalini*. The energy that moved within this channel was neither sudden nor harsh, as it can be experienced when the channel first opens. For me, it was like fresh air flowing through an expansive space. I found that it opened more if I sat up straight, and that I could sit up straight better if I continued to run energy in that channel. In this ceremony, there was still some sense of stuck energy in my pelvis, but it diminished and left entirely as I sat up and encouraged the energy to flow in this way. I continued to do this practice throughout the rest of the ceremony when I could sit, and I worked to sit as much as possible. The plant had provided me an experience of tasting, losing control, and coming back into control. My experience in this ceremony was a direct mirroring of the teaching of the earlier ceremony. It felt extremely important to have the experience along with the concept.

I begin to use a breathing practice that I had developed some months before. As I breathed in, I imagined my heart-field opening to and drawing heaven in. As I breathed out, I imagined my field encircling the earth, coming up through the center of the earth field, and opening again to heaven. With the inbreath, I felt myself taking in the patterning provided by heaven. With the outbreath, I felt myself passing that heaven pattern into form, into manifestation at the level of dense matter.

Then I saw that there were two ways to breathe out. One can breathe out internally, where one completes the circuit of an internal concentration of energy. The other way is to breathe out into the world, which is the function of creation. I saw how intention could be blown into the world. Then I saw how the breath could be focused and more refined. Then I saw that the finer focus could be reduced into words, for example, which convey design. The design is from heaven. Words that do not convey heaven's design do not manifest heaven's design. In such cases, the breath is wasted. If the words do not connect, there is a waste of heaven's energy. At the end of this short tutorial in the breath's role in manifestation, I heard the almost deadpan professorial punctuation on the lesson: *do not waste your breath*. Don't waste your breath, the professor was implying, with idle conversation, with ideas that do not connect, with activity that does not create. Creation requires the connection of heaven's design with the density of earth matter, and breath is literally the intermediary by which the process is initiated as we give voice to the ideas that reveal that design.

In those moments, I could feel my soul coming forward more strongly into the now-receptive personality. I heard *give the soul to the day, and the body back to the night.*

What could that mean? I sensed that I was being told to reverse a prior unconscious reversal. In our ordinary consciousness, the soul awareness remains buried beneath a culturally dominated and rather unconscious surface personality. Lying dormant in the heart, the soul finds its connection to heaven and earth through night dreams, since the unattended heart's imagination is unavailable to it during the waking hours. It is our more body-dominated personality that is awake during the daytime. Just as the soul is relegated to expressing its nature through night dreams, the body is relegated to expressing its nature through day dreams. The body's nature is of the nature of the earth—powerful beyond our ordinary imaginations, sexual, fecund, and more. By day, in our unconscious states, the soul is denied control of our activities, and the body is denied its primordial and unconsciousness connection with the earth.

Perhaps the ayahuasca field was suggesting that by allowing the soul to control the personality, the soul can take the day, collaborate with the body's power, and do the work of the soul. By allowing the body to go loose in the sleeping state, it has the opportunity to visit its own deep and dark nature, and to recover its own energy and power in the earth realm. By unskillfully allowing the body personality to form our primary identity, we have separated it from its earth source. The body needs this connection, and that connection occurs in the merger with its larger nature. By giving the body to the night, we allow it to remerge with the earth in dream state. By giving the soul to the day, we allow it to guide the union of the body and soul, and the connection between heaven and earth, which is served by this union.

The ceremony would continue two nights later.

The Column that Connects Heaven to Earth

Prior to the fourth ceremony, I asked Jungle whether one always needed to come to ceremony with a question. He said to come with *una menta blanca*—an open mind. I formed an intention to come to the fourth and last ayahuasca ceremony in that way. Again, my energy was calm during the day leading up to the ceremony, and my body receptive. My body's fearful anticipation of the drinking was almost gone.

My primary intention this time was to keep focus. I wanted to sit up during the ceremony. Jungle gave me less ayahuasca this time. After I drank, I sat until the plant arose in my body. I purged, and discovered that my lunch had not digested. I had not taken enough water during the day.

The plant vision came, and I remained sitting and focused. Throughout the plant vision, I was able to watch and taste but not lose control of my consciousness or focus. I could move in and out of it with much better control. In time, it subsided, and a space of clarity remained in which I could begin to listen for the voice of the field to speak again.

The voice spoke again. The gist of its communication was that my work—perhaps the work of humans—is to learn to navigate through the heart. I clearly heard, felt, and saw that the other senses, including the mind, must see through the heart. Yet, the message was not coming through with the same clarity of prior communications. Still, it was clear that heart navigation was at the center of the communication. I struggled to give this some more distinct form with my mind, which wasn't working. I continued to return to the breathing pattern that centered upon the heart, and this seemed to be the way to navigate through the intensity of the ceremony.

In the prior ceremony, the breathing form that had previously extended from heaven to earth had been reduced to a tiny field within my heart. On this night, I saw the form begin to spin in the heart, and I could see the field—in the distinct form of an electromagnetic field—take shape into a single field that included heaven, earth, and the heart itself. As it spun, I could see the rotation of the field, and later thought I was seeing a merger that might be called phase resonance among these fields. As I watched this spin within me—all of a sudden—the external breath/energy pattern and everything else zipped into the tiny field. So this external view became in my own vision a projection of this internal field. Without understanding what was happening, I sensed that a travel vehicle was forming within the space of the heart-field, and that this development could be at the heart of the process of organizing all perception through the heart.

I was able to continue sitting erect through the ceremony. My attention was next drawn to a huge vertical column of light. Again, I heard the words *arc of the covenant*. It was only then that I remembered that Er saw this column of light. I felt it coming through me. Now I felt it extend through my central energy channel from heaven to earth. Er's story began to connect the dots, and I could begin to see the huge reach of his simple story.

Then I heard that *the power of the body comes from the earth, just as the design/ program information comes from heaven*. I felt that body responding to the soul, feeling the love relationship develop. I saw and heard that *the body comes entirely from the earth, but is separate from the earth field like the soul comes from heaven, but is separate from the whole of consciousness*. The body is a drop of earth, just as the soul is a drop of heaven. A drop of the ocean is still the ocean, but remains in some way distinct from it. This was coming to me as experience, just as the thought would gel in my mind. I could feel it, and I could think it, while feeling the distinct difference between these two modes of apprehension.

With that, the ayahuasca ceremonies came to an end. The huachuma was next.

The Arc Experienced

The buzz about the huachuma was that it would be a way to transition from the ayahuasca experiences back to a state more suitable for getting on the airplane that would take us out of the jungle on the next day. It would be a soft experience, I was told, one that would take place during the day and encourage a gentle connection with the plants and trees.

We met at 7 am. My prior experiences with huachuma involved shamans cooking their own mix from the San Pedro cactus, resulting either in a thick, dark brown liquid that looked similar to the ayahuasca, or a lighter version that was like drinking bitter Jello. Both elicited a bit of a gag reflex. I was surprised to see that Jungle was spooning green powder—dried San Pedro—out of a plastic bag into a water glass. The men were told to drink two glasses full. The women received one. I took this to be a rough accommodation for the average difference in body weight. Jungle told us that we should try to hold it down for two hours before purging, and to avoid purging if we could.

This grainy green mix went down easily for me, although many were complaining about the taste. I went to the *maloka* and laid down. As time passed, I experienced a little nausea, but I was able to hold it without purging. The two hours were hard and, as time passed, I began to tremble. I put this down to neurological effects that reflected the challenge my body was experiencing with this strange invader. One of my prior experiences of years before with the huachuma was similar but more extreme, as what seemed a trembling neurological response lasted for hours. I told Jungle about it, and he gave me something made from a tree outside the maloka to settle me down. As I continued to lie on a mat in the maloka, I began drumming on the floor with my hands. The wood was very resonate and began to hum with sustaining overtones as well as resound directly from each blow of my hands. Jungle came in and drummed with me briefly on a large Remo hand drum. Then he handed me the drum.

I am not a stranger to drums. Drumming is part of the shamanic tool kit. I accepted the drum and began to shuffle around the maloka to the rhythm of a drummed heartbeat. The heartbeat is always a good place to start, and I was looking to get calmed down some. I thought it would be more polite as well, since two of my companions were also laying on mats in the maloka. They cleared out pretty quickly, perhaps sensing that it would be good for all us for me to be left alone. Whatever the reason, I was glad for them to leave. I wanted to be alone. There was a sense of agitation arising in me quite strongly, despite the heart rhythm of the drum. My movement around the maloka began to respond to the drum, and the drum was responding to whatever was arising in me.

Within a few more minutes, the drumming began to feel almost compulsive. I was feeling manic, and the drumming seemed a perfect way to channel and express it. Before very long, I began to sense that these sensations in my body were not entirely about me.

I was not alone.

Throughout my shamanic experiences, and in some ways during the vision quests, there have been clear visitations by archetypal figures, from animals to other beings. Today, there were three—one very familiar animal spirit, one familiar archetype that occupies an animal form as well as a huge cosmic presence, and a third that is entirely and always cosmic in her reach. It took a little time for them to emerge distinctly in my awareness, but it became clear that the drumming became a way in which I related to them and them to me. I understand that this description does not explain much of anything, and I doubt that any understanding I have formed is big enough to capture the essence of what was then taking place in the maloka. I felt finally that I was doing what I was doing because it had to be done, and that I had little choice in the matter, other than to run away, if that was even possible in the moment. I don't think running away occurred to me.

I was feeling an extraordinary power. Between drumming sessions, I found myself performing a spontaneous qigong. I could see the power radiating out from my hands like ripples from the side of a pond move out in concentric half circles. As I did that, I could begin to see how the energy was available to me in the body, and how it could be managed and directed. I returned to the qigong several times that day.

I was continuing to feel exclusive. I had the sense that the power that I was manifesting was far too strong to bring around people.

Later that day, I heard myself explaining to someone that I had come to Peru feeling split, and that the world was splitting. The drumming was the way in which I brought myself back together, and in that way drummed the world back together. It felt as though my dance *was* the dance between earth and heaven, not a symbolic representation of such a dance. All of these very powerful energies that had come to me at various times over many years. Now they were coming together at the same time and in the same place, not so much with me, but through me in order to dance with each other.

In some way, the connection between my own soul and body had become the connecting link between heaven and earth, and had become the manifestation of the column of light that Er had seen after four days journey from the meadow. It felt like a synchronous connection that four days of journeying with the ayahuasca had preceded this experience. The arc that joined me together had given space for the arc—the light column—that joins heaven to earth, through me.

My subsequent and sober sense was that this dance was a small but deeply experiential demonstration within the frame of my body of the human function that connects heaven with earth. It is our role to make that connection. When we do it, we feel the power of that connection—the power to know, to be, and to create. It was breathtaking, to say the least. It seemed that, if I had had to kill something with my hands, it could have happened. The power was that strong. At the same time, the power to kill felt held and transformed with the power from another dimension, which was the power *not* to kill, and the power to create. I simply do not have words to express more than that.

Later in the afternoon, I began to experience a deep sadness. I could still feel the strong influence of the huachuma in my body, but it had diminished. Again, as though I was witnessing myself from outside my body, I heard myself talking about the sadness that came with putting the infinite into small bottles. To bring the expansive nature of the divine into the limitations of an unconscious human frame felt very sad indeed. It felt sad to return to my small body and leave this feeling of cosmic connection, even as I could feel in my own small human body the true joy of experiencing myself in this cosmic frame.

Another way of seeing this strange experience with the huachuma was in the frame of the understandings I received while drinking the ayahuasca. On its own, the ayahuasca was a deeply experiential encounter with a field that transmitted information in a mental frame along with the more physical experience that illustrated it. Compared to the ayahuasca, the huachuma was deeply experiential without an accompanying text, yet full of information of a different sort. The ayahuasca experience seemed to provide instructions by which soul can connect with body for the further purpose of connecting heaven with earth. With the huachuma, I felt myself enacting this dance between heaven and earth in the full consciousness of the depth of the meaning of that—a meaning felt, without any explanation of its import.

My initial projection of the beginning of the week that the huachuma would be disappointing had been blown away. Between the ayahuasca and the huachuma, it felt that the vision of the inner marriage of seven years before was coming to a kind of consummation.

Stage Five Consciousness

Er's story records a seemingly innocuous detail. Leaving the meadow where the souls chose a life to enact upon the earth journey, the souls journey for four days, seeing on the fourth day a column of light in the distance. On the fifth day, the souls reach the column of light, where they engage with the Sisters of Fate beneath the Spindle of Necessity. In this simple and brief manner, Er foretells that we move through four stages of consciousness before we suspect the arc that stretches from heaven to earth in the form of the column of light, and that we encounter the column in the fifth stage of consciousness, where fate finally yields to destiny. So the template of our own soul journeys is fully found in this brief myth.

And just as the soul's engagement with the pillar of light is not an end, but the marker of a journey begun, the experience of the arc from heaven to earth in Stage Five Consciousness is not an end, but the beginning of the unfoldment of the soul's destiny now consciously guided by the soul within the deepest chamber of the human heart-field. There, the soul joins with the body and engages the covenant that is the condition of the arc's presence.

A covenant is a promise. The arc is a connection between two, making the covenant a mutual promise. When the masculine commits to the feminine, and the feminine to the masculine, there is a promise that allows and creates the arc of connection. From the connection can arise the agreement that is the merger of the mutual promises. The masculine and the feminine commit to each other and promise to hew to each other as the means—the sole means—by which the soul's work can move forward. So the arc is the energetic connection that arises from the intention to connect that gives rise to the agreement to connect. The covenant is the agreement that arises from the mutual intentions evidenced by the mutual promises. That intention is to enter the unknown in the knowing that it is the responsibility of the emerged soul to act out its destiny by bringing its own special gifts to the work of relationship—relationship between soul and body, human and human, human and earth, soul and heaven, and heaven and earth.

All relationship inherently involves the same process, and it is that process that we have come to the planet to learn in order that we may do the dance of creation by which consciousness evolves. The basic skill set that underwrites that journey and the dance is the same regardless of the unique gifts of an individual soul:

- Control attention.
- Bring it to the heart-field.
- Restore attention to the soul whence it came.
- Engage with matter, starting with the body.
- Follow the lead of the heart as it navigates toward that which resonates with the soul's design.

This engagement of soul with matter through the heart is the consummation of the relationship of soul with the body *in* us, and the consummation of the relationship of heaven and earth *through* us. That consummation is the beginning of the dance.

As I write this, and look back at my own life, it is no surprise that I've learned so much from relationships. It is how we learn.

Could it be that what the ayahuasca was saying was all about relationship, and that everything *is* about relationship? Could it be that the ayahuasca is suggesting a shift of focus of the spiritual work on the planet from the search for connection to the reach toward relationship? Is that the essence of a Stage Five consciousness?

CHAPTER SEVEN

FINDING THE HEART OF THE EARTH

In Chapter Seven . . .

Integrating
The Ceremonies Continue
A Conversation with Don Eladio
The Third Ceremony
Finding the Heart of the Earth
Integrating Again
In Present Time: Constants Amidst the Mystery
The Stages ReVisioned, Simply

Integrating

A SURPRISE AWAITED OUR RETURN to the States.

My partner fell ill. It took about a month for her to recover. When she regained her feet, she decided that she had to leave the city for the mountains. Her already considerable sensitivity to the chaotic energies that are an inevitable part of the city environment, she said, had increased as a consequence of her experience with the ayahuasca.

I had work to finish in the city and felt that I couldn't easily leave. This challenged our relatively young relationship. It was apparent that she also sensed another issue in our relationship itself that was making it difficult for her to stay, but she was little able to articulate it. Although I could feel her frustration and my own, I couldn't get my mind around its source. Whatever it was, it needed space from the prior form of relationship to express itself, and it had now become apparent that she herself needed that space. So, despite an incredibly connective journey together in Peru— one which had inspired us to plan a joint return in just a few more months—we instead found ourselves separated and feeling that the relationship might have come to an end despite our mutual preference for the contrary. Our discussion was brief. She left quickly.

The next several months were extremely difficult for both of us. Each of us missed the other deeply, and we both wrestled with disappointment. We met twice, each time experiencing the deep connection that we knew to exist and each time parting in frustration from our inability to translate the connection into a plan for relationship and from the reactivity that arose in our discussions. Within about six weeks after our initial parting, we agreed to end the relationship formally, with ceremony.

The ceremony seemed effective in the moment, aided by our intention to let go of the energetic connection between us. In a short time, however, it was apparent that the ceremony had done nothing to abate the deep sense of connection or the frustration, which continued to dog us both. We communicated briefly from time to time. She proposed another meeting. I declined. I told her that I no longer had the energy to continue to talk. It felt too heavy for me.

Just a few days later, I found myself pacing the floor, completely distracted and unable to work. I didn't relate my state directly to the circumstance with her, although the relationship was on my mind. That night, in bed, I found myself uncharacteristically unable to sleep. In the middle of the night, I felt a blow to my chest. The sensation was so dramatic that my reaction literally bounced me out of bed. I landed upright on both feet, with fists clenched. It was a state of emotional arousal with which I was simply unfamiliar. And I was sure that it had to do with her.

When the sun rose, I called her and asked whether something was happening with her. She told me that she had spent the prior day coming to the difficult decision to end our connection. She, like me, viewed our connection as having an energetic expression that extended from one heart-field to the heart-field of the other. She said that, after a day of reflection, she pulled the connection loose—literally disconnecting it, like pulling an electric plug from the socket. When she told me what she had done, I knew that I had experienced that pulling in all its intensity.

The pain we experienced was sobering for both of us, helping us to appreciate the depth of the connection that had continued despite our ceremonial effort to end it. The experience helped to underline in my mind the distinction between connection and relationship, and how one can occur without the other, as well as how neither connection nor relationship automatically gives rise to the other. Our new sense of the strength of the connection—one that neither of us had experienced in a lifetime of many other relationships—provided an immediate dose of motivation to approach relationship again. We agreed to meet on the following weekend.

Still, I found myself struggling. I wanted to see her again. And I knew that there was something she had identified in my behavior that was making it difficult for her to be in relationship with me despite her inability to articulate it in a way that I could understand. I began to search for any projections that I might have imposed upon her—projections that created the kind of expectations that might make it more difficult for me to simply accept who she is, and might challenge her ability to be who she is in my presence. For three days prior to our weekend meeting, I continued to self-reflect. I found no projections. I believed that I was accepting her as she is, without expectation or demand for something else.

On Saturday morning, I got in my car to drive the two hours to the small community where she lived. As I was driving, my mind continued to whir, searching for what might have triggered her unarticulated sense of an issue in our relationship. Suddenly, I realized that there was no projection on my part, but that there was something else every bit as challenging.

I realized that I was regarding her with the lens of my mind—the mind that separates, analyses, scrutinizes, judges, and categorizes. It doesn't matter that those ordinary mental functions can be done without projection or expectation. It's just that the nature of the lens itself is intrusive. It *feels* violative. And, for both the viewer and the viewed, it feels separating, because it is the nature of the lens to observe by the very mechanism of separation and distancing.

I realized in that moment that I needed to shift lens, and that I needed to bring her within the view of the lens of my heart—the heart that touches, participates, connects, accepts, allows, and knows. It was the way that I had come to connect with her in the first place, before mind recaptured a greater control in the relationship dynamic. I knew that this was not about shifting my feelings, but shifting the way in which I looked, and that different feelings would follow. Emotions are always secondary to how we see. If we see with the heart, the emotions will be far more positive than those emotions that follow a scrutinizing with the mind. What is radical in this understanding is that what we see is not what determines our response to what we see, but *how* we see that determines our response to what we see.

And there is another subtle distinction in this. While the heart sees and senses through the dynamic of a pre-existing connection, what she and I experienced as a particular strong connection is different from the heart's own capacity to connect. While there is an inherent connection that exists with everything, the connection varies in strength. The heart uses the existence of connection in general to sense its way to those places, things, fields, and people where the connection is particularly strong—strong because there is a particular soul resonance with something in particular amidst the infinity of connection. Conversely, the lens of the mind cannot see the connection at all, except in the abstract form of theory. The mind's dangerous substitute for soul resonance is an emotion-fueled projection that is secondary to the fear that we will be unable to discover and experience a sense of connection.

By the time she came into view at our agreed meeting place, I had managed to find my way back to my heart. She sensed the shift instantly, and she responded. We found the feet upon which the relationship could stand and began the process of walking forward, again. It was clearer to me now why she had needed space in our relationship. What had felt suffocating to her was the scrutiny of being held in the lens of my mind. In light of her own reaction to that scrutiny, the only way for her to get space was to create a physical distance. When she experienced my shift of perspective—the being held before the lens of the heart—the felt sense of spaciousness followed, even within a physical space that we shared. Within a couple of months, we were back together and on our way to Peru. It felt as though the ayahuasca had opened a door, and that we had found the way to walk through it. Ayahuasca had brought us more deeply into our hearts, but it was difficult to hold our attention there as we returned to the disconnected environment of the States. Shifting to the heart lens in the context of our familiar home environment—and understanding the necessity of doing that—was the integration. The best way to see the States—and our relationship with it—had been to leave it.

What seems increasingly clear over the course of several ceremonies is that the ayahuasca offers a healing, but that it is up to us to receive it in a meaningful way. Receiving the healing seems always to involve a process of dissembling prior life patterns that do not serve us. The ayahuasca's approach to this dissembling seems to focus first at the physical level, where we have unconsciously held energetic patterns that represent the body's *interpretation* of past experience. These interpretations are often held in the body as defensive postures that seek to prevent the recurrence of earlier trauma. These interpretations have flowed in large part from that *mode of perception* that sees ourselves as separate, isolated, and vulnerable, and concludes that we will not survive without a high degree of control over our circumstances. I have suggested in earlier chapters that this is an inevitable interpretation of our life experience when we view life through the lens of the mind. The body holds these interpretations unconsciously. A shift of perspective that occurs within the mental frame without a shift at the unconscious physical level—like a different understanding of prior life traumas—doesn't seem to release these physical holdings by itself. There must be some opening and release directly at the physical level. Gifted healers facilitate this physical release, and ayahuasca seems to be extraordinarily effective at that level.

When we surrender to the experience of the ayahuasca, we find that the ayahuasca—whatever else it does—brings us to an experience of viewing our lives through our hearts even when we have not intended that. It might do so more quickly when we cooperate by bringing attention to our heart-fields in the presence of the ayahuasca. By sensing the strength of our connection with the plant directly through the heart lens, we open to the strength of the connection—or its absence—directly. This may be the very definition of surrender. I sense that it is in this way that the ayahuasca is capable of a complete discharging of an historically held pattern. This release can occur in the course of one or just a few ayahuasca ceremonies, resulting in a release that is dramatic because of its speed compared to the years that we often spend with traditional psychotherapy. With that dramatic release arises a sense of freedom. That felt sense of freedom comes with a blast of new energy that represents a doorway. This door opens to the immediate opportunity to experience a psychological dissembling—one that results in an understanding that tracks the heart-based perception. Because the heart lens provides a view that we are connected and supported, rather than separate and vulnerable, a new mental understanding that coincides with the body's release of its prior interpretation can bring about the combination of changes that together amount to a "healing." There is ultimately no healing if a release in the body cannot be mirrored in the mind by a release and reformation of the mental patterning that has held the trauma in the body.

It is the same with the plant-facilitated process as with any other growth process that involves the release of an old pattern. Unconscious patterns of somatic holding and thinking are brought to the surface, if only in a flash of vision or insight, and then released in a moment. When that release occurs, what was released must, in turn, be replaced by a new way of seeing the world, how we connect with it, and how we relate to it in order to prevent the old pattern from "reconstellating." Integration of a healing depends upon finding a new perspective. A door is opened, but it is up to us to walk through it by learning to see the world differently.

What I have suggested in this book is that we are able to walk through that door when we bring a heart-centered soul perspective to an experience. The soul perspective, as I have emphasized throughout this book, is not merely a mental construct, but an experience that is grounded in holding our attention within a heart-centered soul. The shift, for most of us, is away from a habitual orientation to thoughts or feelings that are secondary to our viewing the world through the lens of the mind, or from more deeply dissociated out-of-body patterns of holding attention.

My partner and I experienced an almost euphoric feeling of opening with the process of these ayahuasca ceremonies. We had the sense of something having been released. But it took further work, at the mental and emotional levels, to integrate the release. We felt fortunate to have found our way to an integration.

It was now time for the next step, whatever that might be. Shortly after the end of our five-month separation, we headed back to Peru together.

The Ceremonies Continue

Arriving again at the airport in Iquitos, we rode the ten kilometers by motortaxi to the retreat center. Jungle and Sara—the shamans that we had worked with previously—had moved on. Instead, we met Don Eliadio—an ayahuascaro who spoke no English but spoke enthusiastically and at length in Spanish. Our interpreter continued to abbreviate Eladio's longer speeches. We heard from Eladio that he had trained and worked as a shaman in the Amazonion tradition for over thirty years. He was perhaps in his late forties or early fifties, with a youthful energy and an easy self-confidence. Clearly a man no longer of the indigenous jungle culture that had fostered his training, he carried two cell phones. His manner of dress was casual and Western. In ceremony, he assumed a full costume, itself an updated combination of feathered headdress with poncho over white satin pants and shirt. Elements of his costume reflected a connection with the tradition of the Shipibo people, although that was not his own tradition.

That evening, in our first ceremony, my experience was flat, without visions. I had come back to the jungle determined to taste the plant, but not let it control me. My first thought during the ceremony was that I had tried to control too much. Some further reflection led me to conclude that, in fact, my consciousness had been re-acclimated to American culture and the mind-centered habit of consciousness formed there. As a consequence, it was difficult to be present to the plant at all. It would take some work and time to transition back.

The next morning, our group met in circle with Don Eladio, who wanted to hear our experiences and comment upon them. I related with disappointment that I had had almost no experience in the ceremony. Eladio replied that he had watched energy spiraling downward like a whirlwind about my head. "The ayahuasca likes you," he said. "It will move through you like a healer. It is not interested in everyone, but it is interested in you. The healing will come first, then you will get what you want."

I was unsure what to make of this. I sensed that the ayahuasca was teaching me something, and that it was being far gentler with me than with the young men with whom we were doing ceremony. Talking with them, I heard that each of these men seemed to be working with the sense that they had not been adequately loved by their parents. Ceremony seemed to amplify the pain of that perception, suggesting to my mind the degree of resistance each had to letting go of their habitual way of looking at how love is experienced in our lives. I had worked with that issue years before.

Feeling dropped on our heads by our parents seems to be the common perception of a mental, postmodern generation. I had finally let my own parents entirely out of the calculus of my feelings of my own loneliness, and the ayahuasca had helped me years earlier to discover my own heart and a sense of direct connection with the cosmos. The issue was simply no longer present in my body as it was for these young men.

Now, returning to the ayahuasca, I still found myself purging in a rigorous fashion, but it was no longer intimidating or frightening. I had come to accept that as a stage in the ayahuasca's gift of healing other and deeper issues, and in opening to the information that the ayahuasca field held for me. I was more intent upon keeping the ayahuasca in my body long enough to allow the visions to follow. It all felt like hard work, but I wasn't having to struggle like these younger men. I would have found a head cold more unpleasant, if less rigorous in the moment. In contrast, my younger companions were having no visions, or horrific visions, and were unable to purge, or were purging for periods that exhausted the body. Don Eladio's remark that I would get what I wanted helped me to focus on what I did want. I realized that I was unsure what I wanted from the ayahuasca. I didn't have any desire to become an ayahuascero. I wanted more information, but I had no particular plan for how to use it. All I knew was that my heart had drawn me here and was holding me here for something yet to come. Eladio's remarks helped affirm in me the strength of the connection I was feeling with the ayahuasca.

During this discussion with Don Eladio, we learned that he had been with the retreat center only for a couple of months. Eladio and the center had agreed on a trial relationship of three months before deciding on a longer relationship. It was in that getting-acquainted context that we listened as Eladio observed that he thought it was a mistake for the center to offer ayahuasca as the initial ceremony to a group such as ours. Eladio said that while ayahuasca does a deep cleansing of the body as part of its healing process, it cannot reach everything that needs to be cleared. Instead, he said, we should be starting with a tobacco cleanse. While ayahuasca is the mother of the plants, Eladio said, tobacco is the father.

After some discussion with the owners of the center, Eladio announced that he would be offering a tobacco cleanse the next day. He assured us that we would all be having "better" ceremonies after that. I listened to that discussion with some trepidation. I sensed that everyone else in the maloka was also feeling apprehension about ingesting tobacco juice, not to mention following it on the same day with the next ayahuasca ceremony. Jungle tobacco is reputed to have much more nicotine—I heard nineteen times as much—than our more tame North American variety. The mere thought of putting this in my body and following it with ayahuasca was making my gut tighten.

We gathered the next afternoon to drink the tobacco juice. This was not done in a ceremonial fashion, but in an informal and perfunctory manner. Don Eladio poured the tobacco juice into a cup for each of us, to which he added Nescafe and sugar. The mixture had about the same gag index for me as the ayahuasca. He asked us to keep it down for as long as possible, which turned out to be about forty-five minutes for me, although most of my companions were purging rather quickly. Later, I discovered that my forty-minutes was much longer than necessary. Both just before and after the purge, I had an extraordinary episode of sweating, perhaps more than I've ever otherwise experienced. By the time that the vomiting did occur, the tobacco was well into my body. The purge was easy, much less rigorous, I thought, than I was used to with the ayahuasca. Don Eladio offered Boldo tea to those who had purged immediately. For some reason, I assumed I didn't need it since I was holding the tobacco down for a longer period of time. Later, I realized that my failing to drink the tea prevented me from washing out more of the tobacco. I wound up not drinking anything until later in the day—my error—and found myself feeling sick and having to lie down. When I did think to drink water, I purged again and immediately felt better, but not well enough to get back on my feet until hours after the ayahuasca ceremony started. Nor could most of my companions, and the ayahuasca ceremony was attended by only two of our group.

I experienced anger around missing the ceremony. I felt like the second ceremony was lost, like the first. Reflecting on the anger, I could see that I had brought high expectations to the jungle. Going back and forth from anger to reflection, along with the stimulation of the tobacco, kept me awake for most of the night. What came up for me was the fear that I wouldn't be able to "cross the bridge." For years, my most frustrating recurring dream is that I have shown up too late for class and that it is over. In the dream, as in my life, there are so many distractions. Don Eladio later said that he saw himself as a bridge. In the morning, I asked for a meeting with Don Eladio.

That morning, my partner related that she had had an incredible journey in ceremony with Don Eladio. In her vision, she said, she saw a pair of mechanical rotating wheels. She asked them to heal her. Upon her request, the wheels turned 90 degrees and came into her chest to work on her. She said that she felt that this engagement was at the level of the plant—which she called the "DMTs"—rather than what laid beyond the plant. As this process came to completion, she said that she was allowed to see into the "matrix." There, she sensed that the ayahuasca field—what lies beyond the plant itself—is the intelligence moving through other fields. These other fields seemed to respond to the instruction of the ayahuasca field. There was conversation, she said, with the ayahuasca field in which she was given access to the field itself, and a form of protection. At the outset of the communication with the field, she indicated that the field communicated in a high-pitched, digital form that she was unable to understand. She asked for the field to communicate in a manner that she could understand, and the communication that followed took a telepathic form that formed into familiar words. As she told me this story, she told me that it was her sense that the digital communication was a "star language."

My partner's reference to a star language reminded me of prior experience with a shamana who, in a huachuma ceremony about six years prior in Cusco, spoke a lyrical and beautiful language that struck me as a language that did not come from the earth. I could not understand a single word of it, yet I found myself translating the gist of the shamana's speech into English, as though the meaning were quite clear to me. I recall that the speech and the translation went on for fifteen or twenty minutes. I had a similar experience with the same shamana a few weeks after that first ceremony.

When my partner and I shared our experiences with each other, she commented that she was told that she is seeing the back of the clock, while I am seeing the face of the clock. I wondered whether she is seeing the fields unmasked, in more digital forms, while I see in forms that seem archetypal—such as serpents—which one is tempted to assume are masked fields. What I gathered from my own communications with the ayahuasca field is that it works in the frame of a reality that our ordinary brain-dominated lens of perception cannot apprehend. When we approach that reality with less than a heart-surrendered lens, what we see may reflect our own fears and expectations, but only in some respects and at some levels. What we see also reflects, perhaps to a greater degree, the nature of who we are and what the field chooses to show us, perhaps on the basis of what is relevant to our own respective soul work.

My sense is that my own soul nature works more closely with the density of matter, nearer to the level of manifestation than is the case with my partner's nature. It appears to me that her clairvoyant nature takes her to the more subtle, higher-frequency fields—those that might be said to be closer to the level of design information. In a manner of speaking she works more with the heaven fields, while my work seems to be more connected to the earth fields. I'm more involved with the hardware and process of intelligence, and she is more involved with the software and content of intelligence. I work on the wiring. She works on what flows on that wiring. In order for her to work at that level, she seems to need to be less grounded, while my work requires that I be more grounded.

My partner said that she clearly experienced an engagement between the plant and her body at the level of DNA and the cells. In my own ayahuasca ceremonies of eleven years before, I had a similar experience of watching forms work with my body, with the same sense that my DNA was being tweaked. I asked what "they" were doing, and was essentially told *"Be quiet, we are working on you."* My sense is that these examples represent fields that are entirely independent of the body transforming the body so that it can accommodate the presence of the soul and the kind of information the soul needs to help it invite the body into a collaborative relationship with the soul. That collaboration is dependent upon the body's ability to receive higher and more subtle frequencies and the information encoded on those frequencies, which is the same as saying that the body needs to be tuned in order to receive the soul into the body. The soul itself represents the presence of a higher vibration of consciousness within the frame of the lower vibration of consciousness that is the density of matter. This resonate entrainment of higher by lower is the stage for an evolution of consciousness that reveals itself in a constant process of manifestation and creation—a process in which we participate despite the inability of our minds to comprehend its scope or purpose and because of the ability of our hearts to simply know that doing so is the work we are here to do.

A Conversation with Don Eladio

Later that evening, Don Eladio accepted my request for a conversation. He asked how he could help us. We told Don Eladio that we wanted to focus on healing what needed to be healed in ourselves so that we can open to the information that would guide our next steps in our own work. Don Eladio invited both of us to study with him. The conversation was short and to the point. We both had a clear connection with the ayahuasca, he said. The implication of Don Eladio's encouragement to study with him was that we needed to develop a deeper and more skilled relationship with the plant. We talked about our own sense that the postmodern spiritual tourist needs more than the typical tourist ayahuasca experience—that, while these relatively brief encounters have value, participants would benefit from more preparation and a better sense of the need for integration of the experience. I talked about the utility of a soul perspective and the need for attention skills training. We talked about extending the indigenous shamanic model beyond the village setting to a more global perspective, one that could extend beyond "healing" and training the occasional ayahuascero to one that would help non-shamans learn how to communicate directly—without a human intermediary—with those fields that provide the information directly relevant to their own soul journeys.

The conversation was limited by language and time. I had several questions that remained for another time. Was Don Eladio suggesting or assuming that my partner and I—two white people from the belly of the North American beast—should move to the jungle and become ayahuascaros? Don Eladio had said, in one of the morning circles, that ayahuasca is all about healing. But that is clearly not the case. It is apparent that the healing process provides the platform for a information-transfer process to follow—information that is more about soul work than the healing that is the necessary predicate for that work. Traditionally, the purpose of studying with an ayahuascaro was to become an ayahuascaro. I suspect that Don Eladio does not assume that to be the purpose of our deepening relationship with the plant. Eladio also said that he wants to learn from people like us. Because the traditional shaman might easily assume that there is nothing to be learned from the outsider, Eladio's desire to learn suggests an element of the transition that is occurring within the frame of the shamanic encounter between its practitioners and outsiders who come to experience it.

I see Eladio as a "transitional" shaman—one no longer of the narrow indigenous tradition but not yet beyond it, one who can see that the geographical context of the shamanic experience is rapidly changing. Outsiders are coming for the experience and leaving to interpret that experience in another culture. Don Eladio said in the circle that ayahuasca can save the world. That is itself a larger vision than would have likely occurred in a village where the world was infinitely smaller than the encroaching world by which Eladio's vision is being stretched. In our conversations, and the many that are occurring between the spiritual tourists and shamans in many places, the vision is taking form.

During these days that passed between ceremonies, I took time to read the recent book by Sandra Ingerman and Hank Wesselman, *Awakening to the Spirit World: The Path of Direct Revelation*. Their central thesis is that shamanism can be studied for an important purpose other than becoming a shaman. Shamanic techniques allow us, they argue, to access information from the other worlds of shamanic cosmology—the fields—without relying on the limited numbers of traditional intermediaries. That access provides what they call *direct revelation*. We can access that information ourselves, for our own use—for informing our own process of emerging from our own fate into our own destiny. Empowerment always involves transcending the intermediary—whether it be a parent, priest, or shaman. Certainly, the notion of direct revelation transcends traditional shamanic practices in which it is only the village shaman who connects with the fields of information that await just beyond this dimension. Plant medicine processes were acknowledged but not addressed in this work by Ingerman and Wesselman, who are speaking primarily to a Western audience for whom plant medicine use is illegal. Their work is a wonderful compendium of processes that foster direct revelation without plant medicines, and I have experienced the power of that work with Sandra Ingerman, with other teachers, and—in confirmation of the Ingerman/Wesselman message—on my own.

As I considered Ingerman and Wesselman's work, I realized that our own discussion with Don Eladio was proposing to push his traditional work toward the support of direct revelation, with the soul emphasis that drives my own work, and beyond the focus on healing that I regard as a preliminary, but not final, step. Taking that next step requires more than intention on the part of the individual. It requires the cultivation of the skills of attention. By the same token, the means addressed by Ingerman and Wesselman, whether or not those means are amplified or accelerated by the cultivation of a relationship with the plant medicines, require skills of attention. The pathway of direct revelation requires attention skills that allow us to control where our attention is placed, including a shift from our dissociated states, and from our conventional minds and emotions, to the heart-centered soul. Attention skills are the necessary predicate to achieving the presence and surrender that are the predicates of receiving direct revelation. And attention skills are absolutely necessary for the intense work of integration.

That integration requires the work of learning not only how to bring attention to the lens of the heart, but how to direct the lens of the heart as a tool of navigation for the soul. For postmodern people who are no longer connected to the earth, that integration process now requires that we learn how to direct our heart attention not only to our own souls, but to the body and to the body's body—the earth itself. None of this work of attending the soul is ultimately meaningful without the would-be student developing a sustainable relationship with the earth. As people return from their transformative encounters with these transitional indigenous traditions, there is a need to integrate not only within, but without. Not only do we need to transform our personalities in the direction of soul qualities, we need to transform our relationship with the earth upon which we live. The destiny of this work is not found in the creation of "urban shamans," a phrase I have heard many times as my American colleagues attempt to find a way to use their study of shaman techniques. It is found in a larger expression yet, one that has not yet fully revealed itself to this movement in the human psyche.

The Third Ceremony

I spent much of the next day following our conversation with Don Eladio preparing for the third ceremony by holding my attention inward. My intention was to ask for help in moving my own attention more deeply into my heart.

I went to the maloka about an hour before the scheduled beginning of the cer-emony in order to focus on that intention, in hopes of holding tightly to it as my body met the force of the plant's arrival. It felt a little paradoxical to hold tightly to an intention to surrender, but that was the best I could muster. I felt less apprehension and more confidence as my turn came to walk across the maloka to take the cup of ayahuasca from Don Eladio's hand. On this evening, it tasted almost sweet, although there was still a little gag reflex as I drank it. It settled well, but I purged within just a few minutes, perhaps ten or so. I became concerned that I had purged too quickly and might not make the connection with the ayahuasca field. To my relief, it was not long before I felt the plant moving within me. The beginning was very soft. A distinct sensuality spread through my body. I remembered that the plant seems quite capable of titrating itself. The dose necessary on one evening may be quite less than is appro-priate for another. So much seems to depend on one's own readiness, and the degree to which the body has already taken in the plant on prior occasions.

The vision characteristic—for me—of the plant itself came quickly, with my attention standing at a slight observational distance as I again held the idea of tasting but not letting it control me. The visions were against the background of the same kind of dark that one experiences in a dance club, though with an internal luminos-ity. As many times before, I saw three-dimensional patterns that were mesmerizingly fluid. These were larger than many before, like luminous rooms divided only by these lucent and translucent shapes. On this occasion, I felt that my perspective of these forms was from a greater distance than many earlier experiences in which I was viewing them close up. During this time in particular, I was on my hands and knees, head hanging down and off the mat, as I stayed close to the purging bowl. In the rigor of the experience, my purging missed the bowl once. At one point, I lost strength in my hands and arms. I heard my head hit the floor like a coconut, but felt the blow as though from a little distance created by some numbness occasioned by the medicine. I felt very much in the sway of the medicine, but the voice of the ayahuasca field was as much there as the plant itself, keeping me present to her.

After a time I can't estimate—perhaps an hour or so—the vision shifted. Now I saw life-like serpents completely covering other shapes, such as the roots at the base of a tree. The feeling of the vision was still dreamlike, but not internally luminous as the earlier part. All of these serpents were colored a rich dark brown, with intricate detailing, much like the rattles that are sold throughout Peru. I never experienced any fear in response to the vision of snakes, and they seem to be present in one form or another whenever a vision occurs. There is only a kind of awe that arises in response to the magical beauty of their presence and movement. I felt entranced, which is the experience that occurs at the edge of dropping completely into the con-trol of the plant. By holding on tightly to my own attention and the sense of self that comes with that, I was able to stay on the edge and not go over.

Shortly after the beginning of the first of these visions, one of the other partici-pants in the ceremony began to scream loudly. Her voice dominated the room for at least a couple of hours. I initially found myself distracted. As I tried to re-gather my attention, I found myself also assessing the situation in the room. Two of the center's facilitators were quickly in attendance, trying to calm the woman and asking her to be considerate of the other participants. She was clearly not in control of herself to a sufficient degree to comply. As my attention was drawn to her, I sensed that she was experiencing an entity possession. As I focused on that sense, a form came into my own vision—something reptilian, angry, afraid. I found myself assessing whether I was at risk. I found no resonance in myself with the entity and concluded that I was not at risk. For a while, I let myself be attentive to her experience with curiosity and compassion, which was mixed with some irritation that she was interrupting my own experience. I noticed that Don Eladio was continuing to do his work in the ceremony with little apparent attention to the woman as he continued to work from the altar and periodically circle the maloka in his usual pattern. I returned to my own vision, happy to find that it was still there. At some point, the woman left the maloka.

I went in and out of my own vision, staying with it, but in an observational mode even as I invited it in for the healing. Apart from the beautiful visions and the purging, I couldn't say that I had an experience that I could directly identify as healing. Nevertheless, at the end of the evening, there was a distinct feeling of strength and confidence. When I spoke to my partner of the young woman, she said that she had also seen an entity and described it in terms that were similar to what I had seen. It seemed to be ancient, distinctly dragon-like with serpentine appendages coming out of the back of its head. And the vocalization it had stimulated in the young woman indicated that it had no interest in leaving.

In circle with Don Eladio the next morning, he made a point of addressing the circumstance with the young woman first. He knew that it had triggered fear among many of us. This is common, he said, "not a big deal." I had the impression that he was aware of an entity but felt that this ceremony was neither the time nor place to deal with it, nor that it was time critical. It felt to me that she had carried it for a significant time. As for my own connection with the plant, Eladio said I needed "more spiritual strength," which he would address with me in the next ceremony. He said that I needed to recognize that this is a long process—speaking again to what he saw as my impatience. And I was relieved to reconnect with the plant after the flatness of my first ceremony and having missed the second.

Finding the Heart of the Earth

Our last ceremony in this series came on the following night. Before the ceremony, a strong memory arose for me. About three or fours years earlier, I had been in ceremony led by Sandra Ingerman. The centerpiece of the ceremony was an individual journey to discover our life's work. This was, of course, not a plant-facilitated journey. Sandra Ingerman is one of the best known American teachers of shamanic journeying. Her usual tool is the drum. In this instance, the setting of the journey was our ordinary classroom transformed by the creation of a ceremony that involved a ritualized entry into the room in which our journey would take place. Each participant was cleansed with the smoke of burning sage, drummed over, and introduced to the room with the ringing of Tibetan prayer bells. The room was darkened, and we took our place there in metal chairs. The moment that I sat to start my journey, an answer came. Words came to mind as clearly as a voice speaking in my ear: *Find the heart of the earth.*

I was surprised. I had never heard the phrase, so far as I could recall. I associated no particular meaning with it. It was interesting information, I thought, and I filed it away. Now, years later, as the impending ayahuasca ceremony loomed in my gut, the memory of the journey with Sandra Ingerman emerged. I had not thought of it for more than a year. Now, I gave a little thought to what *heart of the earth* might mean, but the mind's attempt to conceive how the heart of the earth might be structured got lost in notions of earth soul and EM fields. If dots were about to connect for me, it was not apparent how. I knew it would not help to move into this experience with my mind. It would be critical to let the experience unfold in the space of my own heart.

So I re-set my intention to be open and surrender to whatever healing and information the ayahuasca might bring. As a footnote, I asked that, if the notion of the heart of the earth was meaningful, I would like to hear about that.

Don Eladio gave me a full dose, about three quarters of his cup. It went down as sweetly as ayahuasca ever does—which is not very. The medicine seemed to settle in a better way, and I didn't purge so quickly. Before very long, I began to feel the characteristic warming that announces the uptake of the medicine in the body—one that starts for me in the belly and moves up to the head, followed shortly with some flashing points of light that immediately precede the emergence of visions. It was only some time later that I did the first and primary purge. By that time, it felt as that the ayahuasca had established itself firmly in my body. Purging came and went throughout the first few hours of the ceremony, perhaps five or more times, with final pushes that consisted solely of phlegm—and perhaps energetic releases that could not be so easily observed.

The medicine was strong enough that I felt the need to lie down early on. As I lay there, my right foot moved in rhythm with Don Eladio's icaros and rattling, while my left foot remained still. My right leg soon joined in with the foot, with my knee moving up and down in rhythm while my hip was literally lifted off the mat. I began to have the sense that the ayahuasca was working on my body, with a focus on the right side, during which time I was also seeing a luminescent vision very similar to that of the prior ceremony. The foot and leg movement continued for a couple of hours.

At some point, it seemed that the ayahuasca's rhythmic work had reached a threshold that would allow the right and left to be joined. I felt a spreading of energy from right to left across my lower abdomen, and both sides then began to move in response to Eladio's rhythms. The movement was, for me, involuntary. I could stop it, but only with effort. As soon as I relaxed and surrendered, the movement was back. As this occurred, my observant mind gave some thought to the notion that the right side represented the masculine nature in my body. I also was aware that the primary physical complaint in my body came from my right hip—which a physician had warned me years before would require replacement. As my leg engaged in this dance, I made that connection and asked specifically for my hip to be healed. If the ayahuasca can heal cancer, I thought, why not a mere hip?

As the vibrating continued, I had the sense that the soul of the hip was being restored, and that the work was coming up through the earth. My mind worked a bit with that thought. If souls were a drop of heaven, and soul retrievals touched into the other dimensional fields to reboot the soul's operating system (my thinking went), then it made sense that the operating system of the body—a drop of earth—would get rebooted from the earth itself. I remembered that Sandra Ingerman, in her presentations on soul retrievals, talked about retrieving the soul of an injured body part, without specifying where the "soul" of a part might hide out. I found myself making a new sense of the distinction between body and soul. Perhaps the design of the body is a field that comes from the fields that we call "earth," in the same way that the field of the soul originates in the fields we call "heaven."

The initial vision subsided around the same time that the vibratory work on my body ceased. It was replaced by a vision dominated by the same earth-colored snakes of the prior vision. Again, the preceding vision was lit internally, made of lights forming into shapes. In contrast, the view of the snakes was dimly lit from the outside of the scene, with just enough light to let me see the detailed patterning seemingly drawn onto the background of the earth-colored skin. As before, these snakes were very realistic and in full movement. They covered whatever they were moving on, intertwining in such a way that they left no space to view the terrain on which they moved. My point of view seemed to be just a few feet away. I was a little more sober at this point, no longer preoccupied by the rigor of the body vibrations. The intricate detail in which the snakes were adorned struck me as incredibly beautiful. I again felt myself in a state of awe, with no hint of a fear reaction. *Awe* is the way in which I had for some years come to describe the state of attention that is completely heart-centered. I was there in that moment.

Within moments, my thoughts began to turn to the notion of the heart of the earth.

The question arose in my mind of what to do with that notion. The answer appeared immediately. What became clear was that my relationship with my partner, and the experience of opening my heart and seeing her with my heart instead of my head, was the template for moving forward *into* the heart of the earth. I opened my heart and began to sink down into the earth. The presence of the snakes seemed now to accompany the movement down, as though they were conducting me in a downward flow. I quickly found myself moving away from my mat in order to lie on the wood floor of the maloka—chest down, cheek to the floor, arms spread out, heart pressed to the earth. I felt into the earth, sensing her presence, seeing her beauty. There I found her heart, already open and huge, as though it had been there all along, simply waiting for me to open my heart. How simple!

What I couldn't do with the earth, any more than I could with my partner, was to connect with my head. The head doesn't connect. Only the heart can participate with the subject of the soul's resonance—what we might otherwise call the *heart's desire*. That simple shift let me connect. I began then to feel the earth's beauty without analyzing it, and without trying to understand or judge it. I spent perhaps an hour or so feeling into this connection, in sensuous connection with the wooden floor, my hands often drumming out a spontaneous rhythm that resonated in my body.

During this time, the awareness of the serpents came and went. Unlike the former ceremony, these serpents had now become very large, like the length of my body. I continued to see them outside of me, as it were, covering everything and entwined with each other even as they coiled and moved. I began to sense that their earth color was itself significant, that it was the vibration of the earth in visible form. I remembered in that moment a seemingly innocuous event from earlier in the week. Three Shipibo women had come to the retreat center to sell their goods. Among the textiles created by the Shipibo are skirts that, unworn, are simply rectangular cloths with an embroidered or painted design. My partner had been attracted to a few that had a particularly bright pattern sewn with artificially colored yarns that struck me as distastefully neon in quality. My taste was drawn to another group of Shipibo skirts that were on a background of earth tones and sewn in more subtle and natural colors that left an overall impression of what I was now experiencing as *earth*.

Now, in the vision, I could see that the background color of the snakes upon which patterns were inscribed was the color of a rich dark mud. The intense detail of the patterning reflected a particularly dense form of scratch art that is found on small gourds in Peru, with much more detail than the jungle rattles. I began to realize that the mud color itself was forming the substance of the vibration that was washing through my own energy field. Just as the chakras have characteristic colors—red, orange, yellow, green and so on—that represent the quality of the energies of the respective chakras, I sensed that the earth field emits a vibration that appears to our subtle sense as a rich, deep, dark brown. I had been attracted to it in the textiles, and now I found myself being bathed in it. No wonder I had the attraction earlier. The earth had been calling to me while I thought I was simply shopping.

The serpents began to move visibly into my body. My mind observed quietly as I simply welcomed their presence. They seemed at once to be the form of the earth's healing energy and the form of the energy by which the earth connects, communicates, and creates form. What came to mind is that the earth contains a basic design for form itself, even if that form is directed in its infinite forms of expression by the design programs of heaven. It is as though earth provides a basic operating system for the hardware that we know as *body*, and that heaven provides software that we call *soul*—software that defines soul fate and, at some juncture that we might call Soul 5.0, provides a sophisticated level of software that makes the soul's destiny express. Again, I had the deep sense that the body is of the earth—a drop of the earth, like the soul is a drop of heaven. And, just as the soul can soar in the heaven realms, I found my soul soaring in the earth realms, via the body.

As I write these words, I am reminded of one of the most challenging aspects of this intensely informational experience. The challenge is to remain in the direct awareness of the experience without retreating to a mental place of interpretation. Going quickly to interpretation interferes with the experience itself. The experience unfolds in its own time, and we must let that unfolding occur. Only by witnessing the fullness of the experience can we hope for reaching a point of direct revelation of information in a form that the mind can apprehend. This is the balancing act that I found myself in that moment in the ceremony. What is my own voice, I would have to wonder, and what is the voice that speaks in my own mind but is coming from outside of it. And, in this context, where is the threshold between outer and inner?

What next emerged into my mind was the notion that heaven can only connect to earth in some particularly critical way that *depends upon* a soul that has consciously reclaimed its own life force, energy, power, and attention—various aspects of soul consciousness. Heaven depends upon the soul to discover the fundamental necessity of using the lens of the heart as the primary mode of the soul's navigation upon the planet, including navigation within the body. Heaven then depends upon the soul's use of the heart to cultivate a relationship between body and soul that gives "legs"—power—to the agenda of soul and heaven. Heaven depends even further upon the soul to direct the angle of the heart lens toward the earth. Heaven can connect with earth, it seemed to me, only through an energetic circuit that is the very purpose of the soul/body connection. Could I be making that up? I just couldn't conceive that these were my own thoughts.

As my mind did begin to process that information, I sensed that this sequential unfolding of the heaven energy through the soul felt purposeful, even if that sequential process may remain shrouded in mystery. In connecting soul to the body and then to earth, the soul's agenda is opened to receive the full resources that reside in the earth—its plants, stones, mountains, waters, and so on. As I lay on the floor, it became apparent to me that all of the earth lies in wait to serve the body and soul and more, if we can only learn to connect with our hearts instead of with our minds. It was in these very realms that my soul vision was swimming in the vast heart of the earth.

There were times during the ceremony that I sensed the presence of beings behind me. Each of those times, I was on my hands and knees. Each of those times, I would rise up to my knees and feel around for a human, and found none. I can't say what the presence was, but it felt obvious that something was present, and that it was present in a supportive way.

Throughout the ceremony, Eladio's rattling and periodic drumming seemed to be right next to me. As I would look up to see where he was, I would typically find him to be somewhere else in the room. Whenever he was actually in front of me, I would work to turn my attention to his presence. As the ceremony progressed, I found myself more and more able to rise up to receive his particular ministrations. It was at one of those times that I saw a luminescence in his face, appearing at first as a mask, then, to my mind, as his *cara verdadero*—his true face. Late in the ceremony, as I was able to meet him there with my own true face, I burst into a laughing, joyful state.

Of all of the ceremonies in this sequence, this one was the longest and most intense. I worked myself to my feet late in the ceremony to find my feet and balance. When I could gain my feet, I sensed the ayahausca urging me to go outside to engage with her in a more physical way. I did go outside, and felt the need to urinate, which I did at the root of a palm tree. Then I put my hands on the tree and sensed a palpable force of incredible strength that made me laugh out loud with surprise that I was able to feel it so strongly. The energy seemed to go down toward the roots, rather than upward as I expected it to.

Then I walked a few steps to the place where the ayahuasca vine grew near the maloka. Wrapping my fingers around the vine, I felt the energy pulling upward. Two nights before, I had grasped the same vine and felt energy that remained within the vine like electricity in a cable. Now it began to pour into my hands and arms, lighting up my forearms to the elbow. Quickly, I felt the vine pulling me back into the vision. I didn't feel steady on my legs, so I let it go and returned to the maloka. The vision stopped as I released the vine. I wondered if I had closed a door.

Back in the maloka, I began to play with the energy, holding my hands with the palms facing each other, about eighteen inches apart. I immediately saw the mahogany serpents emerge from each hand, meet in the middle, then intertwine upward and downward into the form of a cross that I have earlier associated as the intersecting of the covenants of the arc.

Integrating Again

Reflecting upon this series of ceremonies and the interaction with Don Eladio, it felt to me that the ceremonies represented a meaningful progression of the ceremonies that went before. As Eladio had said several times, the spiritual journey with the ayahuasca is a process. As he spoke about that, he would use his hand to indicate a movement up steps. With the ceremonies of both the early part of the last decade and those occurring now in 2011, I felt that I was moving up in a step-like manner, each next step dependent upon my having managed the step before.

Not every ceremony moved me up a step, but it did mirror whether I was ready to take the next step. In terms of healing, the effect on my hip was easy to see. Upon my return to the States, I found that I could lie on my right hip for hours while sleeping. Prior to the ceremony, I couldn't lie on the hip without inducing a level of pain that would roll me over in about five minutes. A therapist who worked on my long-standing scoliosis before this trip to the jungle told me when I returned that my body and face were far more balanced and aligned than before the trip. Otherwise, without knowing precisely what needed to be released, it seemed possible to evaluate the healing that may have occurred before only by watching to see what emerged anew following the encounters with the ayahausca. Those encounters that occurred early in the decade brought me to a place of confidence relative to my place in the cosmos. I came to feel connected within myself in a way that had previously eluded me.

Now, in 2011, the most significant pieces for me seem to be the information that followed. One piece of information is that when I saw the serpents, I felt a comfortable and curious connection, one that allowed me to take them in and interact with them in an easy way. Another piece of information is that the ayahuasca has the ability to work with a resistant physical issue, in this case my hip. Another piece of information is that the ayahuasca has continued to give me information about the nature of our journey as souls on the planet—how connection exists, and how an awareness of connection and its modalities precedes the skillful engagement of relationship. Not least, this encounter with the ayahuasca opened the door to an experience of the heart of the earth, something significant in its own right, and also significant as a next piece of information in the now apparent quest to understand the energy structure of the soul and how it fits into the relationship between heaven and earth. I could see that my mind was now forming questions to fit the answers that were coming ahead of my ability to ask bigger questions.

Upon our return to the States, another vision appeared that seemed to clarify what the experience of encountering the heart of the earth might mean. Again, my relationship with my partner became a vehicle for the integration of the changes that were initiated in ceremony. At one point, I found my chest aching in response to an exchange between us that came to anger, divulging the fear that lay beneath. We again found ourselves dealing with an issue unskillfully, allowing reactivity to govern our communication. As I turned my attention to myself and began working with the pain in my chest, I laid down and began to breathe into my heart. I selected some stones from my altar to use to calm my heart. Then I journeyed for information. What appeared in my internal vision were three concentric rings of fire. I saw my body lying within the inner circle, which was just slightly larger than the length of my body. My perspective on this scene was outside of the body, which I was watching. I could see that my heart was penetrated by a long and thick wood-like stake—too large for a spear, but otherwise unrecognizable to me as an object that one might imagine being thrust through a body. Then, I saw a figure walk through the circles of fire and remove the stake. I could feel the pain begin to resolve. I could see a large number of spirit helpers surrounding the outer fire circle, but sensed that they could not reach me directly. Although I felt that I could access these helpers on my own, I wanted to involve my partner in this process. I knew that she also knew how to access this healing support. So I asked her to assist me in "healing" the heart into an optimal state by using her own connections, and asked that she act as a bridge to these spirit helpers. She did. As she and I worked with my condition, I saw the fires increase in intensity, until my body was entirely surrounded by a sphere of flame. I could see that the three concentric circles had become concentric spheres, with my body held—not engulfed—in the inner of these. Our discussion took on a much softer tone after this.

Later, I sat in meditation with this vision and asked questions. What I found was that the three circles evolving into spheres might represent ignitions—ignitions that marked the commencement or bonding of relationships. The inner sphere was the ignition of the connection between soul and body. The second was the ignition between heaven and earth that occurs within the frame of the ignited soul and body relationship. And the third was the ignition between my heart/soul/body complex and the heart of the earth, empowered with the force of heaven. What seems ignited in each case is a standing energy field that consists of the resonate connection between the polarities that form the basis for each of the ignitions: soul/body; heaven/earth; soul-body-heaven-earth.

The *heart of the earth* is not a concept and cannot be captured by one. I mean by the use of those words to indicate a *field* that can be experienced, I suspect, only when the light of heaven becomes focused upon the earth heart through a single soul that has become consciously embodied in the body's heart-field. This ignition of the soul connection with body allows heaven to reach through the soul/body all the way to earth, giving rise to the next ignition, which forms the basis for the creation of sustainable community of humans with the earth—not *on* the earth, but *with* the earth in a skillful and purposeful collaboration. Within this relationship, the earth can support and inform the human imagination in such a way that humans can use the earth elements to forward manifestation in an open-ended process of creativity and play—and perhaps something even more mysterious for which creative play is simply a means.

In the simplicity of the big picture view, one can imagine that the soul comes from heaven like an astronaut who has slept through a journey of many light years and awakens as a stranger in the place of her destination. Leaving the ship that has carried her to this place, the soul astronaut is left with only a space suit. The soul must learn how to navigate by means of this cumbersome suit with all of its awkward parts. Shaking off its long sleep, the soul remembers that it came from another world, establishes communication with its home base, and begins to establish an outpost on this unexplored planet. Finally, a way of connecting with the new planet is discovered. The soul finds a receptive connection, a home away from home, a home that seems seeded with the very necessities that make home possible. The soul astronaut finds that by some prearrangement, all has been provided for its stay. All that is left for the soul astronaut to do is to explore more deeply, supported by earth's nurture—a nurture that deepens as relationship with the planet deepens.

In this big picture view, one can begin to re-examine the traditional notion of the earth as *Mother*. Our old relationship is one of unconscious child, living in the largess of a mother that requires little in exchange for the gift of the child's well being. In earlier times, only a few—the shamans—needed to have the big picture in order to guide the small groups that lived upon the earth. Now great numbers live unsustainably upon the earth, like a hoard of rebellious teens filled with a sense of privilege, taking the earth for granted like beneficiaries of the trust fund they did not accumulate. To survive, a transition is necessary, one in which we not only recognize our responsibility for the husbandry of the earth, but one in which that responsibility is assumed in the form of a skilled relationship. That relationship cannot be commenced until connection is first discovered, honored, and chosen.

The heart can know that our soul is connected to everything by the nature of things. However, we cannot experience the full relationship that is the potential of that connection without making three choices. First, we have to choose to hold our attention within the soul, and that soul within the knowing heart. Second, we have to choose to direct that attention to the connection with the heart of the earth. Third, we have to choose to stand on that connection and develop relationship with intention. Connection exists as our birthright, but it serves nothing until we use it as a foundation for relationship. Relationship, in turn, exists as our continuing opportunity, but it serves nothing until we awaken to our own soul purpose and cultivate relationship with all the skills of consciousness available to us. There is a sequence in our cultivation of relationship. The process of developing relationship begins in the heart, bringing soul into relationship with the heart and heaven; bringing body into relationship with the soul; bringing soul and body into relationship with the heart of the earth; and, finally, bringing soul into relationship with its own destiny. All other relationships happen on that pathway.

CONCLUSION

Before leaving Peru, we shared ceremony with a well-known huachuma shamana in Cusco. This was an opportunity for us to have another experimental encounter with this plant—experimental in the sense of an attempt to find a shaman who has a sufficient relationship with the plant, and in the sense of an attempt to discover whether we could find our own relationship with the plant. Again, my experience was not gentle, although the huachuma is often introduced as a gentle experience. I had another very highly charged day in which I spent most of my time simply managing the energy that was pushing through my body. However, toward the end of the day, while I was still feeling the effect of this medicine in my body, my part- ner and I accepted an offer to be shown the Temple of the Moon adjacent to the place of our ceremony.

The Temple of the Moon is not a site managed for tourism, and there were no tourists in sight as we approached the area of the Temple. The Temple sits within a rather small outcropping of stone atop a ridge above the city of Cusco and near a group of housing compounds. The outcrop is an oblong mound of deeply fissured stone that sits perhaps ten meters above ground level, and perhaps a hundred meters in length and less than fifty meters in width. As we approached it, we were greeted by three workers who were excavating a small site on its perimeter. We walked up one side of the stone mound on natural ledges that served as high steps until we approached the entrance to the Temple itself, which appears as a natural opening in the rock about halfway up the elevation of the outcrop.

The opening to the Temple is narrower than the span of my arms out- stretched. There were perhaps five or six steps that led down into the cave. They seemed a combination of naturally formed and hand-hewn steps. I let my hands trail the walls of the entrance as we stepped down toward darkness. To my right, at about head level, was a natural formation of stone embedded in the stone wall that looked strikingly similar to a serpent several feet long heading toward the cave. The effect of the medicine, despite its intensity, was to focus my senses, and I lin- gered with my hand on the serpent. What stood out for me was the smoothness of the stone, suggesting that innumerable people had run their hands along this ser- pent while entering this cave.

Two or three more steps took me into the darkness of the cave. I moved slowly, keeping my hands on the rock. I let my hand move to the ceiling that was no more than a foot above my head. Again, I could feel the smoothness of stone that reflected the caress of so many pilgrims. I say "caress" because the rock conveys a sense of care and gentleness that my own hands reciprocated in touching the stone. My own heart was in play as I entered into this space, and I immediately felt a response in kind.

Entering into the cave, I could see a second chamber a few feet ahead. On the far side of that chamber was a natural altar of stone perhaps six feet wide and almost as deep. Several feet above the altar was a small roundish hole that opened to the sky. Later, viewing the hole from above the cave, we could see that the light of the moon could shine directly upon the altar or be reflected from an angled stone standing just next to the hole. I entered the second chamber, continuing to trail my fingers along the stone ceiling. What was immediately apparent to me was the aliveness of this space.

As I held my hands on the ceiling, I began to have a multisensory experience. In my internal vision, I could see energy fountaining out of the stone where my hands touched the ceiling. That energy took the form of brightly colored points of energy—like tiny versions of the internally illuminated serpents of my ayahuasca vision pouring out toward my hands. At the same time, I could feel a deep sadness that occupied the cave, one that seemed to reach back for as long as the cave itself was a place of ceremony and pilgrimage. Several times while I moved about within the chamber, I found myself bursting into tears. I could feel the presence of beings that were unseen. I heard myself saying *I know you,* words that emerged from a deep sense of their presence and a familiarity that could be known only by the heart. The mind had no play in this engagement. And, again on the internal, I heard their voice. *Do not break the connection. Do not break the unbroken chain.* It seemed to me to be a voice coming from the ancestors—the long line of humans that have pioneered this adventure of consciousness on the planet.

I felt that the span of this chamber's human occupation represented the long journey of human consciousness and its struggle with *inconscience*— Aurobindo's term for the sleeping human consciousness and all the pain that arises to awaken us from that slumber. The struggle continues. There is the struggle to remember who we are. There is the struggle to learn to become aware of our connection with everything. There is the struggle to learn how to create relationship out of that raw connection. In the midst of this, I felt the strong pull to bring to the altar the mantra that had come to my inner ear in the 1995 vision quest. Dots were connecting. I sang the mantra and filled the small chamber with the sound of my own deep voice.

Sitting at my computer in the States shortly after these last experiences, and just a couple of months before we are scheduled to return to Peru to continue this exploration, I reflected on the most central pieces of information that emerged from my journey and Er's. What is the short version of this story?

One central impression provides the context for everything else that I would say. I realize that the mystery of human consciousness is much larger than I imagined it to be even as I began to have the experiences I have shared in earlier chapters. On one hand, my understandings have become more humble, more tentative, more provisional and open to revision. On the other hand, I found some constants that seem like a solid platform on which to stand as I continue to turn my face, and body, toward the increasingly deep mystery.

These constants are not about the nature of the mystery, the *whys* and *whats* revolving around the bigger picture. Instead, my constants are about the *hows*—how the exploration that the soul journey represents moves forward in what I have called *a soul perspective.* This perspective is not a prescription, but a process.

As Er related, a soul chooses to come to the planet. It chooses a life, wisely or unwisely, depending upon its prior experience. The soul's memory of itself as a soul is stripped away for most souls, setting the stage for the soul's journey of remembrance and, more than remembrance, a journey to discover *and* enact its own destiny in service of some larger and still mysterious scheme. The scheme of setting up a forgetting and a fate that contains challenges from which the remembrance can be elicited also includes a process by which the skills necessary for later evolution may and must be acquired.

The soul—cut loose from its own memory and distant from its home in heaven—must find its home away from home. That home is what I have described not in physical terms, but in some mysterious field that sits at the juncture of time and space, on the one hand, and infinity on the other. It is a portal for the soul. It is not a portal solely to heaven, as we often think, but also a portal to earth. It is a field that has the qualities of electromagnetic, quantum, and photon fields. It is what we most often call the *heart,* and I have called it the *heart-field.*

For the soul to make its home in the heart-field, the personality—itself a mysterious amalgam of various elements and expressions of human consciousness—must yield its hold on attention and give up that attention to the soul, which in turn must hold its own attention in the heart-field. In doing so, the field that is the soul can be *re-membered* in the heart-field. *Re-membering*—the restoration of wholeness—is the very work of soul retrieval, one of the most valuable of indigenous perspectives and one that has remained largely outside of the limited perspective of postmodern psychotherapy.

Once established in the heart-field, the soul can begin to control the fundamental focus of consciousness that we call *attention,* and thereby take control of the personality—which is both the control center of the body and the mirror of the degree to which the soul has accomplished re-memberment. With the personality under more control, the soul can direct its attention to a seduction of the body into a partnership with the soul and the soul's own agenda, which is the discovery and enactment of the soul's destiny for this turn on the planet.

Just as the soul is a drop of heaven that falls to earth, the body is a drop of earth that rises to meet the soul. The body, held by the soul close to the portal of the heart, holds the keys to the earth's storehouse of energy and power, which awaits the soul's discovery of these necessaries. As the body comes into resonant relationship with the soul, two doors are opened. First, the creation of the relationship between body and soul ignites a fire in the heart-field, signaling to those who await in heaven that the heart is ready to receive reinforcing energies. Second, these reinforcing energies ignite a second field of fire—like a strike of lightning that moves from heaven to the ignited heart and on through the body to the body of the earth.

This newly ignited heart-field is now turned toward its greater help in heaven and also opens itself to the heart of the earth. There, the soul enters the earth's warehouse of abundant resources—everything that the embodied soul needs to sustain a journey of exploration. Heaven has pre-arranged this storehouse in such a way that everything that exists on the earth awaits to serve, each with its own gifts of support—for sustenance and survival, for curing, for healing, and for awakenings. By the resonant connection between the human heart-field and the heart of the earth, the soul awakens to how the earth has been seeded to support the soul's journey. The recognition of this pre-existing connection between heaven and earth, and now between soul and earth, provides the platform for a soul perspective that grounds the soul's journey.

And the soul, now connected with the heart of the earth, returns its attention to the heart-field, which it recognizes as a *lens of perception*—a lens through which the soul may navigate with the ultimate epistemological tool of *knowing*. Knowing is an ultimate expression of intelligence that transcends emotion and thinking, also beautiful epistemological lenses of perception in their own right, but lenses that nevertheless require the guidance and direction of the heart lens. The soul discovers that it may look through the lens of the mind, but that the mental lens is dangerous when used by itself, and that the lens of mind must be used in combination with the lens of the heart to bring the full potential of mental insight into play. In this discovery, we can leave behind an old way of looking that we could call *monoscopic* or *parallel vision*—looking through either the heart or the mind, but one at a time. Our skillful next step, once we have discovered the heart lens, is to look *stereoscopically* through the mind and heart simultaneously. A *stereoscopic vision* cannot help but lend more dimension to the outcome than our peering through either lens alone.

The soul recognizes, now from its own experience, that it can journey with its own attention, through the facility of the knowing heart, to other fields—the fields of heaven and earth, the fields that represent the helper spirits, guides, angels, power animals, plant spirits and so on. The soul discovers that it may, with the mere but skillful control of attention focused in the heart, discover those fields that hold the particular wisdoms that guide the soul to its own particular and unique destiny. And for some souls, those particular fields may include the plant *grandmothers*—the master teaching fields that use the *mother* plants that assist in this informational process by their healing powers.

It is not a new insight that everything is connected. But we do not experience that connection until we bring our attention to the connection. We can do that by returning our attention to the heaven fields, as the central force of Asian meditations traditions teach. That is a process that does not require the engagement of either the heart or an embodied soul. A disembodied soul can constellate quite enough attention to discover the phenomenon of connection by returning to its home in heaven. This happens regularly both as a function of skillful direction of attention and as a function of traumatic dissociation. But experiencing connection does not fulfill the soul's destiny. Rather, it begins to create the platform for the soul's emergence from fate. In order to engage its destiny, the soul has to embody, and to discover connection from the juncture of the heart. The soul has to find itself, and re-member itself, in the space of the human heart-field. From there, it has to discover its connection with all that exists in the three-dimensional realm of density. That requires, ultimately, the opening of the heart to the heart of the earth and all of the earth elements. But going that far still remains only a prologue to what is to follow.

The experience of connection is not the same as the creation of relationship. Relationship is a mutual, respectful, reciprocal, consensual exchange of energies and collaboration in work. The common human misconception is that we enter relationship to get connection, because we sense the need for connection and project its source on other people. It is actually the other way around. We need to find first the connection, and then choose what specific opportunities for deepening connection merit the skillful application of attention that begins the process of developing a collaborative relationship. The way in which it works is the same whether we are relating to the earth, a tree, a guiding spirit, or another person. Relationship with another person just requires more, not less, skill. Without collaborative relationship on multiple levels (and multiple dimensions), the soul journey will stall. The necessary skills of relationship are everywhere and with everything the same. All of these skills are heart skills: presence, non-judgment, compassion. We know their names. The absence of an experience of connection and the consequent absence of the skills of relationship are a sufficient explanation for the state of the world.

From a perspective of the evolution of world culture, it is increasingly apparent that the fusion of the gifts of particular cultures on the postmodern stage now make it possible to mix and match and to create new techniques that serve the soul journey. More information is available to an individual from all dimensions than in any recent time in human history. It is not necessary for us to become shamans or monks to access these gifts. The story of this time in human history is that we may all choose from many tools to do the work that opens the portals. We may all become experts in the unfoldment of our own journeys, getting the information we need by means of our own hearts and attention skills.

All of the techniques devolve into just two: controlling attention and learning the infinity of places that we can put it. And with those two, we can learn with just a little more experience that placing our attention in the heart serves to ignite our own soul journeys and lead us to the places—places of the heart and the cosmos—that are the soul's destination and destiny.

But for now, the trajectory of the soul journey is clearly downward, into the loving heart of the earth, which reaches up to meet us with its own infinite openness and a readiness to partner in the further evolution of consciousness, one soul at a time.

Made in the USA
San Bernardino, CA
22 October 2013